FAMILY TREES

FAMILY TREES

A History of Genealogy in America

François Weil

HARVARD UNIVERSITY PRESS

Cambridge, Massachusetts, and London, England

2013

Chapter 2 incorporates the author's article "John Farmer and
the Making of American Genealogy," from the *New England Quarterly* 80,
no. 3 (September 2007): 408–434.

Library of Congress Cataloging-in-Publication Data

Weil, François.
Family trees : a history of genealogy in America / François Weil.
pages   cm
Includes bibliographical references and index.
ISBN 978-0-674-04583-5 (alk. paper)
1. Genealogy—United States—History.   2. Genealogy—Social aspects—
United States.   3. National characteristics, American.   I. Title.
CS9.W45   2013
929.20973—dc23   2012044769

For Justine and Simon

Contents

FAMILY TREES

PROLOGUE

The 2008 and 2012 presidential elections generated extraordinary interest in Barack and Michelle Obama's genealogies. Much was written on the forty-fourth president's African and American roots and on the First Lady's ancestors in bondage and freedom. The president's ancestry simultaneously spoke of Kenya and Kansas. Among others, it included African cattle herders, midwestern farmers, Irish immigrants, southern slaveholders, and likely the first African slave in colonial America, John Punch. Michelle Obama's African American and white ancestors told a different story, one of tangled interracial roots, of violence and choice, and of more porous categories of race than those customarily acknowledged in American public discourse. In connection with the extraordinary event of the election of the first biracial president in the history of the United States, the engrossing fascination with the Obamas' family trees raised several sets of issues that are central to this book.[1]

One is that genealogical knowledge may provide a powerful lens to understand personal and collective identities, as suggested by

Barack Obama's interest in "the tangled roots of his own personal identity" in his 1995 book *Dreams from My Father,* which he defined as "autobiography, memoir, family history, or something else." Public discussions of his and his wife's ancestors indicate that awareness of the intertwined branches that ultimately constitute their family trees can say much about America's past and present.[2]

Interest in the Obamas' ancestry also testifies to the remarkable popularity of genealogy in the United States today, as does the success of *African American Lives* and *Faces of America,* two genealogy television programs developed by Henry Louis Gates Jr. Family history is a favorite search topic on the Internet. It fascinates Americans of all origins and persuasions, who join hundreds of genealogical organizations and spend a significant portion of their time and money researching their roots in libraries and archival repositories or at home on the Internet.

Finally, interest in the Obamas' genealogies raises a different kind of question. It calls attention to the fact that given all the evidence of the importance of family history in the United States, we should know much about its meaning and history. But we do not. In fact, genealogy is arguably the element of contemporary American culture about which we know the least. Although historians have analyzed the significance of other favorite Internet topics, such as gardening, music, sports, and sex, they have been remarkably discreet about family history. Despite repeated calls for cooperation between genealogy and historical inquiry, the history of genealogy remains largely to be written.

Whether genealogy is understood as the science of family relationships and lineages or more broadly as a personal interest in one's forebears (and the term will be used in both senses throughout this book), it addresses one of the most difficult questions in

American history: identity—the genealogists' identity far more than their ancestors'. Genealogists have always been wont to explain what they were after and why. Their voices resonate in the books they wrote, the notes they penned in their family Bibles, and the family trees they drew or embroidered. They often address matters of identity materially and explicitly. They reveal how Americans relied on genealogy to define and reinforce their individual and collective identities, as well as to situate themselves and their families in time by inclusion and by exclusion of others. They discuss how knowledge of their ancestry is a goal in itself or the means for social, economic, moral, or religious results or benefits. They suggest how they relate to the men and women of the past whom they define as their ancestors, and how this relation defines their awareness of themselves and the world they live in. They explain how they found in their family trees a sense of self they longed for. Throughout their genealogical writings and artifacts, they hint at how class, ethnic, gender, and above all racial concerns framed their genealogical pursuits, as did their visions of blood, heredity, purity, and transmission. They delineate the contours of American genealogical culture and consciousness and of its transformations over time.

To be sure, in its relation to identity, genealogy is not uniquely American. Elsewhere in the world, men and women also explore their family roots because their quest and their findings give them a better sense of who they are. This is as true today as it was in the past. Indeed, ancestral pursuits in colonial America partook of a culture of genealogy that dominated early modern Europe, including England. However, by the late eighteenth and the early nineteenth centuries Americans felt the need to invent forms of genealogy more acceptable in their new republican country. They connected concerns for identity with the recognition that genealogy should not be reserved to the rich, the well-born, and the powerful, but could be a legitimate pursuit for any ordinary American. They also recognized that democratization created a popular market for family trees and that it needed to be as scientific as possible to avoid the pitfalls of excessive commercialization. However uneasy it may have been at times, the relation they established among identity, democracy, science, and the market was uniquely American, and although it was loaded with class, gender, and racial concerns, it stood in sharp contrast to the aristocratic and bourgeois nature of European genealogy.

To explain how genealogy became American and evolved over four centuries is a vast topic. Although I am fully aware of the importance of lineage in African and Native American cultures, I chose to focus on the transposition and transformation in America of a European conception of kin and ancestry, and on its interactions with African American and Native American conceptions between the seventeenth century and the present. My interest is in the ways in which an American culture of genealogy emerged over time as Americans—Europeans and Africans who crossed the Atlantic, Native Americans, Asians who crossed the Pacific, Latin Americans who moved north, and their descendants—incorporated this European notion of lineage and family trees into their lives and transformed it. Their motives were diverse. As a cultural practice and a strategy of memory, genealogy was the product of tangled impulses that attest to its plurality of meanings. Some Americans saw in genealogy the means to preserve family unity and kin consciousness; others had religious reasons to explore their roots; still others hoped to reinforce their social pretensions with an illustrious family tree; many put genealogy at the service of their racial and exclusive purposes. Whether born out of a desire for self-understanding or a longing for self-assertion, family trees were a versatile means to cope with geographic, cultural, and social mobility in a rapidly changing world. This book traces the tensions between these competing impulses and the ensuing multifaceted encounter between Americans and their family trees.

Over the course of American history, the contours of four successive genealogical regimes or configurations emerged. The first ended in the mid-eighteenth century; the second (to which I devote two chapters) lasted almost a century until the 1860s; the third (also discussed in two chapters) went roughly from the aftermath of the Civil War to the mid-twentieth century; and the fourth emerged over fifty years ago and has continued to the present. Each was articulated around a particular organization of the impulses for genealogy I have described, with one or several of these impulses setting the tone for that regime. Genealogy never had a single meaning in American history; rather, it had successive dominant meanings. This book's chronological focus reflects my interest in addressing these dominant meanings, as well as the alternative rationales for practicing genealogy with which they competed in each period.

Until the late eighteenth century a private quest for pedigree, lineage, and social status in the British imperial Atlantic dominated colonial genealogy. Other settlers, however, were interested in their roots for moral, affective, and religious reasons, while African slaves struggled to preserve the memory of their ancestors in their time of bondage. Although their widespread kin-related genealogical practices were less visible than dominant pursuits and proclamations of gentility associated with pedigrees, they contributed to the growth of a familial and individual consciousness, as well as to the progressive elaboration of a distinctive American practice of genealogy.

During the antebellum era, after a period of severe attacks on aristocratic genealogy in the name of republicanism, Americans began to practice genealogy out of egalitarian, moral, and familial concerns. Men and women of the middling classes, including some free African Americans, participated in the transformation of American family trees as they viewed genealogy as a science that would help them reinforce their sense of self and the significance of the family as a moral, civic, and social unit. Their vision of genealogy in the new republic sharply contrasted with the lineage pretensions that in part were inherited from the colonial era and displayed by an elite minority of antebellum Americans, and in part were the product of greed and gullibility exhibited by estate claimants who aspired to fame and fortune.

From the 1860s to the mid-twentieth century, racial purity, nativism, and nationalism successfully dominated the quest for pedigree and gave genealogy more contemporary ideological relevance than ever before. The language of race, heredity, and later eugenics invaded the genealogical sphere, helping many white Americans describe themselves self-consciously as Anglo-Saxons and claim racial and social superiority over others. This new language was so pervasive that many of these "others" (African Americans and European migrants) came to share some of the tenets of racialized genealogy. In this new context the market for genealogy experienced tremendous, though unregulated, growth, which in turn helped develop frauds on a scale unknown in the United States until then. Some reacted and attempted to regulate the field. Other Americans, true to alternative visions inherited from the antebellum period, persisted in connecting genealogy to moral, religious, and democratic concerns, but by the late nineteenth century they were in the minority.

Only when the racial and nationalist foundations of genealogy were undermined in the middle of the twentieth century did the configuration of the genealogical interest in the United States change once again. It took decades, the civil rights movement, and the new interest in ethnicity and heritage for American genealogical culture as we know it today—popular, multicultural, and multiracial family history—to settle in. As the family history market has developed with the advent of the computer revolution and the Internet, genealogy has become a major component of the American economy of culture. In the age of DNA, the return of biological evidence to genealogy also raises new, fascinating, and troubling questions about the identity of individuals and groups within American society.

The present interest in Barack and Michelle Obama's ancestries and other signs of family history's popularity, then, are products of the long and complex history of the ways in which Americans relate to their ancestors and view themselves in time. I hope that this book, a "genealogy of genealogy" in American culture, will enlighten this history.

❧ I ❧

LINEAGE AND FAMILY
IN COLONIAL AMERICA

The letter that arrived in England from Massachusetts in 1725 was unexpected. It bore the signature of the minister of Boston's New Brick Church, William Waldron, a third-generation colonist whose genealogical curiosity had led him to seek help and information. Both Waldron's grandfather, a participant in the great migration of the 1630s, and his father had been respected political and military figures in New England. His older brother Richard followed in their steps, became a judge, and later held the coveted office of secretary of the province. As a second son, William Waldron predictably chose the pulpit. Born in 1697, he graduated from Harvard College in 1717 and was ordained pastor of the New Brick Church in 1722. In 1725 he sent a letter to England.[1]

"It was a very pleasant surprise to me to receive a Letter from you, who no doubt are of the same Name and Family with myself, tho' a letter in it be transposed," Waldron's correspondent John Walrond, a minister in Ottery St. Mary in Devon, England, acknowledged. "You and I are of one Family, Faith, and Profession." He might have added that they were both interested in genealogy.

To answer his New England kinsman's questions, the English minister made inquiries in neighboring Somerset, where Waldron's ancestors originated. He also offered genealogical details about his own branch of the family. The family seat, he explained, had been located in Devon for about 600 years, and most Walronds had remained in the region: "I never could find any of our Name, in all England, but in the Western Countries." Two branches, however, had left England: one "went, as Merchants to Barbadoes, grew rich, and was in the Government there"; the other one was the New England Waldrons.

John Walrond assured his Boston correspondent that he would keep looking into their genealogy and serve as his de facto genealogical agent in England: "I wish you had let me know into what Family your Grandfather married, for that might perhaps have given Light into the Enquiry; however I will examine farther, and take the first opportunity to inform you, as I can get Intelligence." He also provided him with information about the family's social status and volunteered an etymology for their family name, as well as a description of their coat of arms: it was "three Bulls Heads, as you'l see by my seal on this Letter."[2]

William Waldron and John Walrond's epistolary exchange affords a glimpse into the genealogical consciousness that existed in the Atlantic world during the colonial period. The two men lived in societies where genealogical preoccupations, inquiries, and reasoning were common. As Walrond's letter suggests, two meanings of genealogy coexisted at the time: the dominant one was related to social status, claimed or actual, while the other was a form of kin bonding. Walrond's emphasis on his family estate, coat of arms, and antiquity of name disclosed his proclamation of gentility. He assumed with good reason that William Waldron shared his interests and aspirations in Boston. For both men, a family tree suggested anteriority, lineage, and distinction. It served as a social marker in a world organized around notions of deference and difference.

At the same time, John Walrond expressed a revealing sense of kinship with his correspondent. He felt close to his newfound New England distant relative and made sure to sign his letter "Your affect[ionate] Kinsman and Serv[ant]." For him, as for many American colonists, some of humble extraction and modest social aspiration, genealogy suggested a psychological, intellectual, and affective relation to time, ancestors, and family. Although they were less visible than the dominant, status-related search for pedigree, widespread kin-related genealogical practices developed during the eighteenth century in the British Atlantic world and contributed to the progressive elaboration of a distinctive American mode of thinking about and practicing genealogy.

❧   ❧   ❧

American colonists participated in a vigorous Euro-Atlantic genealogical culture and consciousness, connected to a conception of individuals situated in Christian time. The Bible's emphasis on genealogy had long stimulated Europeans to think of their ancestors and kinsmen in genealogical terms. By the time of John Walrond's answer to William Waldron, genealogy had experienced a succession of remarkable developments during the Middle Ages and the early modern period.

Genealogy was originally the prerogative of kings and princes. The oldest surviving royal genealogies in Europe go back to the sixth century A.D. for Gothic sovereigns, to the seventh century for their Irish, Lombardic, Visigothic, and Frankish counterparts, and to the eighth and ninth centuries for Anglo-Saxon and Carolingian kings. Not until the mid-eleventh century did the practice of genealogy affect princely courts. By the twelfth century the growth of an ideology of lineage induced lesser nobles to set down their pedigrees in order to lay claim to land and establish political authority. At first, medieval genealogists were monks working in monasteries to compose the charters that established their aristocratic benefactors' rights to land; later the high nobility used the services of secular clergy to produce the pedigrees they needed.[3]

Whether authentic or fictional, origins mattered. Time and antiquity strengthened contemporary pretensions and ambitions. Thus many royal and princely courts throughout Europe claimed Trojan origins. In eleventh-century Normandy genealogists imagined a Trojan lineage for William the Conqueror's ancestor, the Viking chief Rollo. A century later in England, Geoffrey of Monmouth's *Historia Regum Britanniae* adopted and reinforced a Trojan account of British origins already presented three centuries earlier in the *Historia Brittonum*. Genealogy provided legitimacy to kings and princes, higher and lesser nobles. The recording of a pedigree was a political act and a testimony to the genealogist's obedient creativity. France's Capetian kings and the Wittelsbach dukes of Bavaria manipulated the catalog of earlier dynasties into their own genealogy to root their legitimacy in a much deeper history than their own lineage could provide.[4]

By the fourteenth century the upwardly mobile commercial bourgeoisie of medieval cities imitated the nobility and proudly displayed their ancestral lineage. Many Florentine bourgeois composed personal record books after 1350 to keep track of their investments and their lineage. At a time when life was extremely fragile, these narratives constructed a family identity, reinforced a lineage's political and patrimonial claims, and helped family members define their situation vis-à-vis the marital requirements of canon law (who was a cousin and who was not, whom one could marry and whom one could not).[5]

Late fifteenth- and early sixteenth-century Europe saw a remarkable growth of genealogy that lasted for over two centuries. Members of the nobility needed pedigrees in order to defend their status and privileges against bourgeois upstarts and in response to official investigations of nobility. Spanish inquiries to establish membership in the gentry, French efforts to probe nobility, and the visitations of England, which members of the College of Arms undertook between the mid-sixteenth century and the late seventeenth century, all stimulated genealogical interest and productions within aristocratic and gentry families.[6]

At the same time, successful merchants and other members of urban bourgeoisies launched genealogical pursuits in order to conform in their own specific ways to the dominant aristocratic model. Building on medieval traditions, sixteenth-century bourgeois turned account books and books of hours into family records where they consigned household data, memorialized family events, and inscribed pedigrees. In some remarkable instances they composed illuminated genealogical books and chronicles. All these private records associated genealogical consciousness and celebration of social aspirations, ancient roots, and power.[7]

The extension of status-related genealogical pursuits beyond the nobility—a major legacy of the Middle Ages and the early modern period—raised difficult issues of control and authenticity. In German or Italian cities political fragmentation prevented any effort to regulate genealogical claims and pursuits. The context was different in centralized or centralizing monarchies like England, France, or Spain, where access to nobility was an important source of income. To oversee the process, new genealogical bureaucracies developed in England, France, and Spain by the late sixteenth and early seventeenth centuries, raising the stakes of the genealogical enterprise but also contributing to the vogue of genealogy.[8]

Pedigrees became state matters at a moment when the nature and meaning of genealogical truth changed. Genealogies that had formerly been considered true were suddenly unbelievable. Even as older ways to produce traditional pedigrees survived, science challenged tradition and became a dominant mode in genealogy by the late seventeenth century. The new, critical genealogy was the product of its time. Instead of finding a lineage's original and fantastic ancestor, it was now more important to discover the depth of one's nobility and prove it. This required erudition rather than imagination, science rather than tradition.[9]

European states encouraged these developments, especially among their new genealogical bureaucrats. Demands for critical evidence and authority could be heard in France—where the offices of royal genealogist and judge of arms were created in 1595 and 1615—and in England, where the nature of the College of Arms, formally chartered under Richard III in 1484, changed significantly over the sixteenth century. Until then the heralds acted as masters of ceremonies at tournaments and served as messengers and diplomats. Now this traditional diplomatic role gave way to genealogy and heraldry. The new genealogists were often interested in history and antiquarianism. French genealogists like André Duchesne were historians of royal and aristocratic families. In England, members of the College of Arms knew how to search the Tower Record Office and look for evidence in medieval charters. The publication of William Lambarde's *Perambulation of Kent* in 1576 and the creation of the Society of Antiquarians in 1586 symbolized the new interest in local history, antiquarianism, and genealogy.[10]

During the first half of the seventeenth century, the combination of antiquarianism, the visitations the heralds were instructed to conduct on a regular basis to certify or disprove the pedigree rolls of the gentry, and the need to establish land titles sparked a remarkable proliferation of gentleman genealogists and antiquaries in England. The gentry needed pedigrees to confirm their claim, and the visiting heralds empowered local deputies to paint arms, thus helping spread heraldry and genealogy outside the College of Arms into English culture, from Ben Johnson and William Shakespeare to Andrew Marvell.[11]

Particularly significant was the publication of heraldic and genealogical tools that would serve English genealogists and their colonial counterparts for over two centuries. Heraldry books like Gerard Legh's *Accedence of Armory* and John Guillim's authoritative *Display of Heraldrie* (six editions between 1611 and 1724) could be found in many private libraries. William Dugdale's *Baronage of England* found worthy successors in Arthur Collins's *Peerage of England* (1707), Thomas Wolton's *Baronetage* (1727 and 1741), and Joseph Edmondson's 1764 *Baronagium genealogicum*.[12]

The rise of critical genealogy was no guarantee of authenticity. The late sixteenth and seventeenth centuries are famous for the fabrications produced by officers of arms and genealogists throughout Europe. In 1930 the acid-tongued British genealogist J. Horace Round divided the pedigrees of that period into "those that rested on garbled versions of perfectly genuine documents, . . . those which rested on alleged transcripts of wholly imaginary documents, those which rested on actual forgeries expressly concocted for the purpose, and lastly those which rested on nothing but sheer fantastic fiction." Undoubtedly all could be found—for a price—in England and elsewhere in Europe. In particular, many beneficiaries of the profitable royal trade in, and subsequent inflation of, honors that developed in late Tudor and Stuart England needed a pedigree to give legitimacy to their newly bought dignity, especially after the creation of the rank of baronet in 1611.[13]

To a certain extent, the American colonies inherited these European traditions and this practice of genealogy, but their colonial situation added one important nuance. Genealogical expertise remained largely lodged in metropolitan centers like London and Madrid. There were no pedigree experts, antiquarians, or institutions empowered to validate heraldic or genealogical claims in the Spanish and British colonies in the Americas. Genealogical claims were easier to make in the colonies, but the intervention of the imperial metropolis was required to validate these claims. In this, as in other matters, Euro-American colonists lived on the periphery of empire.

※　　　※　　　※

Not until the eighteenth century did status-related genealogical inquiries by Euro-American colonists reveal the growth of a genealogical consciousness in the form of pedigree or family trees. William Waldron's letter to his kinsman John Walrond in 1725 signaled such an interest, as did similar letters sent twenty years later to England by William Browne of Salem, Massachusetts, and Thomas Lee of Stratford, then president of the Council of the Colony of Virginia. Browne made inquiries about his British relatives during the 1740s and 1750s because he was making out "the Pedigree" and had "a regard for the several branches" of his family. Lee was interested in the ancestry of his grandfather, Richard Lee, who had arrived in Virginia in 1640 and apparently had believed that he was descended from the ancient Lee family of Coton Hall in Shropshire. John Gibbon, who paid a visit to Richard Lee in 1659–1661 and later became an officer of the College of Arms in London, noted that the Virginia Lees used the Coton Lees' coat of arms. Third-generation Thomas Lee did so, but he felt the need to learn more about his family's lineage, wrote to Lancelot Lee of Coton about it in the mid-1740s, and received a detailed answer about common ancestors.[14]

Until the 1670s status-related genealogical consciousness usually took the form of heraldic devices bearing a family's coat of arms (seals, gravestones) and of inscriptions on tombs. Armorial wax seals were by far the most common heraldic object in seventeenth-century English North America. Although in England, as in the rest of Europe, coats of arms were used by commoners as well as gentlemen, in the colonies they served to signal gentility and suggest deference.

In Virginia arms were probably much in use among the first generation of Virginia colonial leaders in the 1610s and early 1620s, but the disappearance of that group led to the emergence of a planter group that dominated Virginia politics and society until the Restoration. Unlike their descendants', these new immigrants' interest in genealogical matters is not well documented. Many were sons of up-and-coming English families, with names like Byrd, Carter, Ludwell, Mason, Filmer, and Culpeper. Some of these families belonged to the gentry, but more important, these men were well connected in business circles often long associated with Virginia. Their families had invested earlier in Virginia land, and several of them had come to the colony to assume and manage the family interests. Others had migrated because of the Civil War or after tensions with their English families. Many succeeded on their own without family support. Economic achievement reigned supreme, and few of them allowed themselves dreams of gentility on the Virginia colonial frontier of the mid-seventeenth century. Nonetheless, immigrant Virginians used heraldic symbols before the 1670s and 1680s, a sign of their lineage consciousness, albeit limited. One inscription on a grave in Abingdon Churchyard in Gloucester County said as much in 1658:

> To the lasting memory of Major Lewis Burwell
> Of the County of Gloucester in Virginia,
> Gentleman, who descended from the
> Ancient family of Burwells, of the
> Counties of Bedford and Northampton.[15]

Few similar traces of lineage consciousness have survived for New England and New Netherland. In the Dutch colony the glazier Evert Duyckinck painted stained-glass windows bearing the coat of arms of successful colonists, like the fur trader Rutger Bleecker, in New Amsterdam and Beverwijck (Albany) churches. In Massachusetts colonial leaders like the Winthrops used seals bearing the family's coat of arms, and John Leverett's portrait (painted when he was a colonial agent in London between 1655 and 1662) displayed his coat of arms.[16]

In the 1670s signs of status-related genealogical consciousness became far more numerous. Some colonists were satisfied with a private knowledge of their social status. Along with a drawing of a coat of arms, the Virginia planter Thomas Carter inscribed the following epitaph of his father-in-law Edward Dale in the *Book of*

Common-Prayer he used as a genealogical record: "He descended from an Ancien family in England & came in ye Coll[on]y of Vir[gini] a after the Death of his unhappy Master Charles First." When Charles Carroll migrated from Ireland to Maryland in 1688, he brought with him a "little Irish Manuscript Book" containing his family's genealogies inscribed in Gaelic.[17]

The Stuart Restoration and the stabilization of relations with England, the economic growth of New England and Virginia, the creation of new colonies in Carolina, Pennsylvania, and New York, and, above all, imperial developments convinced many colonists that their future lay in the British Empire. A growing number of New Englanders took to using English titles that indicated an elevated social station. Coats of arms had a similar function of representation, establishing rank for all to see. As cultural provincials deeply enmeshed in the Atlantic world, the colonists knew that they had to conform to English cultural and social standards. Until the Revolution they looked to England for confirmation of their social status, as well as for solutions to the primitiveness of their surroundings. In the late 1720s the Plymouth schoolteacher and Indian missionary Josiah Cotton regretted that he could "give no certain information" regarding his coat of arms but noted "that one of our name in England had a spread Eagle &c (which denotes Learning) for his Coat of Arms" and advised his "descendants if they pretend to any to assume that except they can discover one more proper." When the prosperous Quaker merchant Isaac Norris of Philadelphia ordered a coach in England in 1713, he first decided to add his coat of arms, then reconsidered and settled for his initials, "IN." Decades later, on the eve of the Revolution, a Virginian still ordered from London "a genteel chariot . . . with the coat of arms of our family."[18]

Colonists took advantage of renewed efforts by the British government to extend its control over the colonies by developing patronage and privilege. The Irish-born William Johnson, for instance, who moved to New York in the late 1730s, became an Indian agent, and carved a vast domain for himself in colonial New York, was created a baronet in 1755. His interest in heraldry went back to the late 1740s, when he decided to use a coat of arms. Once a baronet, he commissioned his portrait and chose a seal and an appropriate motto, *Deo regique debeo* (I owe God and the king). In 1763 Sir William displayed a renewed interest in his coat of arms, which he ordered painted and engraved in New York City. Heraldry served to symbolize Johnson's remarkable rise to colonial and imperial eminence.[19]

One result of the colonial elite's avowed desire to become part of a transatlantic imperial establishment was the emergence of a rich and diversified number of objects related to lineage. By the 1670s and 1680s many wealthy Boston merchants, distanced from the Puritan tradition, imitated Restoration England in the armorial displays common on portraits, seals, gravestones, and silver. At the end of a life of distinguished military and public service, Major Thomas Savage had his portrait painted in 1679. The coat of arms that graced the painting served to confirm Savage's social rank and status in a manner reminiscent of English aristocratic portraits of that period. In New England, as in Old England, in addition to underlining a family's wealth, power, and status, portraits served a memorial and genealogical purpose.[20]

The Virginia planter William Fitzhugh's correspondence bears testimony to the significance of family portraits on the colonial frontier. Fitzhugh was born in 1651 into a mercantile family of Bedford. His father was a woolen draper, and the Fitzhugh family, which was not of the gentry but had given several mayors to the city, had a coat of arms. Fitzhugh moved to Virginia in the early 1670s, married into a prominent family a few years later, and was elected to the House of Burgesses in 1677. Although he considered returning to England at one point in the mid-1680s, the ambitious draper's son turned Virginia planter soon abandoned the idea and stayed in Virginia until his death. Nonetheless, he renewed contact with his English kin and decided to procure a family portrait and the Fitzhugh coat of arms. "I should heartily be glad of your Picture, & our Coat of Arms, fairly & rightly drawn," he wrote his brother Henry in early 1687. A few months later he insisted: "As in my last I intimated & desired your Picture, & our Coat of Arms, if you could not get an advantageous opportunity, of giving me your own wish'd for company."[21]

Gravestones served a purpose analogous to portraits. In Tudor and Stuart England they played an important role, not only marking an individual's resting place but also memorializing him and indicating his social status. "Sepulchres fhould bee made according to the qualitie and degree of the perfon deceased that by the Tombe eueryone might bee difcerned of what rank hee was liuing," the English poet and antiquary John Weever suggested in his 1631 treatise *Ancient Funerall Monuments.*[22]

In tidewater Virginia, where stones were scarce, gravestones were imported from England. About two-thirds of the surviving stones were left unengraved, but one-third displayed a coat of arms. In their wills many Virginia gentlemen requested that their heirs have an inscription and a coat of arms engraved on their tombstones. Lieutenant Colonel Adam Thorowgood (ca. 1635–ca. 1685) was particularly specific when he wrote in his will that his wife Frances—a granddaughter of Sir George Yardley, the governor of Virginia from

1619 to 1627—was to "cause a toombe stone to be sent for with the Coate Armes of Sir George Yeardley and myselfe and the same Inscription as upon the broaken tomb, and the same to be layd over my Grave and the other over the grave of my mother upon brick."[23]

About 200 heraldic gravestones of the colonial period in New England have survived, the works of more than twenty-five local carvers. Apart from Leonard Chester's 1648 tomb in Wethersfield, Connecticut, most heraldic gravestones go back to the last quarter of the seventeenth century and the eighteenth century. At first used by colonial leaders like Governor John Leverett and Major Thomas Savage, heraldic stones became quite common in New England and New York in the eighteenth century.[24]

One related activity that developed in New England was the heraldic funeral. Samuel Sewall mentioned such events repeatedly in his diary. For instance, when Katharine Winthrop died in 1725, Sewall remarked—displaying his heraldic knowledge in passing, even though he never used a coat of arms himself—that "the Escutcheons on the Hearse bore the Arms of Winthrop and Brattle, the Lion Sable." Rich Bostonians modeled their burials on those in England, where funerals of elite families were heraldic events, complete with banners, escutcheons, or pennons during processions. "Funeral achievements" (also called hatchments) were often displayed during these funerals; these "achievements" had a diamond shape and a black background, like the one that the heraldic painter Christian Remick represented hanging on Thomas Hancock's house after his death in 1768.[25]

Nonetheless, portraits and gravestones were comparatively rare. Much more common during the colonial period were heraldic seals and silver. Seals served to close a letter and identify its sender. By the late seventeenth and early eighteenth centuries they were frequently in use among colonial political and mercantile elites—men like Governor Joseph Dudley of Massachusetts, Judge Richard Waldron of New Hampshire, the merchant David Jeffries of Boston, Governor Thomas Dongan of New York, the Scotland-born bookseller and future postmaster of the colonies Duncan Campbell of Boston, Major Ichabod Plaisted of Portsmouth, and Colonel John Husher of New Hampshire.[26]

Engraved silver also spoke of its owners' social status and lineage consciousness. It became popular in the North American colonies after the Restoration. In the late seventeenth century Virginia planters had no option but to order their engraved plate from England. In 1688 William Fitzhugh instructed his London agent to send him engraved silverware "& let it all be thus marked WFS & that Coat of Arms put upon all pieces that are proper, especially the Dishes, plates & Tankards &c that I have sent enclosed & blazoned in a letter to Mr. Hayward." Fitzhugh commented about the silver's social and memorial value: "I esteem it as well politic as reputable, to furnish my self with an handsom Cupboard of plate which gives my self the present use & Credit, is a sure friend at a dead lift, without much loss, or is a certain portion for a Child after my decease."[27]

Unlike Virginians, late seventeenth-century New Englanders could resort to native-born or immigrant craftsmen for plate or engraving. Boston goldsmiths Jeremiah Dummer, John Coney, and the English-born William Rouse catered to an ambitious clientele of New England political and mercantile leaders who operated according to the new imperial system of values and aspired to imitate the manners and lifestyle of their England counterparts. Dummer, his fellow craftsmen, and their many eighteenth-century successors artistically engraved tankards, candlesticks, skillets, sugar boxes, plates, and cups with the arms of their clients—families with names like Lidgett, Pickering, Saltonstall, Brown, Colman, Checkley, and Stoughton or newly arrived merchants like John Foster of Buckinghamshire. Similarly, New Yorkers like the Albany brewer Leendert Gansevoort owned Queen Anne silver tankards that often bore the engraved arms and monograms of their owners—a sure sign that they belonged or at least aspired to the colonial elite.[28]

During the eighteenth century the practice of adorning silverware with one's coat of arms gained even wider acceptance. One author describes the last three decades before the Revolution in Boston as an age "of aristocratic refinement," illustrated by talented craftsmen like Paul Revere Jr., who was soon to achieve a different sort of fame.[29]

✻   ✻   ✻

The lack of heraldic and genealogical regulation in the American colonies created real business opportunities in the late seventeenth and eighteenth centuries. To be sure, on three occasions at least, there had been talk in England of regulating the use of coats of arms in the colonies so as to preclude the selling of fictitious pedigrees. In 1609 the Council of Virginia requested the College of Arms "to record the names and orders of rank of a colonial aristocracy," but nothing came of this. In 1660 colonial use of armorial bearings created a debate on whether a member of the College of Arms should be constituted "only King of Arms of all his Majesty's Plantations in America." The petition was denied. Finally, in 1705 Carolina's Lords Proprietors appointed the College of Arms's York Herald, Laurence Cromp, "to devyse, give, Grant and Assign . . .

Such Arms and Crest" as he thought "most proper." Cromp, however, never made any visitation to the colony. Thus a cottage industry of limners, engravers, stonecutters, and decorators could develop unimpeded in the major cities.[30]

In New York heraldic painters were fairly numerous and advertised their services in local newspapers, particularly after 1740. By the 1770s competition was keen for the heraldic market. Sebastian Gueubel, a coach painter and gilder who settled in New York in 1771, painted "All Sorts of Flowers, Coats of Arms, &c. in the neatest manner." John Hutt engraved coats of arms and crests on plate, as well as "Arms neatly painted on vellum." Several craftsmen advertised their work in a detailed manner that suggests that they had to persuade potential clients. Joseph Simons knew that his clients aspired to English gentility, and he assured them that he would engrave their arms "after the Manner of the Herald's office, and as neat as in any part of England." William Bateman claimed to have had "the honour to do work for the first nobility and gentry in London to their satisfaction."[31]

In Boston the painter-stainer Thomas Child specialized in "funeral achievements." Child was part of a growing milieu of heraldic artists. Nathaniel Emmes, a stonecutter and real estate speculator, was probably the most celebrated gravestone maker in Boston, where he made, among others, Bartholomew Gedney's tomb in King's Chapel (1738). Emmes was in demand as far away as New York, where he engraved John Dupuy's stone in Trinity Church with an armorial coat.[32]

Charleston and Philadelphia silversmiths, engravers, and painters also vied in the heraldic market as early as the 1730s. There, as in New York, the 1760s and 1770s were times of intense heraldic activity. James Poupard of Philadelphia acknowledged this fact when he announced in 1774 that he had hired an immigrant stone-seal engraver from London because there were many local gentlemen who wanted "their coats of arms, crests, cyphers, &c, cut in stone."[33]

Since there was no heraldic regulation in the colonies, clients could choose coats of arms as they pleased. William Bateman said as much when he claimed to own "a book of heraldry" where "gentlemen who want their coat of arms engraved by him, and do not know them, may search the book gratis." Colonists could rely on family tradition to choose coats of arms. William Fitzhugh had assumed the arms of the celebrated Barons Fitzhugh, and after his death his descendants gave his estate the name Ravensworth, which was the baronial seat. When his brother Henry sent him a seal in 1687 with the (different) coat of arms he used in England, William Fitzhugh strongly disagreed. Had Henry's wife "writ it had been our Coat of arms, I should have allowed the mistake not esteeming her conversant in Heraldry, or skilfull in Coats of Arms," he wrote. Since Henry himself had written "it to be so, I must interpret it either to Credulity or mistake." Conflicting traditions could not be resolved, and William Fitzhugh—perhaps because in him "lay the pent-up ambitions of the gentleman manqué"—continued to use his unlikely baronial arms.[34]

Colonial gentlemen could also depend on advice from heraldic craftsmen or find information by themselves in America. Because almost anything was for sale, they could literally pick their arms. Like William Bateman of New York or Thomas Johnston of Boston (whose inventory in 1767 included a "book of heraldry"), some craftsmen owned books such as John Guillim's *Display of Heraldrie* originally published in 1611, which became more widely available following its 1724 edition. Thus John Singleton Copley's famous painting of the Boston silversmith Nathaniel Hurd (ca. 1765) shows him seated behind two books, one of which is Guillim's *Display*. Other heraldic painters gathered their own source material. John Gore of Boston, for instance, created what later became known as the Gore roll of arms—about 100 coats of arms, mostly of New England families.[35]

By the eighteenth century colonial elites might own books of heraldry or the like. William Byrd of Westover owned William Dugdale's 1675 *Baronage of England*. In Charleston the patrician members of the Charleston Society Library (founded in 1748) ordered James Anderson's 1732 *Royal Genealogies; or, The Genealogical Tables* and Joseph Edmondson's costly multivolume *Baronagium genealogicum* for their shelves. Thomas Jefferson's personal library included not only books about the peerage of England, Scotland, and Ireland but also Dugdale's *Baronage* and Gosling's 1714 *Laws of Honour*.[36]

Some colonial gentlemen attempted to validate their heraldic claims by procuring pedigrees and coats of arms in England and ultimately registering them at the College of Arms. The procedure was long, slow, and costly, and its results were extremely uncertain, especially for those colonists who were not entitled to the coat of arms they had adopted. Accordingly, few colonists chose that road, and those who did had good reasons to do so. For Edmund Andros, an Englishman who served as colonial governor of New York and of the Dominion of New England, it was the logical thing to do: in 1686 he registered his arms and pedigree at the College of Arms, five years after he was knighted. William Byrd of Westover had his pedigree recorded in 1702 at the College of Arms because he aspired to gentility.[37]

In February 1771 Thomas Jefferson, who had lost many personal and family papers when his father's house had burned two years earlier, wrote to a fellow Virginian who was traveling to London, Thomas Adams, and requested his help on several business and personal matters before concluding: "One farther favor and I am done; to search the Herald's office for the arms of my family. I have what I have been told are the family arms, but on what authority I know not. It is possible there may be none. If so, I would with your assistance become a purchaser, having Sterne's word for it that a coat of arms may be purchased as cheap as any other coat."[38]

A few colonists wrote to the College of Arms in London, often to be told that no family pedigree could be found and that further investigations would be necessary.[39] Others took advantage of a visit to Europe to inquire directly. The most famous of these early genealogical visitors was Benjamin Franklin, who traveled from London to Wellingborough, Northamptonshire, with his son William in 1758. There the Franklins met Benjamin's elderly cousin Mary Fisher, who could recall the departure of Benjamin's father Josiah for New England in 1685. From Wellingborough Benjamin and William Franklin went to Acton, where the Franklin family had long lived, and looked at the parish registers and the gravestones. Next they went to Banbury, met another cousin there, and saw the gravestone of Benjamin's grandfather Thomas. Upon his return to London, Benjamin Franklin received a transcript of the registers at Acton and exchanged correspondence with Mary Fisher. His visit had taught him what he probably already knew, that "our poor honest Family were Inhabitants of that Village near 200 Years." A second comment pointed to the weight of a sense of lineage even among colonists of modest social background like Franklin: he was, he remarked, "the youngest Son of the youngest Son of the youngest Son of the youngest Son for five generations." Unlike most colonists who went to Europe searching for their roots,

Franklin was not looking for a noble lineage, nor did he try to forge one.[40]

A far more typical colonial genealogical investigator was Henry Laurens, the South Carolina planter who became the president of the Continental Congress. Laurens was the grandson of a Huguenot exile who had resettled first in England, then in New York, and finally in South Carolina in 1715. In 1772 Laurens traveled to La Rochelle, France, in search of the family coat of arms and noble cousins. His quest was unsuccessful, and since he was informed "that there was none of my Name in that City, nor any Register of Family Arms," Laurens despaired of tracing his ancestry. He was delighted, therefore, when a French potential kinsman wrote him two years later. In his answer, Laurens emphasized that his father "had been very Careless concerning his Ancestry," destroying many family papers seen "as incapable of producing any real benefit." Moreover, the older Laurens had "no inclination to gratify his Vanity by a retrospect of any little Grandeur which might have existed, before he was born, among his Fore fathers." Laurens seized on this explanation to "account for the deficiency of my knowledge in the history of our past Generations."[41]

Thomas Lee's son William pursued his father's investigation into the family roots while he was a merchant in England in the early 1770s. He got in touch with the Reverend Harry Lee, a brother of his father's 1745 correspondent and the warden of Winchester College. "I shall send the Family Pedigree . . . , which I hope will give you a clear Insight of the Family," Warden Lee wrote in 1771. A few months later, William Lee, then aged 32, wrote a detailed memorandum about the descent of Richard Lee the emigrant. In a text full of references to gentility, he enumerated the offspring of Richard Lee, "of a good family in Shropshire," including his son Richard II, who "married a Corbin into which Family his Predecessors in England had before married." William Lee then turned his attention to the third generation. One of his uncles, Richard III, was "a Virginian Merchant" in London who "married an heiress in England"; another had settled in Maryland, "leaving a very numerous Family that are now branched out at large, over the whole Province, and are in plentiful circumstances"; his father Thomas had "married a Ludwell of whose genealogy I must give a short account being materially interested therein." Finally, William Lee mentioned his brothers and himself, "William (the writer of this account)," who "in 1769 married in London Miss Hannah Philippa Ludwell." Searching for his family's pedigree confirmed Lee's social status and aspirations to gentility.[42]

✻   ✻   ✻

In colonial America genealogical interest took other, less visible forms than William Lee's pursuit of gentility. Kin-related genealogical consciousness was linked to changes in the conception of family and to the growth of family and individual consciousness at the time. Although many members of the colonial elites were interested in genealogy for both status-related and kin-related reasons, the latter form was not limited to social and cultural elites but bridged class and race barriers.[43]

Although awareness of kinship and kin consciousness is difficult to document because of its oral nature, it was very much present among Africans brought as slaves to British North America during the colonial period and their descendants. Many of them "carried in their minds detailed genealogies that reached back generations, sometimes to an African root." African-born Venture

Smith remembered his ancestors, and Mary, a slave in late eighteenth-century Maryland, knew that she was descended "from Negro Mary, imported many years ago in this country from Madagascar."[44]

Through oral transmission, knowledge of family history could pass from one generation to the next over a century. Mary and William Butler, two enslaved cousins who petitioned the Maryland courts in 1770 for their freedom, knew that they were descended from a slave who had married a free white woman, "Irish Nell," in 1681. Charles and Patrick Mahoney traced their descent through their mother Nelly, grandmother Sue, and great-grandmother Sue to their great-great-grandmother Ann Joice, who had been brought from Barbados to England and then from England to Maryland by Lord Baltimore around 1680. As in similar suits for freedom, the Butlers emphasized descent from "Irish Nell" in their depositions, hoping to secure freedom and ultimately succeeding. One witness for the Mahoneys, Henry Davis, explained that "it was the report of the neighborhood" that if Ann Joice "had justice done her, she ought to have been free." In other cases Anthony Boston explained that he was "a descendant of Violet, the daughter of Linah, the daughter of Maria, or Marea," according to him "a Spanish woman," while Eleanor Toogood claimed descent from a white indentured great-grandmother. Toogood also knew that her ancestor had married a former slave; that her grandmother Mary Fisher had married "a negro man named Dick, a slave"; and that her mother Ann Fisher had already petitioned the courts in 1734 for her freedom and lost. Not only did her genealogical knowledge help her define her identity, but it also contributed to her sense of a possible "future in freedom." In these and similar suits set in late eighteenth- and early nineteenth-century Maryland, plaintiffs relied on direct testimony and hearsay evidence to prove their lineage. Their depositions suggest how successfully many slaves managed to preserve their family history over a century of bondage.[45]

Slave naming practices sometimes expressed genealogical awareness as well. Slaves of the Carroll family of Maryland chose to maintain family ties by giving children the names of their parents and grandparents, a practice that preserved names from earlier generations until the Civil War. The children of two eighteenth-century South Carolina slaves, Windsor and Angola Ame, also named their own children after their parents, thus connecting "grandparent with grandchild, second generation American-born to African-born."[46]

For a large number of white colonists as well, genealogical consciousness meant a direct or indirect knowledge of their kin. Thousands of surviving wills afford a glimpse into what colonists knew about their kin. Indirect knowledge was passed on in the family, either orally or in writing. Colonists of various social backgrounds thus developed and preserved genealogical memory in their families.

When they inscribed family records in Bibles, account books, diaries, almanacs, birth certificates, or commonplace books, colonists had diverse purposes. Most notes were oriented toward posterity. In their simplest form, colonial family records could be a simple sheet of paper or a couple of sheets sewn together. One early eighteenth-century record read: "The names and births of the Children of Samuel Dunbard of Bridgewater who was born in the year 1704 and Matilda Mabatiah his wife." Colonists seldom elaborated on their reasons for creating such records, but we can speculate that their first goal was practical. Church registers were unsystematic and unreliable. Like probate records, they focused on individuals (when they were born, were baptized, married, or died), not family units. Private family records did just that.[47]

Colonists often commenced a family record when they married or had children. The frequency of widowhood and remarriage made family records even more useful. John Granbery and Abigail Langley of Virginia recorded their marriage and the birth of their children in a booklet closed by a small clasp that also served as an account book. When Granbery died in 1733, Abigail married Robert Hargroves. She inscribed the names of her children with him, her father and mother's deaths, and the births of her slaves in the book. A Virginia physician, Philip Turpin, similarly transformed an account book into a family record where he entered the names of his successive wives and his children with them. Preserving family details along with business transactions, as many colonists did along the Atlantic seaboard, underlined the original record's practical nature.[48]

Family records also held moral, religious, and affective value. Puritans believed, in the words of William Stoughton, that "the books that shall be opened at the last day" would "contain Genealogies among them," and that "a Register of the Genealogies of New England's Sons and Daughters" would be "brought forth." In *New-England's True Interest,* an Election Day sermon delivered in 1668 and printed two years later, Stoughton used genealogical reasoning as one rhetorical and moral strategy to emphasize Puritan religious duty. One of "the Grounds of the Lords Expectation," he emphasized, was "the Extraction of a People, or their descent from such Parents and Progenitors." Because "Religious Parentage and Descent" mattered, the future acting governor of Massachusetts and presiding judge at the Salem trials underlined the importance of Puritan ancestors ("the Remainders of the Ancient Stock amongst us," he called them) for his own generation. Knowledge of ancestors reinforced the Puritan family and provided models to emulate and respect.[49]

Family pride surfaced at times among Puritan luminaries. Cotton Mather's *Magnalia Christi Americana* (1702) includes an "Attestation" by John Higginson, the minister of Salem, who celebrated the importance of the Mather family for the religious history of Puritan New England and expressed the wish that "God grant that such Mathers may continue to arise, and sons of sons, and children born to them." By far, however, genealogical pride was second to the notion that family records provided indirect moral guidance to second- and third-generation Puritans struggling with the magnitude of change in seventeenth-century New England. Likewise, Quakers, Moravians, Mennonites, and other sectarian colonists valued knowledge of family history for its moral dimension. Because families were central to many colonists, they understood that ignorance of ancestors would weaken their commitment to their kin.[50]

Colonists who relied on family records to strengthen kin and generational continuity logically inscribed and preserved genealogical information in their most treasured possession, the family Bible. "I purchased this book for 3 Gilders, and I love it more than all the world, in Wittenberg, Germany," one eighteenth-century immigrant wrote in German next to the indication of his marriage and dates of birth of his fifteen children. Many Protestant immigrants of English, Dutch, French, Swedish, or German origin likewise took the sacred book with them across the Atlantic. Settlers bought, offered, or received Bibles as a personal, family, or wedding present whose religious meaning was enhanced by its genealogical significance.[51]

Colonists used Bibles for genealogical purposes in different ways. Family records were inserted on a separate leaf or inscribed on the inside cover of the book or a specific page. Sometimes the record's form or language revealed the affective importance it held for its owner. Eighteenth-century members of New York Anglo-Dutch colonial elites like Kilian Van Rensselaer and John Schuyler, who routinely spoke and wrote English in their commercial and political transactions, systematically inscribed genealogical information in their Bibles in Dutch. Sectarian Germans sometimes penned family registers in their Bibles in calligraphic script called Fraktur. In both instances Bible records revealed a connection among family history, ethnicity, and identity that obviously mattered to their owners. More generally, Bible records emphasized the importance of the family as a close social unit maintained over time.[52]

So did family documentation recorded on furniture, pottery, portraits, and needlework. Although the beginnings of a genealogical art of the family were still tentative until the mid-eighteenth century, late seventeenth- and early eighteenth-century New England chests marked with their owners' initials or full names served to pass on to posterity names preserved in what were some of the most precious possessions of a family.[53]

Genealogical notes in diaries and commonplace books added a moral dimension and an elaborated emphasis on the self. Colonists used these books to record maxims, proverbs, anecdotes, thoughts, scraps, book titles, notes, and quotations. Ministers reproduced passages and ideas they would memorize and use in their sermons. Many of these commonplace books contained detailed genealogies of their keepers. Besides dozens of pages of notes and thoughts, Seaborn Cotton, a minister in Hampton, New Hampshire, and a son of the celebrated Puritan divine John Cotton, filled about twenty pages of his commonplace book with genealogical information that he wanted to remember. He mentioned his father's death and his own marriage in 1654, the day and hour of his children's births (and deaths when that was the case), his first wife's death, and his remarriage. Keepers of commonplace books often emphasized their genealogies' memorial function by entitling that section of their book "Memoranda" or, as the Reverend Samuel Brown did in the early eighteenth century, "A memorandum of the remarkables of my life." The frequent juxtaposition or interlacement of moral and genealogical notations in these commonplace books suggests that their keepers did not separate moral fashioning of the self, individual insertion into a genealogical continuity, and family identity.[54]

As they were transmitted from one generation to the next, family records of all types took on added psychological and affective significance during the eighteenth century. They remained oriented toward posterity but also served as markers of remembrance and genealogical memory of earlier keepers. They helped colonists press the claims of kinship and extended the definition of what constituted a family toward an ever-deeper past. Abigail Granbery's family record covered two generations—Abigail's and that of her daughter Mary Granbery Cowper, who inherited the record—and half of the eighteenth century. Seaborn Cotton's commonplace book bridged two centuries and three generations from Cotton himself to his son John to John's son-in-law Nathaniel Gookin. Maria Carter Beverley and her husband Robert Beverley gave the Bible that contained their genealogical record to their daughter Lucy when she married into the Randolph family. The exceptionally detailed genealogical record that the patriarch Josiah Chapin began in 1726 at age 92 covered much of the colonial period and three generations from the first of Chapin's three marriages in 1658 to the death in 1777 of his granddaughter Deborah Chapin Nelson, who took over the task of recording the family record after Chapin's own death. Record keepers were often conscious of the memorial implications of generational transmission and emphasized family connection over time. "I Daniel Brown was born dec 31th 1769," Samuel Brown's descendant Daniel intoned when he became the keeper of the family's commonplace book and family record—echoing his ancestor's opening words ("I Samuel b was Borne att Newbury September 5th Anno 1687"). Lucy Beverley Randolph, now 71 years old, commented in 1842 that "by my calculation, this sacred book is 111 years old." Her calculation was erroneous (the book was 95 years old and had been given to her mother 89 years earlier), but her comment suggested her Bible's special meaning as a genealogical heirloom.[55]

In contrast with family records oriented toward posterity, ascending genealogies were rare but not unheard of during the colonial period. Because of the difficulty of genealogical pursuits at the time and the additional challenge created by the colonial context and transatlantic distance, such genealogies usually did not reach beyond a writer's father's or grandfather's generation. Hannah Deane, a Taunton, Massachusetts, woman who dictated an account of the Leonard family to her grandnephew Zephaniah Leonard in the early 1730s, is a rare example of a colonist who knew the names of her great-grandfather, grandfather, grandmother, father, mother, uncles, and aunts and their lives.[56]

Authors invoked family circumstances, moral and religious exemplarity, and curiosity as rationales for their genealogical explorations of their forefathers. Daniel Denison of Ipswich, Massachusetts, wrote a detailed genealogical account to his grandchildren in 1672 so "that you being left fatherless Children might not be altogether ignorant of your ancestors, nor strangers to your near relations." Because he felt that his son's death had interrupted a generational transmission of genealogical information that needed to be restored for moral and religious reasons, Denison "thought meet to acquaint you with your predecessors, and your decent from them." Starting with his own father, he went on to describe their ancestry "by the father side" before he gave a briefer but rare account "by your Mothers side." His grandchildren, he concluded, "need not be ashamed of [their] progenitors, who have in many respects been eminent in their times"; rather, they should imitate the "piety and goodness" of their "Godly Ancestors" and never "degenerate from those Roots from whence you are sprunge." As they grew old, some first-generation Puritans like Denison relied on genealogy to help transmit moral and religious values to their descendants.[57]

Others did not initiate genealogical pursuits but were requested to provide information by their children and grandchildren—second- or third-generation colonists who demonstrated genealogical curiosity on their own. On January 1 1698/99, 60-year old Samuel Smith of Hadley, Massachusetts, wrote to his son to satisfy the younger man's questions about his own father Henry, a minister in Wethersfield, although he was "possessed of but little of the Information for which you seek." When the celebrated New England diarist Samuel Sewall wrote a similar genealogical letter in 1720, he credited his son for having "often desired, that I would give you some account of the family of which you are." Sewall, who had been interested in his ancestors when he was a younger man and had done research when he had gone to England in 1689, was able to go back three generations to his great-grandfather, a linen draper in Coventry. Sewall's letter did not appease his son's curiosity, and the younger Sewall pressed for more information a few weeks later.[58]

Samuel Smith's and Samuel Sewall's sons felt a psychological need to mine their fathers' memories before the passing of generations and the growing chronological distance from the beginnings of colonization created amnesia. Colonists established ascending genealogies in growing numbers in the eighteenth century, especially after 1750, and they offered more detailed and candid rationales for doing so than previous generations. An early example is that of Josiah Cotton of Plymouth, a schoolmaster, Indian missionary, compiler of an Indian dictionary, public servant, and a nephew of Cotton Mather and Seaborn Cotton who chose to include an account of his "Predecessors, Relations, Posterity & Alliances" in his 1726 manuscript memoirs. First, he considered that genealogical knowledge conveyed moral values. "I am willing that my Posterity should know from whence they are descended," he argued, "that they may imitate the virtues & avoid the Errors of those who have preceded them." Besides, genealogy reinforced kinship and ensured that descendants would "manifest that Friendship & natural Affection to those of the same Blood, which Nature & Religion do require." Finally, Cotton felt a genealogical duty both to his ancestors and his posterity because he had outlived his contemporaries. Since it had "pleased HEAVEN also to lengthen out my Time beyond all the Sons of my Father's House," Cotton would "therefore revive their Memory & bring those to view who are gone out of sight & otherwise may be forgotten."[59]

Many eighteenth-century colonists shared part or all of Josiah Cotton's motives for collecting his family tree and often added one, personal curiosity. The Quaker merchant Jonathan Mifflin Sr. wrote an account of his family in 1770 and revised it before his death. One Rhode Islander explained that he had "undertaken to write this small Book for myself, that I may remember my Fore-Fathers, and not forget them." Robert Bolling of Virginia wrote a family genealogy, "Memoirs of the Bolling Family," in the mid-

1760s because, as his nephew later explained, "it had been neglected by his ancestors," and Bolling had concluded from his own interest in their genealogy "that at some future day others might be equally interested in what pertained to himself and bretheren."[60] Bolling's contemporary and fellow Virginian Jaquelin Ambler began his family record in 1774 because his eight brothers and sisters were dead by then and he wished to memorialize their lives.[61]

Genealogy-minded colonists knew all about the traps and troubles of genealogical investigations, given the paucity of documentation and the lack of genealogical networks in the colonies. In the absence of the American equivalent of European antiquarians and local historians (except for a few isolated pioneers like the Reverend Thomas Prince in Boston), middling colonists were left to themselves. Impediments undoubtedly hindered many, but some colonists made remarkable genealogical progress. Benjamin Ballou, a young Rhode Island farmer, faced many obstacles when he decided in 1774 to gather his family genealogy. Although he inquired carefully, he could "find out but little" of his ancestors' traces. Not knowing "any one who hath undertaken this work, or have any Account of them," Ballou concluded that it was "high time to write what little I know about them." He was able to trace his direct line back to his ancestor Mathurin, who arrived in New England in 1634. "His wife's name is unknown to me," he regretted, but he learned the names of their daughter and five sons—what he called "the first stock of the Ballous."[62]

Like Benjamin Ballou, many colonists displayed a keen but private interest in genealogy on the eve of the Revolution. Genealogies were manuscript heirlooms that were meant to remain in the family as they circulated from one generation to the next. To be sure, there is the exception of the *Memoirs of Capt. Roger Clap* (1731), arguably the first printed genealogy in colonial North America. Clap was an early colonist who had arrived in New England in 1630. He died in 1691 and left his children a remarkable manuscript that contained his personal narrative of migration, as well as moral and religious advice for "instructing, counselling, directing and commanding his children and children's children"—but no genealogy. In the late 1720s Thomas Prince, minister of Boston's Old South Church and a noted historian, was presented Clap's manuscript. He decided that it was worth printing and he added a "short account of the author and his family" composed by a descendant, James Blake Jr. Clap's *Memoirs,* however, were not published because of this genealogical appendix but because of his exceptional account of life in early New England.[63]

Publication, as opposed to private elaboration, of a family genealogy had to await not only a general consensus on the moral and pedagogic virtues of genealogy (which already existed by the 1730s) but also the relative growth of private genealogical pursuits in the mid-eighteenth century and a changing ideological and political context in the last decade before the Revolution. In 1771 the publication of the *Genealogy of the Family of Samuel Stebbins* suggested that times were changing. The book's author was a middling merchant, innkeeper, and schoolmaster of Kensington, Connecticut, Luke Stebbins. His reasons for undertaking genealogical pursuits were traditional. Genealogy reinforced religion and kinship among descendants, he proclaimed, "as it may give demonstration of the power, faithfulness, and goodness of God to their ancestor." Genealogy was also pedagogical: "Where their Ancestors have led pious and religious Lives . . . , it may excite in their Decendants a laudable Ambition to imitate those Things that were excellent, praiseworthy and amiable in them."[64]

But Stebbins's statement was nonetheless exceptional. What distinguished his genealogy from others was that he saw fit to print it. This was a radical departure from colonial and European genealogical cultures. Published genealogies in Europe were usually produced by the aristocracy or aspiring bourgeoisie, while in the colonies the gentry never felt the need to publish their family trees, especially in the absence of an institution of genealogical regulation like England's College of Arms. Europeans of middling status and no visible social aspiration, like Luke Stebbins, would never have decided to commit their family tree to print. Publication of the *Genealogy of the Family of Samuel Stebbins* was clearly an exceptional initiative in 1771, but it was a highly significant one. As a cultural and political process of creolization and gradual separation from England transformed colonials into Americans, so European-bred colonial genealogical cultures and practices evolved into new modes of searching for and reflecting about one's ancestors. By the 1760s the genealogical norms that dominated the colonial period—with its visible, status-based, gentry genealogy and its more private, kin-related, moral and religious genealogy—were under attack. The Americanization of genealogy was in progress.

❦ 2 ❦

THE RISE OF
AMERICAN GENEALOGY

I am endeavoring to make out a memoir of our family before it is entirely lost," Leverett Saltonstall told his younger sister Anna in December 1815. "It is astonishing how little is preserved of some of our ancestors." A few weeks later he wrote again, apologizing for "troubl[ing her] once more." Having judged that she had "the most curiosity upon the subject of our family," he submitted queries about their genealogy while appealing for her utmost discretion. "These questions are not for publick information," he warned. "I should be unwilling it should be generally known that I have been engaged in this inquiry, because it would by many be attributed to vanity—by all who sprang from obscurity. Vanity it is not—tho' I confess some pride, and it is a proper feeling."[1]

Saltonstall's need to justify his endeavor testifies to genealogy's ambiguous status in the new republic. A descendant of a distinguished colonial family, Leverett Saltonstall understood that the practice of genealogy was usually associated with the colonial gentry's attempts to secure social status within the British Empire. In the context of postrevolutionary America's future-oriented egali-

42

tarianism, genealogy had no rightful function but challenged the dominant republican ideology.

By the mid-nineteenth century, however, the search for roots had become acceptable and even popular in the American republic. "Sober and practical America" was "the largest present producer" of genealogies, an observer noted in 1856. "The number of family records, or genealogical monographs," was "much larger in America than in aristocratic England." The celebrated British genealogist Sir Bernard Burke concurred, claiming that "Massachusetts [was] more genealogical than Yorkshire." Thousands of Americans were exploring their pedigrees, and Boston, unlike London, could even sustain "a magazine devoted exclusively to genealogy."[2]

This transformation of the genealogical landscape had no equivalent in Europe, where the pursuit of pedigrees remained dominated by a concern for social status and distinction. In contrast, antebellum America's passion for genealogy originated in the growing significance of the family as a moral, social, and political unit in the new republic. Genealogy allowed Americans to deal with the tensions imposed by ever-changing economic and family settings, and with the physical and affective distance and distress caused by geographic mobility. As the nation matured and as pride in its origin grew, pedigrees also helped Americans understand their local and national history and situate it in larger ideological and memorial contexts. This entire process democratized the practice of genealogy, in effect creating a new genealogical regime dominated by middle-class, family-related, republican moral concerns while reinforcing many Americans' sense of self as individuals and citizens.

❖   ❖   ❖

A major outcome of the revolutionary era was the "changes [it brought] in the realm of belief and attitude." To be sure, relations to hierarchy and deference shown had been shifting for some time in British North America, but it was only after the Revolutionary War that the triumphant republican ideology privileged the common good, equality, and citizens' virtue. Although social distinctions were not disputed, participation in public life was to be determined not by rank but, as Thomas Shippen of Philadelphia put it, by "capacity, disposition, and virtue."[3]

By the 1780s it was clear how far the new republic had gone in its effort to break free of prerevolutionary assumptions about the connection between lineage and social eminence. In 1783, as a means of offering ongoing fellowship and mutual assistance, a group of prominent officers of the Continental army formed the Society of the Cincinnati. According to the society's constitution, membership would be hereditary, passing down to each man's "eldest male posterity, and in failure thereof, the collateral branches, who may be judged worthy of becoming its supporters and Members."[4]

Even though George Washington agreed to serve as its president general, the Cincinnati—soon numbering some 2,300 members organized in state societies in thirteen states and in France—aroused public furor. True to the spirit of revolutionary-era pamphleteering, critics like Aedanus Burke of South Carolina charged that the society created "a race of hereditary patricians or nobility." Burke predicted that "a hereditary peerage" would "be settled as firmly in each potent family, and rivetted in our government, as any order of nobility is in the monarchies of Europe." In sum, the society's creation was a divorce "from our open professions of republicanism." In March 1784 the legislature of Massachusetts condemned the Cincinnati "for tending, if unrestrained, to *Imperium in Imperio.*"

Resistance to the society was particularly strong in New England, but the president of the Cincinnati's Rhode Island branch, Nathanael Greene, acknowledged that "all the inhabitants in general throughout the United States" were opposed to the Cincinnati.[5]

The Cincinnati promptly abolished the hereditary membership provision that had caused the greatest furor and soon disappeared from public view, but the polemic confirmed the new republican climate. Even those Americans who had displayed genealogical curiosity before the Revolution knew that times had changed. Interest in ancestors now seemed unacceptably aristocratic. Therefore, when George Washington received a letter from Sir Isaac Heard, Garter King of Arms, with a genealogical sketch of the Washington family, he passed on the information to relatives and corresponded politely with Heard but was quick to point out that he had little interest in the matter. Thomas Jefferson, whose efforts to procure a coat of arms in England in 1771 were described in Chapter 1, opposed the Cincinnati because he thought that American institutions should be built on "the natural equality of man, the denial of every preeminence but that annexed to legal office, & particularly the denial of a preeminence by birth."[6]

Many in the first generation of Americans questioned the compatibility of genealogy and republicanism. They feared that the practice of genealogy would endanger the nation's collective identity. When Jefferson began his autobiography in 1821, he mentioned the tradition in his father's family that it had come from Wales and the fact that his mother's Randolph family traced "their pedigree back in England & Scotland," but he hastened to add, good republican as he had become, "to which let every one ascribe the faith & merit he chooses." Visiting New York City in 1833, the Scottish traveler Thomas Hamilton attended a play that ridiculed "a pompous old baronet, very proud of his family, and exceedingly tenacious of respect," who had the "folly to imagine the attractions of his person and pedigree irresistible." The audience went home "full of contempt for the English aristocracy, and chuckling at the thought that there are no baronets in America."[7]

American genealogists acknowledged the magnitude of the problem. Genealogy conflicted with the demand for equality and the interest in the future rather than the past that saturated American culture at the time. In the public mind, genealogy was associated with a conception of distinction and status that emphasized ancestral worth, not personal worth. It contradicted one of the central tenets of the dominant republican ideology, the idea that individual merit mattered more than birth. Consequently, genealogy was suspect ideologically as long as it remained associated with a quest for social status. One author captured the essence of the genealogy dilemma in the 1850s when he asked how "in this land of equality, where every man is as good as every other, can it be possible that any man believes his ancestors to have been greater and better than himself and his friends?" The answer to the question was so obvious that "to speak of American genealogy" seemed "at first sight a positive misnomer."[8]

An interest in lineage also stood in contradiction with the apparent dismissal of tradition that defined late eighteenth- and early nineteenth-century American culture. From Thomas Jefferson to Abraham Lincoln, Americans liked "the dreams of the future better than the history of the past," as Jefferson once remarked to John Adams. Many Americans agreed with the contemporary emphasis on the nation's future-mindedness and heard Ralph Waldo Emerson's famous call to abandon "the sepulchres of the fathers," stop groping "among the dry bones of the past," and care for the living. "When I talk with a genealogist, I seem to sit up with a corpse," Emerson acidly noted in his diary in 1855.[9]

Both the republican imperative and the exhortation to look ahead put amateurs of family trees in a quandary. Like Leverett Saltonstall, some chose to pursue their interest discreetly. Peter Chardon Brooks, for instance, perhaps the richest Bostonian of the 1830s, acquainted Lemuel Shattuck with his genealogy but requested that his correspondent not disclose the source of his information. Others understood that the tensions and contradictions between the republican emphasis on the youth of the country and the American taste for pedigree could be resolved, but only if Americans imagined acceptable forms and contexts for displaying their genealogical interest.[10]

*   *   *

The family provided such a context. Just as colonials had relied on genealogy to build and reinforce a world of kin, so independent Americans refined, extended, and justified genealogical pursuits within the family sphere. A new conception of the family as a discrete social unit emerged in the late eighteenth century. It was viewed as a refuge from the outside world in an ever-changing environment, a private sphere where one's sentiments and sensibility could be legitimately expressed. As such, the family was invested with more significance than in the past.[11]

In this new domestic environment genealogy was justified as a family-related activity. Americans often emphasized that their genealogical quests contributed to their family's self-knowledge and long-term stability. Explaining his reasons for writing his family history, Joseph Sharpless of Philadelphia insisted in 1816 that the reason was not "a desire of exalting themselves, by publishing to the world, their imperfect and uninteresting history"; rather, "it arose from a desire in some of the family, to have a record preserved" of their ancestors' migration to America. Jedediah Herrick of Maine published a family genealogy in 1846, hoping that it would serve as "a medium of recognition and intercommunication among relatives otherwise strangers and unknown." Family genealogy was becoming a matter of curiosity, knowledge, morality, and remembrance.[12]

Like their colonial predecessors, antebellum Americans wrote the names of their ascendants and descendants in their family Bibles. As the trade in religious books expanded dramatically in the postrevolutionary decades, millions of Bibles entered American households. Throughout the fast-growing United States countless surviving family records reveal the widespread habit of inscribing genealogical details in these sacred and familiar books. To ease record keeping, commercial publishers began in the 1790s to add preprinted blank family records in their Bibles. Isaiah Thomas's 1791 folio Bible included a simple form, but nineteenth-century publishers competing in an increasingly commercial market inserted illustrated genealogical blank forms, which testified to the genre's popularity, in their Bibles.[13]

Other ways to record genealogical memory and convey family documentation evolved as well. During the colonial era genealogical representations had been an upper-class preserve; by the late eighteenth and early nineteenth centuries middling New Englanders revealed an intense genealogical self-consciousness. Calligraphers and engravers created unique or printed family registers as wall hangings for avid customers. Young girls embroidered family trees. Similar attitudes induced Pennsylvania German families to preserve their culture of Fraktur certificates, now often preprinted forms or family registers that were subsequently filled out, hand colored, and illuminated. These diverse objects avowed the family's unity, intensity, and durability.[14]

Younger family members often sought family history from relatives. In 1789 James Ball of Virginia wrote to a nephew that he had given him "as full an account of our Family as my Father's recollection & the papers in our possession would admit of." Manning Redfield took advantage of a visit to his ancestral home in 1819 to inquire about his great-grandfather. Elias Warner Leavenworth's genealogical curiosity was stimulated when he was a senior at Harvard College in 1823 and met a great-uncle with a long memory. Soon the young man and his brother William knew "a very general genealogy of the family," as well as names of other relatives, to whom they wrote during the next five years with inquiries.[15]

Sometimes a tragic event—the loss of a parent or a spouse, for instance—triggered a newfound desire to record a family history. Loyal Case, an 18-year-old Vermonter, wrote his "minutes of his Fathers Family" in 1825 because he was "the only one left of the Family." Within a few months of his brother Ezekiel's death in April 1829, Daniel Webster, fully conscious that he was "the sole survivor" of his family, began an autobiography that traced him back to the seventeenth-century colonist Thomas Webster, the "earliest ancestor" of whom he possessed "any knowledge." Webster knew little of his ancestors and could only surmise that they came from Scotland. Until his wife Ann Logan died in 1843, Anthony Charles Cazenove was not interested in his family history either. One week after her death, however, he wrote a nine-page memoir of his youth in Switzerland, subsequent migration to the United States, marriage, and the birth of his children and grandchildren, hoping to give her life and death a specific context.[16]

Many authors of genealogical memoirs worried lest the knowledge they had of the family's past would disappear with them. "What is known to this, may otherwise be unknown, to the next generation," former U.S. senator Jonathan Roberts of Pennsylvania explained in his memoirs. Rachel Price of Pennsylvania, knowing that she was the only survivor of her family, kept genealogical tables and wrote a history of her Kirk ancestors. Elizabeth Tucker Coalter Bryan of Virginia wished to preserve the memory of her deceased father, Judge John Coalter, by passing on his history to the next generation.[17]

African American slaves shared these concerns, although they seldom committed them to paper during the antebellum era. As Frederick Douglass remarked, "Genealogical trees do not flourish among slaves." Kinship mattered in slave communities, however, and fugitive narratives suggest that many slaves retained memories of kin and forebears in their minds despite forced separation and family disruptions. Genealogical awareness became one of the many strategies slaves used to fight the actual and symbolic violence of slavery. Some named their children after their immediate or distant blood kin and ancestors. Like enslaved Africans during the late colonial and early federal periods, others revealed the extent of their social memory when they were suing for their freedom. One petitioner in 1808 could identify four generations of women ancestors, going back to the early eighteenth century. Another slave in 1834 had genealogical memories of her grandmother in the 1780s. Antebellum trials of racial determination, later records of the Freedmen's Bureau, and interviews with former slaves during the 1930s suggest that these were not isolated instances but forms of genealogical awareness carried by many slaves. Knowledge of a familial past ranged from sketchy to detailed, not unlike that of many white Americans.[18]

While African Americans turned to genealogical memory to re-inforce their sense of self in the context of enslavement, some white Americans elaborated moral arguments in order to justify the practice of family history. In the 1840s a New England clergyman convinced his father and namesake Jotham Sewall, who had been born in 1760, "to prepare a sketch of his life" because "the living may be benefited by the dead." The older Sewall accordingly opened his autobiography with a genealogy in biblical mode in order to emphasize its moral and religious dimension: "My father's name was Henry, son of Nicholas, son of John, son of Henry, son of Henry, son of Henry Sewall, Esq., who was some time mayor of the city of Coventry in England." Because the postrevolutionary ideal family was as much a moral as a social unit, many Americans viewed family history as a morality tale. They did not assume that moral worth would be passed on from one generation to the next through some hereditary mechanism, but many would have agreed with Thomas Coffin Amory's notion that "the virtues & vices . . . of one's progenitors good or bad rightly used may prove of invaluable service to descendants either as an example or a caution." In the words of a New York City clergyman, since "an honourable family connexion" was "a worldly blessing" provided to "his offspring" by "the faith and holiness of some ancestor near or remote," it justi-fied exhibiting such ancestors. Genealogical knowledge provided an education in morality, one orator argued, because the past was "parent to the future." Genealogy had "a far higher object than to gratify an idle curiosity."[19]

Moral arguments opened up the possibility of making private genealogies public precisely on moral grounds. Despite Luke Steb-bins's pioneering example in 1771, most genealogists of the post-revolutionary decades did not publish their pedigrees. Judge George

Thacher of Massachusetts, for instance, devoted himself enthusi-astically to genealogy but kept his work to himself. Beginning in the 1810s, however, a growing number of genealogists committed their family histories to print, often emphasizing a moral aim. Thach-er's nephew James, a distinguished Revolutionary War veteran, published his sketches of the Thacher family in the 1830s because he thought that "the descendants of the Puritan fathers of New-England" had "a peculiar interest in the character and transactions of their ancestors."[20]

Not all Americans agreed with this notion that family history was valuable, and many remained either indifferent to or suspicious of genealogy. "I was not aware that there was importance enough attached to the stock bearing our name to become the subject of a book," William Shattuck wrote in 1853. "The race has been remark-able for nothing that I know of but modesty (I mean past genera-tions)," concurred William Bullard in 1855, "& I would not do vio-lence to this trait by any ambitious biography of those who are gone." Like many other amateurs of pedigree hunting, Jonathan Brown Bright, a retired businessman and broker in Waltham, Massachu-setts, lamented his family's lack of interest in genealogy: "Nobody but myself cares tu pence about it.... They are not genealogists constitutionally."[21]

Members of one group of Americans, however, were often "gene-alogists constitutionally": women. Their role as stewards of family memory grew in the revolutionary and postrevolutionary decades as the ideology of republicanism placed them at center stage. The training of women as stewards of family memory began at a young age. As of the mid-eighteenth century, girls and young women edu-cated in New England schools and female academies painted or embroidered genealogical representations, which they called family records, family registers, or samplers. The growing demand for needlework or watercolor and ink genealogical objects suggested that the transmission of family identity and memory was not solely an upper-class preserve but mattered to ordinary New Englanders as well.[22]

Young women translated these expectations into a language of genealogical symbols and representations. Needlework samplers and other family records bespoke the need to emphasize family unity and the weight of genealogical descent in a period of rapid social change. Thus New England women used symbols like vines, touching hearts, or links. Soon a popular motif was the tree—long a genealogical symbol in Europe but one seldom found in colonial North America. Yet in postrevolutionary New England, by the early nineteenth century, the tree became ubiquitous in family registers, some of which offered exceptionally detailed representations. The family tree of Moses and Lydia Emery of Newbury, Massachusetts, likely made around 1820, represented five generations of Emerys: Moses and Lydia (who had both died before 1800), their ten children, about forty grandchildren, a hundred great-grandchildren, and six great-great-grandchildren.[23]

As they grew older, many women remained active keepers of genealogical memory. "The subject on which you write," Anna Saltonstall explained to her brother Leverett, "I have ever felt interested in." Numerous women devoted themselves to the preservation of family history. Some, like Mary Ann Dickerson, a free African American woman in Philadelphia, kept a family record. Others, like Sarah Thompson and her daughter Rebecca Dunn of Pennsylvania, added genealogical details to their commonplace books. A few even published their family genealogy, as the Vermonter Sarah Robinson, then 52 years old, did in 1837. "The hearts of fathers should be turned to the children, and the hearts of children should be turned to the father," she quoted from the Old Testament (Mal. 4:6), hoping her "little compilation" would "assist to awaken and perpetuate kind and kindred feelings."[24]

Many single women specialized in keeping alive their family's historical and genealogical memory. Perhaps they felt that they were fulfilling a sense of civic obligation comparable to the mission entrusted to married women in the young republic to raise their children as virtuous citizens. Like Ralph Waldo Emerson's beloved "Amita" (his aunt Mary Moody Emerson), these women found in family lineage a source of personal identity as much as a treasure to revere and pass on to younger generations. Many nephews and nieces owed them their understanding of family origins and celebrated, like John Kelly of New Hampshire, the "good old maiden aunt, who kept in her head the records and genealogy of the family" and told him of his family's Irish origin. Despite all his proclaimed future-mindedness and apparent contempt for genealogy ("It is my own humor to despise pedigree"), Emerson knew his debt to the "kind Aunt" who told him "oft of the virtues of her and mine ancestors." His genealogical interests were strong enough that in 1822 he began recording genealogical information in a notebook. Even Emerson could not escape the increasing importance of genealogy in the family sphere.[25]

❊   ❊   ❊

The nation's westward extension and its growing temporal distance from the Revolution reinforced the legitimacy of family-related genealogy. Beginning in the 1760s and accelerating in the 1780s and the 1800s, Americans went west.[26] Westward migration extended kin ties both for those who left and for those who stayed behind. Sometimes quite literally, family records and memories stretched over geographic distance. "As I am not in possession of a record of my ancestors; and as my father settled in Seneca Co. N.Y. in 1795, at a great distance from all other branches of the name, my account must be brief," William Shattuck lamented in 1853. "I cannot find any record, of any papers of my Father's, they were left in my Brother's care, & were carried with us to the West," wrote Elinor Kinsman in 1840. "I presume many of them were left there, as our Furniture & many other things were."[27]

Frontier conditions may not have been conducive to archival preservation, but within a generation or two they did not prevent westerners from developing a desire to track family roots. Jesse Grant's father, a Revolutionary War veteran from Windsor, Connecticut, migrated at the war's end to Pennsylvania and then to Ohio and Kentucky. A tanner by trade, Jesse Grant was an avid and self-educated reader who "took a great interest" in genealogy, according to his son Ulysses. When questioned about his familial origins, Abraham Lincoln confessed ignorance ("We have a vague tradition, that my great-grand-father went from Pennsylvania to Virginia, and that he was a Quaker") but expressed curiosity: "If you shall be able to trace any connection between yourself and me, or, in fact, whether you shall or not, I should be pleased to have a line from you at any time."[28]

Even those Americans who did not go west experienced the effects of increased geographic mobility and distance. This was made quite clear in 1853 by Sylvanus Adams, a cotton-mill agent in Chicopee, Massachusetts, who wrote to a Brookfield correspondent that he was aware of his connections there and felt "quite anxious at times, to trace out the genealogical connection between the different branches of the Adams family." Although Adams was a profit-minded industrialist, he wanted to assess his ties to a rural, family past and keep track of the comings and goings of his now-extended family networks.[29]

Territorial expansion and geographic mobility nurtured family-centered genealogical activities, as did a growing temporal distance from the revolutionary decades. Between the 1780s and the 1820s public memory of the war went from celebrating a small group of heroes fighting a people's war to expressing gratitude to a mass of humble veterans of the Continental army. National gratitude translated first into bounty-land warrants and later into pensions—both affecting potentially thousands of revolutionary veterans and their widows. Although these laws sometimes created controversy and even scandals—the 1818 Revolutionary War Pension Act, for example, led to widespread fraud before it was amended—they stimulated a new genealogical awareness as well.[30]

Applicants, particularly the thousands of veterans' widows who applied for pensions following congressional legislation in the 1830s, had to produce evidence of their claim. In many cases, doing so was easy. Widows had Bible records or family registers in their possession and included them in their applications. Sometimes they had to recover these records from other family members or produce affidavits of their contents. When Elizabeth Anderson's husband died, his family Bible was sold at the settlement of his estate. Fortunately for the Virginia veteran's widow, her son William bought back the book and gave her the family record she needed for her pension application. Other widows had to hire a lawyer and start serious investigations. The same was true for bounty-land claimants. Whether they wanted to occupy the land they claimed or, as most did, to resell it to warrant brokers, they had to prove entitlement, which often meant heirship. The Virginia lawyer Thomas Green worked for dozens of such claimants in the 1830s, collecting affidavits of evidence of military service, searching for heirs, proving genealogical links between them, and drawing family trees in his ledger book.[31]

Claims for pensions and bounty lands reinforced family-centered pursuits, but they also suggested a new relationship of genealogy to the American nation and to civic identity. Genealogies established a claimant's rightful place in the past, as well as his justified reward from his fellow citizens. Family trees helped root individuals in the nation, and thus establishing them became a patriotic pursuit.

❊   ❊   ❊

Even as the republican imperative for self-fashioning and the exhortation to look ahead persisted in the young nation, Americans established institutions that would seek and preserve materials from the founding generation and promote the "shaping of a national tradition." Both the Massachusetts Historical Society (1791) and the New-York Historical Society (1804) had national ambitions despite their local names, as did the American Antiquarian Society (1812). The historians David Ramsay and Mercy Otis Warren narrated the glorious struggle for independence, while Mason Locke Weems's *Life of Washington* (1800) initiated a new historical genre— biographies of prominent Americans—that was to seduce nineteenth- and twentieth-century readers. Fourth of July orations occasioned tributes to revolutionary heroes—powerful stories instilling national pride in the crowds that had gathered to hear them.[32] By the 1810s and 1820s many Americans began to feel "a new sense of the relationship between the present and the past," a simultaneous awareness of distance from and kinship with "what came before." This "paradoxical relationship" not only inspired the literary imaginations of such writers as Ralph Waldo Emerson, Nathaniel Hawthorne, and Henry Wadsworth Longfellow but also stimulated local history (or, as it was then called, antiquarianism) and genealogy.[33]

Antiquarians were mostly New Englanders. Although historical societies were created in such southern states as Virginia (1831), Louisiana (1836), and Georgia (1839), most declined after a few years and had to be revived at regular intervals during the antebellum era. No cohort of southern antiquarians emerged, and the great issues of historical preservation were hardly broached in the South. In the mid-Atlantic states local historians mounted significant efforts in both New York and Pennsylvania, but only in New England did antiquarians form a group remarkable for its size and the volume of its productions. Their domination allowed them to connect local and national history and to argue successfully that New England's history was the history of the nation in the making. In addition to collecting local records, early antiquarians published the first town histories and family genealogies.[34]

By the early 1820s the pioneering labors of the previous decade were followed by more numerous efforts. "We have just discovered that we have ancestors," Nathaniel A. Haven of Portsmouth rejoiced in 1823. John Farmer, his New Hampshire antiquarian friend, agreed that there was "a spirit of historical research and inquiry excited, which we have seen at no former period." Daniel Webster's celebrated oration at Plymouth—delivered on December 11, 1820, almost on the occasion of the bicentennial of the Pilgrims' landing there—marked a turning point. "It is a noble faculty of our nature which enables us to connect our thoughts, our sympathies, and our happiness with what is distant in place or time" and "to hold communion at once with our ancestors and our posterity." Webster not only offered a brilliant justification for local history but also articulated a conception of genealogy that linked history and morality. Although "there often is . . . a regard for ancestry, which nourishes only a weak pride," Webster insisted that "there is also a moral and philosophical respect for our ancestors, which elevates the character and improves the heart."[35]

Echoes of Webster's eloquence at Plymouth Rock reverberated throughout New England. The creation of new historical societies in Rhode Island, Maine, and New Hampshire in 1822 and 1823 registered the shifting climate. In New Hampshire, for instance, the success of the Plymouth bicentennial persuaded local antiquarians to link the founding of a historical society and the celebration of the 1623 arrival of English colonists in what later became New Hampshire. There, as elsewhere, the antiquarian impulse nurtured genealogy. Many genealogists of the 1820s and 1830s were antiquarians first, who began creating networks. Central to this process was John Farmer of New Hampshire, celebrated nine years after his death of consumption in 1838 in the initial issue of the first genealogical journal in the United States as "the most distinguished Genealogist and Antiquary of this country."[36]

In 1829 Farmer published *The Genealogical Register of the First Settlers of New England,* the first genealogical volume published in America that extended beyond one person or a single family. It quickly established Farmer as America's leading genealogist. Some 352 pages long, the *Register* included "the names of a large portion of the First Settlers, of the most prominent, as well as the more humble," in hundreds of entries arranged in alphabetical order.

Alongside magistrates, ministers, colonial deputies and representatives, and graduates of Harvard College, it listed the freemen
admitted to the colony from 1630 to 1662, as well as "the names of
all such Emigrants, both freemen and non-freemen, as could be
collected, who had come over to the several colonies before 1643."
A fellow antiquarian commented, "It is considered a wonderful
book—a monument of patient research to the compiler."[37]

Even more important than the *Genealogical Register* was Farmer's
remarkable talent for promoting the cause of genealogy and antiquarianism. Because of his precarious health, correspondence was
his lifeline. He maintained a list of his correspondents and kept
careful records and statistics of letters he wrote and received concerning the ancestors of his contemporaries. He constantly prod-
ded his correspondents to support antiquarian and genealogical
enterprises and worked to draw New England antiquarians and
genealogists into a network of the like-minded. When Joshua Coffin wrote Farmer about his projected genealogy, Farmer hastened
to pull John Kelly into the search for missing material: Coffin
"states that he has a genealogy of the Coffins from 1580 to the present time, including about a thousand names," he wrote. "He wishes
to know something respecting Rev. Peter Coffin, of East Kingston,
and Charles and Nathaniel Coffin, who graduated at Dartmouth
College in 1799. Can you give any information of them?"[38]

Farmer's genealogical network was considerably enhanced when
in April 1825 he issued a circular letter that described his proposal
for a "General Biographical Dictionary" and requested assistance
from his correspondents. Letters soon poured in from various
quarters, sometimes lacking genealogical information but more
often offering encouragement and materials. For the next four and
a half years, preparation of the "dictionary" drew New England

genealogists together in a common enterprise and stimulated interest in ancestors among individuals who had never considered the matter before. "I approve of your undertaking," Samuel C. Allen wrote from Greenfield. "It has multum in parvo" [much in little]. The Boston lawyer Francis Jackson explained that he had passed on Farmer's circular with a request for genealogical materials to Patrick Tracy Jackson of Waltham and Lowell fame.[39]

Some New Englanders were pleased to discover that their own family history was of interest to others. Edward Bangs, who had written a memorandum about his ancestry, was surprised when James Savage requested the material for Farmer's intended *Register,* never having supposed that it "could be of any other consequence than as a matter of curiosity to our own family." Like Bangs, Ralph Waldo Emerson went to some length to satisfy Farmer's demands. He sent him a sermon by his ancestor Rev. Joseph Emerson but lamented that "the rev. preacher considered the spiritual wants of the Malden yeomen & not the antiquarian curiosity of Dr Farmer or of his own great grand nephew & your poor servant." Emerson also reported that he had made inquiries of a relative and had questioned his aunt Mary Moody, "who is a very accurate person generally."[40]

Many other New Englanders requested family information from Farmer or provided it to him. When the *Genealogical Register* appeared in the late fall of 1829, regional interest in genealogy increased. Farmer's friend Joseph Willard accurately predicted when he supervised the printing of the *Register,* "You will incontinently set the *universal Yankee nation* to hunting out their pedigree." Former New Hampshire governor William Plumer called the *Register* "a vast treasury of historical facts," and Lemuel Shattuck termed it "a monument of patient research" and "an indispensable companion in my antiquarian researches." Interest in genealogy did not abate in the 1830s as Farmer envisioned a revised edition of his *Register* and continued to send and receive letters from men and women requesting and submitting genealogical information.[41]

*   *   *

The preparation, publication, and subsequent revision of Farmer's *Genealogical Register* transformed the practice of genealogy in the United States. Antiquarians defined genealogy as scholarship and agreed on a series of guidelines, practices, rules, and goals that defined the contours of their shared investigations. Unwilling to accept what they called "tradition" or "traditionary report" at face value, Farmer and his friends demanded that other "evidence"— that is, primary sources—be consulted as a critical supplement to and corrective of family lore. Antiquarian and genealogical claims must be substantiated, Farmer argued, and he insisted on the production of evidence. Nathaniel Adams's *Annals of Portsmouth*, published in 1825, was "a valuable work," but Farmer could not hide his disappointment. It ought to have included "copious notes" that recorded "genealogical *data* respecting the early families, by which their descendants might trace back in an interrupted line their descent to those who came over at the first." In contrast, Willard's *History of Lancaster* (1826) exhibited "that minuteness & accuracy of detail which could not but gratify one who reads every thing of the kind that comes in his way."[42]

Some of his correspondents apologized for not being able to answer his genealogical queries because, as one put it, "the only information" he had been able to obtain "has been traditional, and in some respects so contradictory as not to be relied on." Antiquarians learned to accept being "thrown into a perfect fog" when they found several individuals with the same first name and could not decide who the right one was. They wondered about the form or arrangement that would best allow a local history or genealogical memoir to provide satisfactory evidence of its claims. Farmer found a pamphlet on a Massachusetts family wanting in this respect: its "chronological arrangement" was "liable to several objections, but principally, that it separates a family into too many integral parts, & requires considerable care in calling out those necessary to make a genealogical series." After a critical look at several town histories—Andover's he found "dry and without arrangement," Dedham's "not popular at home, though it contains many good things," and Salem's "too confused"—Lemuel Shattuck confessed to being "somewhat perplexed in fixing on the plan of my proposed history" because he had "seen none I fully approve." What was he to do with individual genealogies, he wondered? The quest for the appropriate methods, style, and structure had begun.[43]

To the doubtful authority of oral tradition, antiquarians and genealogists opposed the evidence of primary sources, either public records or family papers. Given the paucity and lack of organization of most town records, antiquarians passed on advice and information to one another concerning how best to gain access. In Woburn, where records were "in chronological order," one had "to go over considerable ground to collect together the members of a single family," John Farmer warned a friend in 1823. In Exeter, John Kelly discovered that the registrar was "an old bachelor" who did not expect "that in centuries to come anybody will look back to him as a progenitor" and therefore was "not particularly disposed to encourage genealogical researches." Despite these difficulties, New England genealogists of the 1820s and 1830s made a point of exploring original materials. On one of the rare occasions when he left Concord, Farmer spent some time in Boston using the collections of the Massachusetts Historical Society, to his great delight. Looking at the "folios, quartos, octavos, and all sorts of *os* and *mos,* and yellow, musty and scrawling manuscripts" was, one observer noted at the time, "a real feast to an antiquarian."[44]

A scholarly approach to genealogy meant that results should not only be published but also discussed and criticized. No forum existed for such debates during the 1820s and 1830s except private epistolary exchanges among genealogists. The controversy about the Dudley genealogy is an example. In 1822 a descendant of Governor Thomas Dudley of Massachusetts (1576-1653) claimed that his ancestor was the son of the Duke of Leicester. John Farmer was skeptical—available sources listed Dudley as the son of a Capt. Roger Dudley—and he shared his concerns with his friend John Kelly, who also doubted the new finding. In subsequent years Kelly and Farmer exchanged jokes about the claims of "the *would-be* Earl of Leicester." In 1826 Farmer returned to the Dudley genealogy when he was preparing the *Register.* Governor Dudley probably "came from an honorable family in Northamptonshire," he concluded, not from nobility. "How mortifying it is, to a man ambitious of being considered as descended from the nobility of old," Kelly chuckled, "to have a prying antiquarian peeping into his genealogy, and proving, by musty old records, which should have been burned up long ago, that his ancestors were carpenters instead of 'barons bold.'"[45]

Antiquarians read and criticized one another's work. In true scholarly fashion, Farmer asked James Savage to go over the manuscript of the *Register.* During the fall of 1828 and the early months of 1829, Savage sent him long letters filled with corrections and suggestions. Farmer envisioned his work as a contribution to science and felt "some satisfaction to receive the approbation of competent judges." Farmer and his fellow antiquarians debated the book's title, considered how and by whom it should be printed, followed the manuscript through its various stages of publication, and ruminated about sales and marketing. After consulting with his friends and various printers, Farmer decided to publish his work by subscription. On 2 November 1829 Joseph Willard, who had supervised the whole process with what he called "almost parental tenderness and affection," announced the volume's publication. Farmer knew that his book was "*unique* in its character," and he hoped that "no one will condemn it without examination." He fully understood that his book had become a model and a reference— "the Revised code of genealogical descents," as Willard phrased it—for all future work. It opened up new perspectives and possibilities for future genealogists.[46]

Willard's expressions conveyed more than intellectual appreciation. Their common interest in genealogy created bonds of sympathy and sometimes of affection between antiquarians. They called each other "brother," "Mi frater," "my dear Antiquary," or "my truly good Friend." They exchanged information about recent or forthcoming books, especially those written by one of "the brethren." A few women joined Farmer's "growing network of antiquarians and genealogists," like Mary Clark, a Concord woman whose interest in genealogy was deeply rooted in her fondness for "mouldy things" and her strong moral and religious identity. Farmer's friends shared anecdotes and narratives of antiquarian discovery: "To one, like yourself, familiar with historical research," Alonzo Lewis of Lynn wrote Farmer, "it is unnecessary to say what satisfaction it affords, after having ransacked fifty libraries, spelt out the hieroglyphics of fifty antiquated records, and read all the gravestones for fifty miles, for the purpose of ascertaining a single fact—to have it suddenly imparted from an unexpected source." Answers to one's letters were eagerly awaited: "If you are dead, busy, or absent, say so," Lewis asked Farmer after he did not receive a response to a "long letter, containing the 'Second Chapter' of the account of the Farmers."[47] A corresponding society of like-minded souls had discovered their passion for family roots and initiated the genealogical project that would engage their fellow Americans thereafter.

❦   ❦   ❦

John Farmer and the early antiquarians with whom he corresponded helped redefine the meaning of historical time for their contemporaries. Although many Americans continued to focus on the future, they came to appreciate, and often to cherish, the past, especially as it related to their families. The ensuing depth that genealogy added to antebellum Americans' sense of time was usually limited to their ancestors' colonial experience. Alonzo Lewis spoke for many when he acknowledged his failure to trace his pedigree beyond the arrival of his immigrant progenitors to the colonies: "I have been able, with the utmost clearness, to trace my ancestors for five generations, up to their arrival in America, with the births and deaths, of all except the first."[48]

Antiquarians' interest in family history prompted recognition that new efforts would be required to develop their discipline. To do so, antiquarians established the first genealogical society and the first genealogical periodical in the United States—the New England Historic Genealogical Society (NEHGS) and the *New England*

Historical and Genealogical Register—in the 1840s. In their view, none of the existing historical societies met their needs. New England's oldest and most important organization, the Massachusetts Historical Society (MHS), was an elite institution with limited, exclusive membership and a focus that did not include genealogy. Because most genealogists were also antiquarians, some were members or corresponding members of the MHS, but they were not numerous. James Savage, then the president of the MHS, was an obvious example, as was Lemuel Shattuck. The American Antiquarian Society (founded in Worcester in 1812 by Isaiah Thomas) also did not serve the direct interests of genealogists, given its larger mission to collect Americana and encourage the study of the American past.[49]

The men who met in Boston in October 1844 to discuss the creation of a new organization did not fully agree on its goals, but all were passionate genealogists. John Wingate Thornton and Samuel Gardner Drake wanted the new society to blend history and genealogy; Charles Ewer favored genealogy and heraldry; only Lemuel Shattuck thought that the institution should be devoted exclusively to genealogy, perhaps because he was a member of the MHS, unlike his associates. Even as they chose the name New England Historical and Genealogical Society, they left the matter of its mission undecided. In March 1845 the General Court of Massachusetts granted the organization a charter, but under pressure from the MHS, its name was changed to New England Historic Genealogical Society.[50]

Over the next two decades the NEHGS grew slowly. Its founding 5 members had become 87 at the end of 1845, 143 a year later, and 449 in 1855. By no means was it an elite, exclusive society. It was controlled by the network of antiquarians and practicing genealogists who had created it. The NEHGS's first president was founding member Charles Ewer; a former bookstore owner and publisher who had lost much of his money in unfortunate real estate transactions, he was not among Boston's social elite. The bookseller Samuel Gardner Drake was an erudite antiquarian whose plainspoken personality also excluded him from Boston's upper echelons. The NEHGS operated as a learned society, with monthly meetings where historical and genealogical papers were read. Its most important contribution to genealogy during its early years was launching the *New England Historical and Genealogical Register* in 1847.[51]

In addition to its institutional legacy, that network of antiquarians helped ease the acceptance of genealogy in the United States. By the 1830s and 1840s American genealogy had become more frequently associated with erudite than aristocratic pursuits. Never had so many Americans been sensitive to the state of decay of public documents and private monuments or disposed to consider local lore as a treasured heirloom. When the second edition of Farmer's *Historical Sketch of Amherst, New Hampshire* was published in 1837, the discriminating *North American Review* commended him and his fellow antiquaries for their achievement "in collecting and preserving the fading memorials of our little democracies."[52]

Spurred by their efforts, hundreds of Americans were undertaking research into family history. In many cases the task was passed from one generation to the next. Manning Redfield, for instance, published "a little slip" about his family tree in 1819. Ten years later his kinsman William C. Redfield read it and began an investigation that led to publication of genealogical tables in 1839. In the 1840s John Howard Redfield undertook "a thorough revision" of the family genealogy, sending circulars "to all the scattered representatives of the family," transcribing town and church records, and eventually publishing the results in 1860.[53]

By the late 1840s approximately 45 family genealogies had appeared in print, and the 1850s added another 158. Many more were being prepared with no plans to publish them. Four books written by James Savage, Lemuel Shattuck, and William H. Whitmore symbolized the period's excitement about family histories. In 1841 and 1856, Shattuck published the first how-to books in the history of American genealogy, *A Complete System of Family Registration* and *Blank Book Forms for Family Registers*. He hoped to help ordinary Americans research their genealogy while teaching them how to maintain their records correctly. As "no proper system of registration" existed at the time, he had "prepared a system for his own use" and decided to make it available to others. In 1862 the young Whitmore, then 26 years old, published the first edition of his *Handbook of American Genealogy*, "a catalogue" that listed and assessed the books "treating on family history" published in the United States. A remarkable overview of the field's development, it established Whitmore's reputation instantly. Between 1860 and 1862 James Savage published his four-volume *Genealogical Dictionary of the First Settlers of New England*. Although he claimed modestly "to prosecute the genealogical pursuits of John Farmer," Savage knew that his reputation would depend on this book. "One initial letter in this dictionary required a year and a quarter for its complete preparation," he explained. In the final analysis, his *Genealogical Dictionary* was over 2,500 pages long and included "every settler, without regard to his rank, or wealth," who had arrived before 1692. According to the *North American Review*, it was "the most stupendous work on genealogy ever compiled." Savage agreed: "I have made a path easier for others."[54]

By the eve of the Civil War, genealogical curiosity was widespread and acceptable when it was framed in the language of republicanism.

"I disclaim all intent of magnifying individuals," claimed James Savage in the mid-1840s. "The humblest artisan or laborer, who partook in the glorious work of peopling our N.E. world, should be secure of his commemoration as much as Govrs. Winthrop, Haynes, or Eaton." This conception of a democratic genealogy was not limited to its birthplace, New England. "We may rejoice in being able to recite the humble narrative of our patriarch, and his immediate descendants," William Darlington of Pennsylvania noted in 1853, "with a just pride in the traditional family reputation, of plain, unpretending, old-fashioned integrity." True to his word, Darlington celebrated his family's "prosaic annals" and "mediocrity." "Within the last half-score of years," a reviewer for the *North American Review* remarked in 1856, "many modest men have been surprised by the receipt of letters written to them by entire strangers, asking for a communication of all the known particulars of their kinships, pedigrees, matrimonial alliances, and family histories."[55]

These queries by "entire strangers" differed from those of the 1820s in volume, not in content. James Savage worked for years with dozens of correspondents for his *Genealogical Dictionary*. From Sylvester Judd, "the distinguished antiquary of Northampton," he received "several hundred pages of letters." Between 1851 and the Civil War, Isaac W. K. Handy, a Maryland clergyman, sent "not less than two thousand pages of letters" to "persons in all parts of the land" for his projected genealogical study "of the Handys and Their Kindred." Henry Bond, a Philadelphia physician, antiquarian, and genealogist, addressed hundreds of similar letters between the mid-1830s and the mid-1850s. His correspondents often went to significant lengths to help him—writing letters, looking into family Bibles and records, searching court and town records, and talking to family members. Carlos Coolidge explained that he had postponed an answer to Bond's request because of his impression that he had "no memorials, or entries, of the facts you wished to ascertain." However, he had changed his mind and had undertaken "a thorough ransacking operation upon all means and resources in my possession." The result was impressive: he sent Bond eighteenth-century family records abstracted from his father's family Bible. Bond's correspondents were sometimes "very ignorant" of their pedigree but started genealogical research at his insistence. George Bowman, for instance, confessed in October 1853 that he could not "go back beyond [his] grandfather," but he then wrote to an uncle, visited a grandmother, consulted her family record, and sent five letters to Bond on the subject between March and August 1854.[56]

At times, answering Bond's letters became a collective enterprise that spread genealogical interest among family members. Nelson A. Bixby assured Bond that he had received his request but needed to contact relatives who lived in the West before he could answer. Six months later Bixby sent the information the family had collected. George A. Bond, a former tanner in Rome, Michigan, explained that his father had helped him collect the requested genealogical information. Women sometimes answered in lieu of their brothers, fathers, or husbands, although Mary Bond asked Henry to excuse her "boldness" for answering in lieu of her husband. Mary Bowman, a Pennsylvania woman, explained that her brother had never felt "an interest in the matter" and was about to answer Bond in the negative when she offered to take over. She, on the other hand, was interested in the past: "The customs, habits, manners, of these days made a strong impression on my memory, and I have always had a very great respect for New England, and felt proud of my Puritan decent."[57]

In several instances family members decided to create family associations and to organize family reunions. A newspaper reported in 1850 that it was "getting fashionable and profitable" throughout New England for those who could "trace their genealogy through a long ancestral line to a common parentage, to hold family meetings occasionally." Family reunions apparently began in the 1840s. The descendants and relatives of Holland Weeks of Vermont met in 1841 "to spend a few hours in social, mutual, unrestrained, & friendly intercourse," but also "to trace our genealogy from some of the first settlers in New England down to the present time." Other meetings followed in 1847, 1850, 1855, and 1860. The Haven family of Lynn, Massachusetts, met in 1844 to celebrate "the second centennial anniversary" of the landing of their ancestor. Reunion proceedings were published afterwards, and a second gathering was held five years later. Although many family reunions took place in New England, there also were some in Pennsylvania and New York.[58]

These reunions sometimes led to other projects. Henry W. Cushman, a Massachusetts businessman, politician, and genealogist, gathered "a few of the descendants of Robert Cushman, the Pilgrim," at Plymouth in mid-August 1855. Participants were expected to "stand on Plymouth Rock where our ancestors first landed in America," "make arrangements to erect a monument in Plymouth to the memory" of their ancestors, and perhaps "form an Association of their descendants for that and other purposes." About a thousand family members attended. The Cushman Monument Association was born in September 1855 and began to raise funds for the proposed "Granite Monument, 26½ feet in height, with inscriptions in bronze," which was completed and inaugurated in late 1858.[59]

✳   ✳   ✳

Henry W. Cushman succeeded in his plan to "erect a monument," but raising funds was difficult. Despite his repeated pleas and the contributions of some 300 family members, the Cushman monument left a deficit that underlined the still-incomplete insertion of genealogy in the market economy. Many genealogical artifacts, like the samplers embroidered by hundreds of New England young women as part of their school curriculum, were unique and carried no market value at the time. Existing markets for genealogy were local, and profit was limited. Like William Saville, a Cape Ann man who was at times town treasurer, town clerk, and schoolteacher, most genealogical artists who drew, painted, or engraved family trees had other occupations.[60]

The democratization of genealogy, however, suggested that it had a future in the market. Genealogical artists like Saville and others in New England, the mid-Atlantic states, and the South developed models they could reproduce to satisfy local customers, and engravers began to preprint genealogical registers or records for individual use. Ambrose Henkel of New Market, Virginia, printed genealogical broadsides. Richard Brunton engraved family registers in Connecticut and later in Massachusetts from the 1790s to his death in 1832. Brunton and fellow engravers Benjamin Blythe of Salem, William B. Annin of Boston, and Peter Maverick of New Jersey used copper plates for runs of about 100—an indication of the limited size of their market.[61]

By the 1820s and 1830s the printing firms of Daniel W. Kellogg in Hartford and Nathaniel Currier in New York City used the cheaper technology of lithography instead of the more expensive copper plates to develop business. Through direct and mail-order sales,

Currier and Ives family registers soon invaded American homes by the thousands, while Kellogg blank family trees were printed in magazines with large circulations. These same firms captured the market for other family-related objects, such as the lithograph memorials and mourning prints that flourished in the 1820s.[62]

Such mass-market family artifacts had little in common with the books published in growing numbers, mostly for their kinsmen, by amateur genealogists and antiquarians. In the 1850s many printed genealogies were still very similar to the one pioneered by John Farmer in 1829 for his *Genealogical Register*. Subscription printing was the rule, and money was often an issue. Lack of resources and severe personal conflicts imperiled the New England Historic Genealogical Society in the 1850s. The society's journal barely survived the decade. The readership's small size and the rugged personality of editor Samuel Gardner Drake endangered the *New England Historical and Genealogical Register* on several occasions. One sympathetic observer did not hide his pessimism. "It is a question whether the 'Register' will be published another year," he regretted in the early 1850s. "The society has no funds to carry out any project—is slightly in debt, and its Library closed for want of a Librarian."[63]

There were, however, signs of change and development elsewhere. Commercial publishing houses like Case, Tiffany and Company of Hartford and Dutton and Wentworth, Henry W. Dutton and Son, Crosby and Nichols, and James Munroe and Co. of Boston began to print genealogies. The Albany publisher Joel Munsell (1808–1880) began a distinguished career in the late 1840s as the country's premier genealogical publisher, publishing individual family histories and projects like Whitmore's 1862 *Handbook of American Genealogy* and saving the *New England Historical and Genealogical Register*, which was about to discontinue publication, in late 1861.[64]

The commercial enterprise of genealogy even extended to genealogical work itself. To be sure, most antebellum genealogists did not make any money from their work, and family genealogy was too much a moral activity to suggest profit. It was time-consuming, however, and it did not take long before some genealogists offered their services to rich but time-pressed pedigree hunters. Although this practice was rare during the antebellum period, it emerged as Americans attempted to trace their roots back in England. James Savage, John Farmer, and other early antiquarians had made epistolary inquiries in Great Britain as early as the 1810s; Savage used a tour of England in 1842 to collect genealogical data for friends like Lemuel Shattuck and for himself. In general, however, transatlantic research was difficult and costly. Israel Daniel Rupp, the historian of Pennsylvania who started a genealogical correspondence with German Rupps in the 1840s, was an exception. Many Americans had no idea where to look for records. New Englanders were long "content to reach the cabin of the Mayflower" and "to find an ancestor there." By the mid-1840s, however, demand had grown so much and had begun to extend so far back that it created the need for genealogists-for-hire.[65]

The first such professionals who worked for American clients in England were Britons, but the most important one was an American expatriate, Horatio Gates Somerby. Born in 1805 in Newburyport, Massachusetts, Somerby moved to Boston in the early 1820s "to learn the art of decorative painting." His true interests, however, lay in genealogy and heraldry, and when he visited England in the mid-1840s, he decided to make genealogy his profession. Until his death in 1872, he resided chiefly in England, becoming the first London correspondent of the New England Historic Genealogical Society while serving as secretary to the board of trustees of the

Peabody Fund established by his friend George Peabody. American genealogists who did not want or could not travel to England hired him to research their ancestors.[66]

During the 1850s and 1860s Somerby traveled throughout England on behalf of his American clients, filling notebook after notebook with information copied from parish registers, wills, and newspapers. He billed his employers for his time, travels, and the fees he paid to procure documents. Ordinary clients asked him to make genealogical investigations for a certain amount—one mentioned 30 to 50 dollars in 1856, another 100 to 200 dollars, and so on. Somerby usually asked for a retainer. He kept track of his expenses and accounts carefully, acknowledging the sums he received, sending detailed bills to his clients, and occasionally reminding them of what they owed him. Some rich Americans, like Abbott Lawrence or Lewis Tappan, were willing "to pay all charges" and were billed accordingly. "Many families in New-England are indebted to his researches for their first knowledge of their English ancestors," John Bradbury eulogized in 1874. By the 1880s, however, many of his rich clients' pedigrees were found to be fraudulent, the fruit of Somerby's imagination rather than his research.[67]

The figure of Horatio Gates Somerby suggested how far American genealogy had come since Leverett Saltonstall requested his sister Anna's discretion about genealogy in 1815. By the eve of the Civil War, family trees were familiar and legitimate in the United States as long as genealogists had their family or a moral and civic purpose in mind. In effect, genealogy underwent a process of democratization that had no equivalent in Europe. "What was diffidently essayed years since by a few," John Farmer's faithful friend Joseph Willard concluded, "has now become the pursuit of many."[68] At the same time, antebellum American genealogy bore the seeds of its own contradictions and ultimate demise. As entrepreneurs plied the trade for blank family registers or investigations on demand, democratization stimulated commercialization and helped develop a market that slowly undermined its presumed moral foundations. As countless middle-class individuals searched for their ancestors, patrician Americans sought to develop different genealogical strategies to distinguish themselves from their fellow citizens and to challenge the notion of democratic genealogy.

❧ 3 ❧

ANTEBELLUM BLOOD AND VANITY

Herman Melville's novel *Pierre; or, The Ambiguities* (1852) opens with a remarkable assertion of "the great genealogical and real-estate dignity of some families in America." Pierre, the hero, is the scion of a prestigious lineage and the heir to a Hudson Valley mansion and domain. He is a representative of those Americans who could easily "compare pedigrees with England." Among them were the many New England families who could "trace their uninterrupted English lineage" far back in history, the old planter families of the South, and the manorial families of the Hudson Valley, like Pierre's. Withal, the narrator concludes, "Our America will make out a good general case with England in this short little matter of large estates, and long pedigrees—pedigrees, I mean, wherein there is no flaw."[1]

Melville's mordant irony hints that the antebellum democratization of genealogy did not completely displace the colonial taste for status-based pedigree. Melville knew it firsthand, for his father Allan Melvill (the family added the final *e* in the 1830s) liked to boast about his aristocratic ancestry despite his impeccable re-

78

publican family credentials. Allan Melvill's father, Thomas, migrated from Scotland to New England in 1761, attended the College of New Jersey (later Princeton University), and became a friend of Samuel Adams and a player in the revolutionary events of the 1770s (he took part in the Boston Tea Party and fought in the Revolutionary War). Thomas Melvill later became a U.S. congressman and a distinguished member of Boston's postrevolutionary elite. Allan Melvill's patrician father-in-law, Peter Gansevoort of Albany, was an even more formidable figure, a Revolutionary War hero who had risen to the rank of brigadier general.[2]

Despite this patriotically perfect family background, Allan Melvill was obsessed with his lineage and decided to prove his "long pedigree." One year before his son Herman's birth, in 1818, he sailed to Great Britain for business and genealogical reasons. In St. Andrews he rejoiced to have found traces of his ancestors in the university's records. Visiting the Melville family seat, he met with the Earl of Leven and Melville and tartly wrote to his wife that "this whole property should have come to my father as heir at law." Melvill did some genealogical research that allowed him to write a few months later to the Earl of Leven and Melville about their lineage connection and announce the news to his wife. "It appears evident," he wrote to her, "that I am sprung from a gentle & a royal line of ancestry on both sides from my Father & Mother." On the paternal side he boasted of an ancestor who was "Brother to Queen Margarett wife of Malcolm Carnbee who came with her from Hungary in 1060"; on his mother's side he found another ancestor who "was Brother to a Queen of Norway." Melvill's interest in lineage did not abate in the 1820s even as the New York dry-goods merchant struggled to avoid the commercial failure that finally hit him in 1830. When he sent his son to live with his brother-in-law

Gansevoort in 1826, he described the 7-year-old Herman as an "honest hearted double roosted Knickerbocker of the true Albany stamp" who "would do equal honor in due time to his ancestry, parentage, and kindred."[3]

      ❦   ❦   ❦

Allan Melvill suggested how genealogy could be associated with an aristocratic sensibility. This temptation did not dominate antebellum America, but it was powerful enough to be noticed by some Americans and many foreign visitors during those decades. Catharine Read Williams, the author of a novel set in New York during the Jefferson administration, *Aristocracy; or, The Holbey Family* (1832), deplored that "the spirit of aristocracy" was so prevalent among all classes of American society. Her novel, a satire of Federalist pretension, described the rise and fall of Augustus Holbey during the Jefferson administration. Holbey's parents, a Scottish drummer and a camp woman, had deserted the English side during the Revolutionary War and removed to New England, where they became innkeepers. As little Augustus grew up, his parents began to regret that they had left England, where he could have been educated as a gentleman. Augustus went to college and then moved to Philadelphia, where he could "boast of his *English ancestry*, without the fear of detection." In Williams's tale, Holbey entered politics as a Federalist who attacked his opponents without scruples and ended as a traitor to his country. A would-be aristocrat in a republican country, Holbey was a failure, but also a representative of American status ambitions.[4]

Williams obviously had little regard for such individuals, whom she considered a menace in a republican society. In the mid-1840s her *Annals of the Aristocracy* denounced the "spurious, upstart, mongrel kind of *nobility*" who had forgotten their modest beginnings and displayed contempt for middling-class Americans. Williams explained that she intended to reveal the vanity of their pretentions by publicizing their true origins. Others criticized Federalists who claimed to be "the nobility of the land" and imitated "the ridiculous peculiarities of that purse-proud caste in other countries"—tracing "back their pedigree with as much family pride," and displaying equal contempt for "admixture or association with the people at large."[5]

American interest in aristocracy, lineage, and hereditary status was a commonplace in the writings of foreign observers of the United States. The viscount François-René de Chateaubriand derided American "plebeian nobles" who spoke constantly of "their ancestors, proud barons, bastards apparently and companions of William the Bastard." As the French writer and diplomat, whose *Memoirs* opened on his truly aristocratic pedigree, noted ironically, "They display the knightly blazons of the Old World, enriched with the serpents, lizards, and parrots of the New." When Frederick Marryat, an English Tory who toured the United States in the late 1830s, visited the White Sulphur Springs (now in West Virginia), he felt there "how excessively aristocratical and exclusive" Americans could be.[6]

The Austrian-born commentator Francis J. Grund, in his perceptive social satire *Aristocracy in America* (1839), emphasized how Americans worshipped European nobility, and he ridiculed a New Yorker who had bought portraits in Europe "in order to form a whole gallery of ancestors." Of particular note were the many Americans who enjoyed the company of Old World aristocrats and came home from their European tour displaying heraldic insignia and despising equality. "No people on earth are more proud of their ancestors," he concluded, "than those fashionable Americans who can prove themselves descended from respectable fathers and grandfathers."[7]

Grund was convinced of the long-term success of democracy, but he recognized that an aristocratic conception of genealogy survived in Jacksonian America. Whatever its long-term fate, aristocratic genealogy concerned a visible set of antebellum Americans. Lineage consciousness delineated the contours of proper society, excluding the many and comforting the few in their social pretensions. Descendants of elite colonial families, at least those who had not chosen the Loyalist cause too visibly during the Revolutionary War, relied on genealogy to help them wage a culture war against democratization, cultivate nostalgia, and preserve exclusivity. John Randolph of Roanoke, for instance, the formidable and eccentric Virginia conservative, studied his ancestry carefully and knew all about his descent from Pocahontas. Shortly before he died in 1833, he startled a visitor by giving him "a very minute account of his own genealogy, up to William the Conqueror."[8]

A map of antebellum aristocratic genealogy would have revealed exceptional concentrations in the major port cities of the colonial period (from New England to Georgia), as well as in the manorial Hudson Valley and the plantation South. One commentator observed in the mid-1850s, "Virginia has her first families; New York her Patroons and names of ancient honor; and New England has had Winthrops, Wyllyses, Adamses, and Phillipses, leaders by ancestral prescription in politics and society."[9] In cities like Philadelphia and Charleston, aristocratic genealogy often reflected disgust with the country's evolution and a bitter realization that both cities were inexorably overshadowed by rivals. Replete with feelings of relative decline, elite Charlestonians and Philadelphians chose to emphasize lineage distinction, which fed their sense of alienation from contemporary America. Most antebellum observers agreed with a visiting Englishwoman's remark that "the Philadelphians claim being the first in rank in society of any town in the States." Nowhere was "there so much fuss made about lineage and descent" as in Philadelphia, another British visitor noted. Society was divided into sets of persons who did not mingle. Although it was difficult to ascertain "the grounds of their distinctions," there were families "whose claims [were] universally, although perhaps unwillingly, acknowledged."[10]

Philadelphia's title to lineage prominence was widely recognized since the 1790s, when the city had enjoyed the status of state and federal capital. "Among the uppermost circles in Philadelphia," the Irishman Isaac Weld remarked at the time, "pride, haughtiness, and ostentation are conspicuous." According to Weld, Philadelphians approved of the creation of "an order of nobility" in the United States, "by which they might be exalted above their fellow citizens, as much as they are in their own conceit."[11] Although Philadelphia's political status changed after the transfer of the federal capital to Washington and the Republican triumph of 1800, the city's upper-class families struggled to preserve their aristocratic tone and behavior. *The Hermit in America,* a satirical account of Philadelphia published in 1819 by the Philadelphia socialite Robert Waln, contained similar references to the superior countenance of local elites. At a supper party, one participant was described as belonging "to a pretty numerous class" that believed that it was entitled "by birth" to hold "a situation in the first ranks of society." Patricians prided themselves on the exclusive character of their coteries.[12]

Money alone did not give access to society. In his *Notions of the Americans,* James Fenimore Cooper explained that Philadelphia did not produce "a better bred, or a more enlightened society" than New York, but that it was "less interrupted by the intrusions of that portion of the world which is purely commercial" than New York society. "Claims are canvassed, and pretensions weighed," the Scot Thomas Hamilton observed in the early 1830s. "Manners, fortune, taste, habits, and descent, undergo a rigid examination."[13]

Charleston was Philadelphia's rival in terms of exclusive society. Hamilton noted that Charlestonians were "in private life aristocratic and exclusive," proud of "a descent from several generations of respectable ancestors." Sir Charles Lyell, visiting Charleston in 1842 and 1849, reported he had "heard its exclusiveness much commented on," because families "whose ancestors started from genteel English stocks" kept to their aristocratic circles. The celebrated painter Charles Fraser concurred that Charleston's society was the country's most exclusive at the time. For good reasons, then, many Charleston patrician families, like the Manigaults and the Hugers, maintained close ties with Philadelphia throughout the antebellum era. Charlestonians and Philadelphians felt that there was an aristocratic community that shared a sense of privilege, entitlement, and cosmopolitanism.[14]

Charleston and Philadelphia patricians expressed exclusive forms of genealogical pride that placed them above other Americans. "I am somewhat proud of my family," the lawyer and gentleman farmer Sidney George Fisher confessed in 1837 as he pointed to his ancestors "on both sides" who for several generations had "held the stations of gentlemen & men of property & education." In his view, being a descendant of such distinguished ancestors was "something in this country of parvenus." His distant relative, W. L. Fisher, boasted of owning various documents that conferred genealogical and social status. "Of my father's family," he noted, "there are several manuscript accounts in my possession, about a century old." His mother's family, the Logans, was "for many years distinguished in Scotland, and connected by marriage with some of its noble families, of which many particulars are related."[15]

A genealogical connection to European nobility mattered because it attested one's long-standing social status and because the European reference suggested refinement. "What a race the English are!" intoned Hugh Swinton Legaré. "They are without exception, the highest specimen of civilization the world has ever seen." In Washington Irving's words, American aristocrats admired Europe with "a hallowed feeling of tenderness and veneration, as the land of our forefathers—the august repository of the monuments and antiquities of our race—the birth place and mausoleum of the sages, and heroes of our paternal history."[16]

In contrast, Philadelphia and Charleston patricians often felt at odds with the recent evolution of their country. In their nostalgic view, the political revolution of 1800 that ousted the Federalists and the transfer of the federal capital from Philadelphia to Washington boded ill for the country. Andrew Jackson's accession to power in 1828 only reinforced these feelings a generation later. Sidney George Fisher, for instance, thought that the United States of 1836 was nothing to be proud of. Americans had "no past, with its thousand recollections, associations and monuments"; they had "no distinct national character" and were divided into sections with interests "so distinct and often so conflicting." Finally, they were "poor, and coarse and unrefined," and they lived in a country that suffered from "slavery, and southernism and Yankeeism, and western barbarism, and lynch law, and mob law and democracy."

The only remedy lay in claiming an individual and collective connection—genealogical, political, and cultural—to England: "There are so many things to disgust & feel ashamed of," he concluded, "that I really think the true way is to insist on our claim of relationship to England & feel proud of her glory and greatness."[17]

In the meantime, lineage consciousness helped maintain high social standards. Insiders knew one another and one another's families, and they were careful to collect and pass on genealogical information from one generation to the next. Charleston's aristocrats prided themselves that "but one inscription" indicated the place of the family grave, "for we were as one," and they hung ancestral portraits by John Singleton Copley in the halls of their townhouses, as the New England–born Charlestonian author Caroline Gilman suggested in her 1838 *Recollections of a Southern Matron*. Joshua Gilpin researched his family tree while he was in England in the late 1790s and mid-1810s and gathered the information together in 1835. His brother Thomas published Joshua's and his own findings in book form in 1852.[18] Deborah Logan's diary opened in 1808 with an address to her "posterity" that insisted that "some person in every family" should "make it their concern to keep a Book in which they would record such facts as come under their Observation, together with their experiences of various kinds, and such accounts and notices of their families as they would either recount themselves or had received in tradition from their ancestors." She copied "an old mss in my possession" that gave "an historical account of the Ancient & Honourable family of Logan of Restalrig near to Edinburgh," and added information on her own parents and grandparents, Lloyds and Norrises. Her "book" served to signal distinction, pass it on, and prove it to her "posterity."[19]

Although nostalgic uses of patrician genealogy took center stage in antebellum Charleston and Philadelphia, they remained comparatively marginal in more dynamic economic places like Boston and New York. In the Hudson metropolis aristocratic pedigree hunting concerned former colonial and federal elites and their descendants who felt left behind by the pace and magnitude of commercial development and displaced by an emerging new mercantile upper class. According to a contemporary insider's opinion, the old elite valued "the cultivated and refined, but without the slightest reference to a pecuniary standard," and demanded that applicants display "the unmistakable evidences which, the world over proclaim the gentleman by sentiment and education." Culture and ancestry were prized above money. Old New Yorkers "abhorred everything vacillating." Economic stability and an "unvarying mode of living entered strongly into the Knickerbocker notion of family pride or aristocracy." George Templeton Strong, the Whig lawyer and diarist, saw the development of "a fluctuating mushroom aristocracy" in New York with considerable fear.[20]

For these families, genealogy represented a conservative refuge to cope with undesired change and to find solace in the memory of ancient lineages. Patrician New Yorkers like Allan Melvill attempted to root their family trees in noble ground, recover the history of New Netherland and colonial New York, and create exclusive institutions that would preserve social distinctions. Some imitated the New York lawyer Henry Sands, who gathered information about his ancestry in a manuscript volume, "House of Sands from the Earliest Antiquity to the Present Time." Washington Irving, who as a young writer repeatedly satirized the pedigree consciousness of aristocratic New Yorkers in *Salmagundi* (1807) and mocked them in the pseudonymous Diedrich Knickerbocker's

History of New York (1809), in 1835 become one of the founders of the Saint Nicholas Society, which was very attentive to Old New York and its traditions.[21]

By the 1840s New York bluebloods began to feel the need to make public genealogical information that had formerly remained private. *American Genealogy,* a book published by Jerome Bonaparte Holgate in 1848, included seventeen genealogies, mostly of such New York families as Van Rensselaer, Livingston, Beekman, Hoffman, De Lancey, and Roosevelt. James Riker, the son of a New York merchant and landowner, started to research his family genealogy and the history of Newtown, New York, in the mid-1840s, two undertakings that resulted in the publication of *A Brief History of the Riker Family* in 1851 and *The Annals of Newtown, in Queens County* the following year. *The Annals of Newtown* included several dozen pages devoted to the town's "genealogical history" and insisted on many families' noble origins: the Rapelyes "possessed large estates in Bretagne"; the Brinckerhoffs belonged to the patriciate of the Flemish city of Ghent; the Rikers originated in Lower Saxony, where they owned land in freehold tenure, thus enjoying "a state of allodial independence, at that day regarded as constituting nobility"; the Polhemuses wore a name "with a distinguished place" in the Netherlands; the Luysters came from "a very reputable Dutch family"; the Fishes and the Ways were ancient English families; the Van Alsts descended from a manorial family in Flanders; the Van Duyns were an ancient titled Burgundy family; and the Debevoises had "a highly respectable and well-educated French protestant" emigrant ancestor. Almost all these families used coats of arms.[22]

In Boston postrevolutionary elite genealogy was seldom nostalgia minded. The city's upper class, which was substantially transformed by the events of the Revolution, played an active role in innovative economic and cultural pursuits. Successful commercial and industrial strategies paved the way for cultural institutions like the Massachusetts Historical Society, the Boston Athenaeum, and the Lowell Institute, all funded by Federalist and later Whig economic leaders whose temporary hegemony stimulated searches for genealogical confirmation of their social status.[23]

Nathan Appleton is an example. Few antebellum Bostonians demonstrated more business and investment acumen than this New Ipswich native. A successful merchant, one of the earliest and largest investors in textile manufacturing at Waltham and Lowell, a savvy businessman who by 1815 (at age 36) valued his wealth at $200,000 and died a very rich man in 1861, Appleton displayed a keen interest in genealogy from his mid-twenties. He collected materials concerning his ancestors in England and New England, displayed particular interest in their coats of arms, and probably went to the family's ancestral seat, Wallingfield, during his business trips to England in 1802 and 1810–1811.[24]

In the late 1810s Nathan Appleton launched a large genealogical investigation. He wrote to relatives in Brunswick, Gloucester, and Salem and asked his brother Eben, then in Liverpool, to collect as much material in England as he could.[25] Eben Appleton later reported that he had traveled to Kent, Essex, and Suffolk, looked over local histories "as well as books of Heraldry—without number," obtained "very little information at the Heralds Office, although frequently there," and consulted "the Library of the London Institution," which contained the best resources on the subject. This research allowed him to compose a "genealogical table," which was "essentially the same as what you have previously had from other sources," but with "some little additions." Eben sent Nathan various coats of arms, pedigrees, and abstracts of parish registers.

He confirmed that there was "little doubt the *name* of Appleton" was "of Saxon origin," and he assured his brother "of the correctness" of the arms they assumed. While warning his brother that none of their ancestors were noted "as great warriors, orators, or statesmen," he managed to convey a vivid sense of the past that could only reinforce Nathan's lineage consciousness. In the church at Little Waldingfield, seeing a helmet "and a sort of coronet, which tradition gives to our family, although I know not upon what ground," he "climbed up and touched with awe the rusty remains of Appletonian Chivalry, and could almost fancy [he] saw by the dim twilight, its venerable possessor watching his armour in this lone chapel, at midnight, as valorous Knights were wont."[26]

Nathan Appleton remained interested in genealogical pursuits for the next three decades, visiting Suffolk himself and financing Isaac Appleton Jewett's *Memorial of Samuel Appleton* (1850), in large part a published version of his own notes since the early 1800s. As congratulations poured in from American luminaries like George Bancroft and Edward Everett and transatlantic readers like Sir Bernard Burke, Nathan Appleton must have felt that his genealogical undertakings secured his social standing.[27]

❉ ❉ ❉

Beyond individual lineage, antebellum patrician Americans became interested in collective identities. Many resorted to a language of race that had little to do at the time with natural science and heredity and much with forms of cultural ancestralism on a regional scale. While Philadelphians deplored the disposition in Pennsylvania "to under-rate the sterling worth of her native Sons," New Englanders spoke of Puritan blood, New Yorkers of Dutch and

Huguenot races, and Virginians and Carolinians of a southern (and in the latter case, sometimes of a Huguenot) race. All debated the particular value of each "stock."[28]

The notion of a "Puritan stock" emerged in early nineteenth-century New England as one of several answers to what many New Englanders perceived as the relative political and cultural decline of their region in the new republic. Pilgrims, Puritans, and their descendants were enrolled in the cause of a New Englandism that emphasized the transmission of moral virtues from the forefathers to the daughters and sons of New England. Fourth of July and Plymouth Rock orators soon discovered that antiquarianism and genealogy were powerful weapons in the culture war they waged against other sections of the United States in the name of their developing northern nationalism. Famous and less famous authors like Jedidiah Morse, Daniel Webster, Timothy Dwight, John Farmer, and John Warner Barber all contributed to the construction of a collective, genealogical idea of Puritans as (generally) virtuous ancestors even as nineteenth-century New Englanders debated, sometimes heatedly, the pros and cons of Puritanism.[29]

Along with writers, orators, and historians, expatriate Yankees took to exporting this New England–centered interpretation of American history outside New England. They established voluntary organizations called New England Societies in order to provide good company and mutual aid in distant places and to celebrate the grandeur of their home region. The first one was instituted in New York City in 1805; others followed in Philadelphia (1816), Charleston (1819), and many other places in the following decades. In 1820 the bicentennial celebration of the landing of the Pilgrims at Plymouth allowed New Englanders and the New England Societies to celebrate New England's past, present, and future. During the following two decades existing societies spread their vision of New England's central place in American history in such a way that when in the late 1830s the federal government commissioned a painting of the Pilgrims, the nationalization of the New England narrative had become a fact and the notion of "Puritan stock" a common reference. Commentators could rejoice "how far the Pilgrim race has diffused itself over the country," not only because of the efforts of the New England writers and orators, but also thanks to the publication of "many genealogical histories of the families of the earlier pilgrims." New Englanders like Theodore Parker and John Gorham Palfrey (the author of a multivolume *History of New England* and a genealogist) shared and spread the notion that Puritan ancestry conferred superiority on descendants, especially over southern rivals.[30]

As it acquired a national dimension, the identification of Americans as descendants of Puritans and Pilgrims was contested outside New England. The antebellum South was "a polyglot culture" of many "tongues and peoples," but the region experienced a gradual process of elaboration of southern identities that had a definite genealogical dimension. Most visible, although never hegemonic, was the emergence of the figure of the Virginian cavalier in the early nineteenth century. It partook of the growth of a sectionalism that emphasized, among other traits, a patriarchal ideal and southern cultural heritage. Writers like William Wirt, George Tucker, John Pendleton Kennedy, William Alexander Caruthers, and John Esten Cooke all helped develop the myth of the cavalier and an aristocratic colonial Virginia gentry. By the 1850s at least some Southerners deemed cavaliers responsible for the origins of American liberty and individualism, in direct refutation of the notion that American freedom had Puritan origins.[31]

Unlike New Englanders, antebellum Southerners seldom translated their genealogical conception of their collective identity into
actual, large-scale, public searches for pedigree. Whatever genealogy
existed remained comparatively rare, isolated, and private. This
began to change in the 1850s as sectional tensions grew. In 1857 the
Episcopal bishop of Virginia, William H. Meade, published *Old
Churches, Ministers and Families of Virginia*. Ostensibly an account of
the Episcopal Church of Virginia, it was organized in chapters tell-
ing the history of each Virginia parish and its old families. Although
Meade carefully insisted that "a renowned and wealthy ancestry"
was no cause for pride, he used genealogical materials communi-
cated by descendants who wished to appear in his account and insisted on ancient families, listing, for instance, the descendants of
Pocahontas and John Rolfe with care.[32]

\ The book's publication provided an opportunity to celebrate
Virginia family trees. The Southern propagandist George Fitzhugh
hailed Meade's books as "a *tableau vivant* of our ancestry" and con-
gratulated the author for his "love of genealogical research, and
his respect for ancestry." In Fitzhugh's view, "Counties, States, and
nations are but collections of families," and knowledge of family
history reinforced society. Not only was genealogy "a most important part of history," but it also had a "conservative effect." Ignorance of one's family history bred "little attachment to their country or its institutions." He argued, "The 'sons of nobody' belong to
no place or country." Genealogical knowledge, on the other hand,
led one to desire to conserve the status quo and to "oppose any political or social revolutions that might involve family, relatives,
connections, friends, and property, in ruin." It also fed patriotism.
"Family pride begets patriotism, and is the only reliable source
from whence it arises." Ultimately, therefore, Fitzhugh enrolled

Meade's book and genealogy in the Southern cause. "May many such books . . . be written, to show that we of the South are one people in blood, in sentiment, in thought, in social organization, and in political interests and institutions."[33]

Genealogical rivalry between New Englanders and Virginians degenerated during the Civil War into a racialized, nationalist reformulation as a conflict between Southern Normans and New England Saxons. Both sides used a language of race loaded with genealogical undertones. The "Puritan stock" was publicly hailed by New Englanders like Wendell Phillips, whose interest in his own genealogy led him to correspond with John Farmer in the 1830s and to contribute to the *New England Historical and Genealogical Register* in the 1850s. "I fear Northerners and Southerners are aliens," the New Yorker George Templeton Strong penned in his diary in December 1860, "not merely in social and political arrangements, but in mental and moral constitution. We differ like Celt and Anglo-Saxon." In the South, men like William Falconer of Alabama and the firebrand George Fitzhugh saw the conflict as a "contest of Race" and wrote about it in the *Southern Literary Messenger* and *DeBow's Review*. Genealogists partook in the debates. In 1864 William H. Whitmore wrote *The Cavalier Dismounted,* a genealogical pamphlet that argued that most Southerners did not have Cavalier origins. He also authored an essay in the *North American Review* in 1865 explaining that during the colonial era more New Englanders than Virginians and Carolinians had the right to use coats of arms.[34]

Like Southerners, New Yorkers reacted to what they perceived as the undue domination of the Puritan narrative over American history. Patrician New Yorkers of Dutch, Huguenot, and post-Puritan English origin begged to differ. "Why is it that we hear so much of 'the Puritan Anglo-Saxon stock,' who first settled on the outer-casing of this continent?" the editor and poet Charles Fenno Hoffman lamented in his address before the Saint Nicholas Society of New York in 1847. By contrast, he deplored that so little was heard of the "bold Belgic navigators," the "devoted Huguenots," and the "brave English cavaliers." Here, the orator insisted, was a "trinity of good blood" that blended "for two hundred years on the soil of New York" and flowed "in the veins of her native-born children."[35]

Such midcentury expostulations were the result of four decades of arguments to defend the particularity of New York's past and encourage native New Yorkers' genealogical and historical pride. Gouverneur Morris's 1812 address before the New-York Historical Society was one of the first and most influential illustrations of the New Yorkers' case. Morris described New York "as a commercial emporium" in the Dutch tradition of political and trade freedom and insisted on the specificity of New York's ethnic complexity. New Yorkers were "born cosmopolite" because their "ancestry may be traced to four nations, the Dutch, the British, the French, and the German."[36] In 1814 De Witt Clinton petitioned the New York legislature on behalf of the New-York Historical Society to request funds to promote local history and archival preservation, including Dutch materials. A few years later Gulian C. Verplanck made the case for the Dutch and the Huguenots. "We have no cause to blush for any part of our original descent, and least of all for our Dutch ancestry," he argued. As for the Huguenots, Verplanck was certain that New Yorkers would agree "in ascribing parts of our character to the moral influence of a virtuous and intelligent ancestry" and therefore "may well look back, with pride, to [their] Huguenot forefathers."[37]

All this served to bolster a New York collective identity. The Saint Nicholas Society of New York, founded in 1835, was a natural place for expression of such feelings. James Fenimore Cooper thought that the society was "one step in asserting the proper rights of the real New-Yorkers on their own ground" because it allowed "the voices of the descendants of the old stock" to be heard. At the society's 1837 anniversary dinner, members toasted "the blood of the Batavian patriot, the Huguenot exile, and the English cavalier" that mingled in the state of New York. The following year Verplanck made fun of Yankee claims to primacy, spoofing "what, according to their tradition, they call 'the landing of the pilgrims.'"[38]

New Yorkers translated this ancestral pride and bonds of affection into historical and genealogical pursuits. Descendants of prestigious colonial families, like John P. De Lancey and Pierre Van Cortlandt, began to search for their ancestors.[39] During the 1840s and 1850s the New-York Historical Society published materials on New York's Dutch period in the second series of its *Collections*. A major enterprise was the discovery and recovery of important sources about New Netherland in the Dutch archives by the American chargé d'affaires to The Hague, the distinguished Albany patrician Harmanus Bleecker, who was also founding president of the St. Nicholas Society of Albany. Bleecker's secretary John Romeyn Brodhead had these sources transcribed and put them to use in the first volume of his *History of the State of New York* (1853); they were compiled, translated, and published by Edmund B. O'Callaghan in his four-volume *Documentary History of New York*, published between 1848 and 1851, and in *Documents Relative to the Colonial History of the State of New York*, an eleven-volume monument whose publication began in the early 1850s.[40]

✻   ✻   ✻

The pursuit of genealogy represented an attempt by marginalized patricians to preserve social distinction and a strategy to elaborate sectional or regional identities, but nouveau riche Americans understood the need to own a pedigree at all cost. Genealogical frauds were nothing new, but they became more numerous than ever in the fast-growing republic, particularly in its economic hub, New York City. Anthony Evergreen, a character in Washington Irving's *Salmagundi*, acknowledged that "treating of pedigrees [was] rather an ungrateful task" in New York. Although De Witt Clinton argued in 1811 that there was "a strong propensity in the human mind to trace up our ancestry to as high and as remote a source as possible," he was quick to acknowledge that in New York, in the absence of "a reliable statement of facts, fable is substituted for truth, and the imagination is taxed to supply the deficiency."[41]

As the city grew in size and riches, the trend accelerated. An observer noted in 1821 that "those who hold the 'vulgar orders' in the most sovereign contempt, *are those who most recently had risen from them*," such as "the daughter of a *lace* pedlar" who "made herself out (by a little 'paltering in a double sense') a descendant of the ancient family of the LACIES."[42] Nothing had changed by the late 1860s. In nouveau riche New York, the journalist Junius H. Browne scathingly pointed out, it was "very natural that ignorant men who have suddenly grown rich should wish others to believe they have distinguished ancestors and patrician blood in their plebeian veins." As a result, "They might pay liberally for a coat of arms when they remember they began life in a coat without arms."[43]

A commentator on the situation of "American genealogies" explained the process in the mid-1850s. "Smith, the parvenu," knew "more of stocks in Wall Street, than of his own ancestral trunk," and could not "write a book." Fortunately, "his cousin of the same

name, some starving minister, or briefless barrister," could. Thus
the two men entered "into a limited copartnership of money and
brains," and soon "the friends of the family" received a "resplen-
dent, hot-pressed octavo, on 'The ancient and honorable Family of
Smith'" as a present.[44]

At least two signs suggest that nineteenth-century New York was
the capital of parvenu genealogy. One is the relative abundance of
contemporary sources that mocked the pretensions of upstart New
Yorkers. Francis Grund's *Aristocracy in America* (1839) was one of the
earliest and most detailed illustrations of the genre. Grund derided "the exclusives" who worshipped nobility until they imagined "themselves to belong to it."[45] By the late 1840s and early 1850s
the theme had become a New York commonplace. "Joseph," the
anonymous author of *New-York Aristocracy; or, Gems of Japonica-Dom*
(1851), ridiculed parvenus who, "never without a book of the Peerage at hand," would adorn their carriage or harness with crests
"got up 'to order'" by "the herald chaser in Reade street, or purchased privately from some Gallic refugee."[46]

George William Curtis's *Potiphar Papers* (1853) also poked fun at
New York's "best society." If it were "fine" to "drive a fine carriage
and ape European liveries, and crests, and coats-of-arms" and "to
talk much of the 'old families' and of your aristocratic foreign
friends," then New York society would be "prodigiously fine." Curtis pitilessly derided the genealogical claims of the newly rich. "I
am lineally descended from one of those two brothers who came
over in some of those old times, in some of those old ships, and
settled in some of those old places somewhere," explained one
such character, Mrs. Potiphar. Another one, young Minerva Tat-
tle, saw her hopes to fit into Saratoga Springs' best society shat-

tered after her rich but clumsy father suggested publicly that they should go to Newport because "all the 'parvenus'" were going and therefore they would have "to go along." Nathaniel Parker Willis's *Rag-Bag* (1855) included gentle but ironic comments suggested by English projects to establish a Canadian nobility "with a Vice-Royal Court at Montreal." Willis wondered "at the effect, on New-York, of a Throne and Court, whose Windsor will be at Niagara!"[47]

A second sign of the importance of parvenu genealogy in mid-nineteenth-century New York was the many facilities offered by the city. As in the colonial period, upstart New Yorkers could buy a pedigree and have "coats-of-arms traced, painted and engraved" on carriages or "dinner, tea, or dessert sets." At least one heraldic office operated on Broadway in the 1850s and 1860s. Called the Heraldry Office and the New York College of Arms, it was headed by Henry Hays, who used the bogus title "Windsor Herald." Hays offered to send "family arms and a sketch forward, upon receipt of $1," and to engrave seals and paint crests "upon carriages." Hays's Heraldry Office regularly inserted advertisements with such titles as "A Fortune Gained for Two Dollars" in the New York newspapers and was apparently "a success." The author of a contemporary social satire asserted that it was easy to obtain "an emblazoned escutcheon" in a city where everything could be "won with wealth, and worn with impudence." As the writer suggested, there was no need to pretend that one's coat of arms had been lost, for the heraldic office knew "as well as you do, and more, that they were never found."[48] Junius H. Browne devoted a full chapter, "Heraldry on the Hudson," of his book *The Great Metropolis* (1869) to the Heraldry Office:

It is supported by the class of absurd people who are aspiring to a recognized position, who have more money than ancestors, and wish to exchange a little of the former for a good deal of the latter. The capital invested in the office is trifling. It requires only two or three men to look serious over a farce; a collection of old volumes full of shields, devices, and mottoes; a lot of genealogical trees hung up on the walls in antique-looking frames, and an uncertain number of histories and chronicles, including Froissart, Burke's Peerage, and kindred works.[49]

The vogue of pseudopedigrees suggested both commercial opportunities and the need for regulation. A young pioneer in chromolithography, Thomas W. Gwilt Mapleson, decided to address both in his *Hand-Book of Heraldry* (1851). At first glance, its purpose was to explain the nature of heraldry. Mapleson granted that some New Yorkers made abundant and irregular use of "heraldic devices" and that "such ostentation" was "folly." Most advance subscribers to his book were members of prestigious New York families (for example, Schermerhorn, Livingston, and De Peyster) whose coats of arms could be found among the forty-six printed by Mapleson.[50]

Although the *Hand-Book of Heraldry* claimed to stand on the side of authenticity, it contributed to the contemporary heraldic fad. Nathaniel Parker Willis mocked this "catechism or primer of pedigree-diness," but he also noted that it sold very well. The *Hand-Book* was a commercial undertaking prompted by the notion that Americans wanted "to know the look of a ticket to aristocracy." Its success suggested that this was a clever strategy, as well as a sign that heraldry had entered New York culture. Next, he predicted, would come the creation of a "Herald's college in New York." His prediction soon became true: in 1860 Albert Welles established the

American College of Heraldry and Genealogical Registry, which aimed at becoming the American equivalent of London's College of Arms.[51]

＊　　　＊　　　＊

Concern for lineage, real or imagined, social or financial, resulted in the multiplication of estate claims relative to both American and English estates. The phenomenon went back to the colonial period, but it became more prevalent during the antebellum era. Some of these claims were legitimate and led lawyers to undertake often lengthy genealogical investigations to determine the rightful heirs. The disposition of the estate of Joseph Ball, a Philadelphia industrialist and businessman who died intestate in 1821, dragged on until a lawyer, Charles DeSelding, contacted all putative heirs in the 1850s and offered to buy their share or help them assert their right to their claim. Many other cases were simply fraudulent and based on phony genealogical claims. Their success, however, testified not only to the claimants' gullibility and cupidity but also to the importance in mid-nineteenth-century America of inheritance, either of imaginary ancestors or of ancestors whose descendants thought that they had been robbed of their legitimate heirlooms. Estate claims thus lay at the promising intersection of lineage consciousness and greed.[52]

The most famous case of all had a long history that went back to a Dutch woman in seventeenth-century New Amsterdam, Anneke Jans. Jans migrated to New Netherland in 1630 with her first husband, who died a few years later. In 1638 she married New Amsterdam's minister, Dominie Everardus Bogardus. When she died in 1663, she held title to a large tract of land on Manhattan Island, which she willed to her children by her two husbands. In 1671 several of her heirs conveyed title to the land to Governor Francis Lovelace. However, one of her sons, Cornelius, did not partake in the deed, and this was the source of all later controversy. In 1705 title to Anneke Jans's former land was conveyed by Queen Anne to Trinity Church, whose corporation's finances greatly benefited from the revenues of the land and later from partial sales as prices of Manhattan's real estate rose.[53]

One of Cornelius Bogardus's descendants, a grandson also named Cornelius, contested the conveyance to Lovelace and Trinity Church in the 1780s. He lost in court, but in 1807 his son John brought suit again and also lost. By the 1820s the Jans-Bogardus claim was a cause célèbre in New York. Cornelius Bogardus's heirs claimed that the conveyance was fraudulent and asked for the restitution of Manhattan land, which by then was worth a fortune. John Bogardus filed a new suit in 1830; he died in 1834, but his heirs pursued the matter until judgment in 1847 in *Bogardus v. Trinity Church*. The case was tried in Chancery Court and received particular attention. The court reporter noted, "Besides the documentary evidence and proofs taken in the usual mode before the examiner, many witnesses were examined in open court during the progress of the hearing, which occupied thirteen days." In the end, judging that there was not "a particle of proof" that "the complainants ancestor, the first Cornelius Bogardus, was ever in possession of the Dominie's Bowery, or ever asserted a right to it," the court decided in favor of Trinity Church in 1847. Vice-Chancellor Sandford wrote in his opinion, "A plainer case has never been presented to me as a judge."[54]

Contested in the Jans-Bogardus claim was Trinity's title to Manhattan land, not the genealogical ties among Anneke Jans, her son Cornelius, and their nineteenth-century heirs. Most antebellum

ANTEBELLUM BLOOD AND VANITY

cases, however, were characterized by a triple uncertainty: about the very existence of a property, about the legal claims to the property, and finally about the genealogical basis of the legal claims. This triple uncertainty encouraged frauds based on imaginary domestic or foreign ancestors and estates. The 1840s saw a great deal of this type of activity throughout the United States. According to the later testimony of Wilson Miles Cary, "In 1840 there was a great stir excited in our family in Virginia by a 'Great Cary Fortune' to which it was said that the Virginia Carys were entitled & wh[ich] was said to consist of large extent of land or rents in London." Family members wrote one another feverishly about their future riches. "Before I got your letter I got a letter giving information that the Cary family had fallen heirs to a title of 14 millions in money," 74-year-old Mary Jacquelin Lee of Durhamville, Tennessee, wrote to her cousin Mary Jacquelin Vowell in 1843. Wilson Miles Cary reminisced, "Agents came out from England in reg[ar]d to the matter but the family never was induced to any concert of action in the case & the affair died out."[55]

In the Jennings case, things went further. Convinced that they had a valuable claim to the real and personal estate of William Jennings of Acton Place, a rich Suffolk man who died intestate in 1798, putative heirs began to organize in the late 1840s. Letters circulated between perfect strangers who discovered their kinship on that occasion. Hansford Dade Duncan of South Carolina, for instance, exchanged several letters with William Chapman Jennings of Virginia in 1848–1849 before he met him in person. Soon he called him "my dear Cousin William," invited him to South Carolina, visited his Virginia relatives, and enjoyed his newfound kinship.[56]

Still, he hoped "to realize the great fortune," and other Jenningses did too. On 15 September 1849, several dozen family representatives met in Nashville, Tennessee, to discuss their options. Two days later the seven-person committee they had appointed to study the family genealogy reported its belief that "some of the heirs to the estate" were among them and could "trace their lineage to Humphrey Jennings, the grandfather of the intestate." Another committee, in charge of drawing articles of association, reminded the audience of past fruitless attempts to establish a link and advised convention members to limit risks by joining efforts; accordingly, they created the Jennings Family Association, which included fifty-six founding subscribers from Alabama, Georgia, Indiana, Kentucky, Mississippi, North Carolina, Tennessee, and Virginia.[57]

Soon the association collected money to send an agent to England in hopes of finding the necessary genealogical links and proofs. For the next few years Jennings relatives exchanged information about the search. When the agent, Colonel F. A. Jennings, came back from England in 1852 with little new information and a demand for more funds, association members did not mince their words. "If the whole American heirs have failed, why not give the information without delay?" one member protested. "I for one wash my hands forever, from any further concern in the matter."[58]

In New England there were several similar cases in the late 1840s and the 1850s. The rumor of a family estate in England began to spread rapidly in late 1846 among New England Chases, including antiquarians like Benjamin Chase of Auburn, New Hampshire, and Joshua Coffin of Newbury, Massachusetts, whose daughter Lucia had married a Chase. Circular and personal letters were sent to many New England Chases. About 600 of them met in Newbury in early 1847 to discuss the possible inheritance.[59] Others were less easily convinced that there was a Chase estate "all ready for some of our name in this country." "I might think more of the report and might feel disposed to do more in aid of investigation if I had not witnesseth the failure of so many money diggers in my time," Moses Chase, a 75-year-old lawyer in Calais, Vermont, wrote skeptically while rejoicing that the planned family assembly "will probably furnish materials for a more perfect history than now exists" of the Chase family. Many New England Chases, however, were more gullible than Moses Chase.[60]

The notion that "a large amount of property had been lying in England" awaiting American Houghtons led first to the creation of a Massachusetts Houghton Association, then of a Houghton Association in 1845–1846, and then to the merger of the two societies after a meeting in March 1847 in Worcester, Massachusetts, with 400 participants in attendance. The Massachusetts Houghton Association sent an agent to England in late 1846 and another in early 1847, with few results. Various rumors about an estate linked to Houghton Street in London, money in the Exchequer, or a manufacturing village in Lancashire all proved sheer fantasy. However, at the Worcester meeting it was decided that a new investigation was "encouraging and prosperous." Members paid five dollars each to finance expenses. The association's recording secretary, F. M. Rice of Walpole, New Hampshire, was chosen as agent and was sent to England in the summer of 1847. Upon his return in the fall, he reported that there was no estate. The association accepted the report and dissolved, although some family members decided to pursue the matter individually, using the services of another claims agent, Columbus Smith. Their efforts also proved fruitless.[61]

By the late 1840s there were dozens of such agents active in the United States and England. For them, genealogy was not a goal but the means to obtain a result. A professional genealogist like

Horatio Gates Somerby was careful to distinguish between his trade and their activities. On being asked to work for a putative heir to a supposed Townley estate, Somerby answered in 1852 that he could not "look up Townley claim on speculation" because he was "too much occupied in other genealogical matters." In any case, he asserted briskly, "[I] have no interest in claims, neither do I wish to have."[62] In contrast, agents specializing in claims had no interest "in other genealogical matters," only in those that made it possible to allow or disprove a claim.

The most famous of these agents was Columbus Smith, the man hired by disappointed members of the Houghton Association in 1848. Smith was beginning to enjoy a modest fame at the time. At age 23, soon after graduating from Middlebury College (class of 1842), the Vermont-born Smith considered moving to Kentucky to teach. Instead, he went to England in 1844 as an agent for the alleged American descendants of Frances Mary Shard, the daughter of an innkeeper in Trenton, New Jersey, who had married first a noble Irishman, Lord Fortescue, and after his death a rich Englishman, William Shard. She had inherited both of their fortunes but had died intestate and without heirs apparent in 1820. While working for the Shard heirs in England and in America during the late 1840s and the 1850s, Smith decided to extend his business and work for other clients. By the mid-1850s, when the English Court of Claims found in favor of Smith's clients in the Shard case, his reputation was established.[63]

Smith's papers offer a rare glimpse into the operations of a claims agent. His first task was to find clients. In the mid-1840s, when Smith was still unknown, this was a difficult challenge. The young man did not hesitate to offer his services to potential clients and advertise his services in newspapers. One such advertisement in 1846 earned him a letter from Orange Brittell of Weybridge, Vermont, who thought that he could inherit a property in England. "From your statement of the case," Smith answered, "I think [it] is a good one & one worth looking into." Joseph Loomis of Syracuse, New York, and Benjamin Chase of Vergennes, Vermont, saw similar advertisements in the press a few months later and wrote to ask for Smith's terms to investigate the story of a Loomis estate and a Townley estate, respectively.[64]

These advertisements, his energy, and rumors about his expected success in the Shard case led to his appointment as agent for several claims, including those of Houghton and Gibbs. In the Gibbs case, rumors of an English fortune led to the creation of a family association at a meeting in Brandon, Vermont, in May 1847, and to Smith's appointment as agent. Smith went to England and began investigating rumors about property in Somerset, London, and Kent. In his report to the association in 1848, he explained that he pursued other leads like the inheritance of a Sir Vicary Gibbs or alleged Gibbs deposits at the Bank of England. Smith also printed advertisements for Gibbs property and met with an Englishman fond of Gibbs genealogy, Sir George Gibbes—all without result. Finally, he reported that he had found a property in Devon, the Manor of Inslow, worth about $500,000, and that he was "convinced that this must be the main property which had caused the numerous reports to be circulated in this country." Many English Gibbses claimed ownership, however, and the problem for American Gibbses was to establish their genealogical right to the property. Smith concluded that American Gibbses had to develop better knowledge of their collective and individual genealogy. His report was printed in 500 copies and distributed to members, and he was compensated for his work and his expenses.[65]

By 1850 Columbus Smith's name circulated widely, and he could afford to change his strategy. There was no need for him to advertise his business in newspapers any longer; letters poured in from all over the country. "Within the last three months," he wrote in March 1850, "I have mailed about 150 letters to various parts of USA and Europe and received through the P.O. over 100 letters within that time, besides newspapers, pamphlets &c." For the period 1854–1864 he listed some 960 correspondents—the largest numbers coming from New York (157), Pennsylvania (100), Ohio (88), Vermont (85), Massachusetts (79), the United Kingdom (67), and Wisconsin (54).[66]

Faced with such high demand, Smith could now choose his clients and dictate his terms. He explained to one prospective employer, "I cannot consent in any case to advance money to make examinations for others."[67] Consequently, he charged his clients for short as well as long investigations. Simply to look into papers related to "the Morris claim to some property in England" that he had brought back from England and had not arranged yet, he requested five dollars from David Morris. He explained to another correspondent, "My business is now so extensive regarding foreign claims I am obliged to make small charges otherwise my whole time would be occupied in giving such information without remuneration."[68]

For long investigations, particularly in Great Britain, charges were obviously much higher. When George Hoskins questioned him in 1850 about costs, Smith answered that an investigation in England was too expensive for an individual. Hoskins was therefore advised "to call a meeting of the family immediately," collect information "concerning the genealogy of the family," and create "an association and raise funds" for the search. Smith was willing to research the case if he received "a small percentage" of the sum eventually recovered and had all his expenses paid for in advance. Family members were, in other words, shareholders: they raised funds by buying scrip—in fact, a lien on the future property or fortune. Buying a five-dollar scrip meant that one would be entitled to a certain amount of money (100 dollars, for instance) from the amount that would be recovered. In the meantime, the money invested in scrip served to cover Columbus Smith's expenses.[69]

Smith carefully prepared his trips to England. Before crossing the Atlantic in the spring of 1850, for instance, he negotiated with several parties interested in the Gibbs and Houghton claims. He not only entered into an agreement with the family associations but also made separate deals with individuals. To John Gibbs, for instance, he explained that since his family seemed different from other Gibbs families, he might want to sponsor a separate investigation. Once his clients had agreed to his terms, Smith began researching their claims in England. He usually worked for several clients simultaneously and kept track carefully of his expenses for each case. During his English trip in the summer of 1850, for instance, he worked on the Gibbs and Houghton claims from June to September but also made more limited searches related to the Goldsborough, Hungerford, and Colburn cases. His work was not faked: for instance, he billed the Goldsborough Association for spending time at the British Museum's library looking at directories to track down a certain man, visiting people who had lived in the same house, working at Doctors' Commons searching wills, sending reports to the association, traveling outside London for the case, and meeting with British solicitors.[70]

Smith also used his time in London to gather information. In a series of notebooks he copied hundreds of notices of missing heirs and next of kin published in English newspapers since the eighteenth century, as well as names found in books of unclaimed dividends from the Bank of England. One volume, for instance, contained all excerpts from the *London Gazette* "from 1854 back to 1728" by year; another one included the same information by name; others included lengthy indexes. Smith thus gathered a huge amount of documentation that he could use for future investigations.

Claim agents like Columbus Smith had a utilitarian and businesslike vision of genealogy that remained marginal in the mid-nineteenth-century United States but received considerable exposure because of the fascination English estates exerted on American imaginations. Apart from the celebrated Shard case, most claims were unsuccessful, and those who profited most from this new genealogical business were undoubtedly the claim agents. Columbus Smith, for one, was a rich man when he retired in the early 1870s, the owner of a beautiful property near Middlebury, Vermont. He, at least, had found the estate he had been looking for.

❖   ❖   ❖

By the 1850s claim agents like Columbus Smith enjoyed a thriving business from persuading American clients that they could legitimately dream of owning a castle in England. Their success testified to the dual nature of mid-nineteenth-century American genealogy—a democratic, scholarly pursuit and a nouveau riche quest for fame and fortune.

William H. Whitmore's *Handbook of American Genealogy* (published in 1862 and reprinted as *The American Genealogist* in 1868 and 1875) reflected this duality perfectly. "The study of genealogy," Whitmore explained in 1868, "must be governed by the tone of public sentiment." Adding that it was "in no way incompatible with

our republican institutions," he contrasted the practice of genealogy in the United States at the time with that at other times or
in other countries, where "it may serve only to foster a mistaken
pride." But in his book Whitmore also listed the many genealogical
reports about supposedly vacant English properties published on
behalf of hopeful American families, attacking their authors
repeatedly and forcefully and fuming that "the whole subject is a
scandal to the science of genealogy." In Whitmore's view, undertakings of that sort remained marginal. He was more impressed by
"the improvement in the subject of our genealogies." Between the
1840s and the 1860s scholarly genealogy had considerably transformed the field. "Twenty years ago nearly every man who knew
anything of his pedigree beyond his grandfather, was firmly possessed with the idea that three brothers of the same name came
over here; every family was confident that it was of noble descent;
nearly every family was positive that it was the rightful inheritor of
an immense fortune in England." This, he applauded, was no more.
"These ludicrous mistakes are now seldom published, and are dy-
ing out of the public faith."[71]

Whitmore's celebration of the ascendancy of scholarly genealogy
during the antebellum era offered a valid estimate of the respective
importance of democratic values and exclusive or pecuniary motives in American genealogy at the time. What he underestimated
as he wrote these lines in the 1860s, however, was the growing influence on American genealogy of a notion that became central in the
late nineteenth and early twentieth centuries: race.

❧ 4 ❧

"Upon the Love of Country and Pride of Race"

The Civil War profoundly altered the meaning and practice of the American genealogical scene. Both literally and symbolically, the conflict tore apart many white families but made it possible for African American families to imagine being reunited and to use genealogy to serve their purpose. In the wake of the war, many whites felt the need to bind up wounds and restore unity—defining reconciliation not by section but by race, nation, and ancestry—at the expense of racial equality. The relation they established among ancestor worship, nationalism, and racism during the late nineteenth and early twentieth centuries made genealogy into a political and social tie for some Americans, as well as a way to exclude others.

As the United States underwent social change of a magnitude unknown until then and struggled between the 1870s and the 1920s with the effects of large-scale urbanization, industrialization, and immigration, the search for ancestors experienced a tremendous surge in popularity. Many Americans became obsessive about their ancestors. At the same time, the meanings of genealogy that had dominated the antebellum era gave way to new ideals and impulses. Americans resorted to genealogy to confirm their sense of individual and collective superiority. In 1856 the *North American Review* could ask how it was possible "in this land of equality" that "any man believes his ancestors to have been greater and better than himself and his friends," but this question lost much of its meaning within a few years. A very different vocabulary and vision, premised on the importance of race, heredity, and nationalism, soon emerged in relation to genealogy. "As members of the great Aryan race," the naturalist George Brown Goode explained in his 1888 family history, "we may justly take pleasure in tracing back our lineage, so far as possible, in that broad stairway of ancestral derivation which is the most illustrious in the world." Alexander Brown, the author of a genealogy of the Cabell family of Virginia, theorized in 1895 that "the interest of people in their kindred is one of the measures of the distances between the races of men," and he added that "the continued existence and prosperity of every nation" depended "upon the love of country and pride of race." For more than half a century after the Civil War, such language became common among genealogists as racialized and nationalist pursuits came to dominate pedigree hunting and gave genealogy more contemporary ideological relevance than in the past.[1]

*   *   *

Central to this evolution were conceptions of race and heredity. In 1925 the Columbia University anthropologist Franz Boas recognized that the notion of racial superiority was "a symptom of the world-wide 'complex' of race consciousness" that had grown during the nineteenth century. He ascribed the grafting of racial superiority onto nationality to "the development of a biological point of view" among Americans, and particularly to "the influence of modern theories of genetics." As Boas noted, the late nineteenth and early twentieth centuries saw the growing racialization of American society and culture. An old vocabulary that emphasized skin color as a marker of racial difference gave way to a new language of race, "a biological point of view" that soon permeated the United States. Late nineteenth-century Americans developed new racial notions in order to include, exclude, and rank individuals. These categories served to distinguish whites from blacks, Native Americans, and Asians and to distinguish between white "ancestors and immigrants."[2]

According to this racialized vision of American society, the Anglo-Saxons stood at the top of the racial scale. They were the proud heirs to a political tradition and racial culture that had its origins, according to English and American Anglo-Saxonists, in the forests of Germany. The English historian Edward August Freeman's influential essay *Comparative Politics* (1873) helped root the notion of an English-speaking race in England and America, bound by "everlasting ties of blood and speech" and deriving directly from Aryan, Teutonic, Anglo-Saxon origins. Anglo-Saxonism, arguably a conception of history and an ideology of race with relatively few followers in the antebellum United States, now reigned supreme. Not only did it attract the likes of the historian Herbert Baxter Adams and the political scientist John W. Burgess, but it also captured the attention of many ordinary Americans who learned about Anglo-Saxons from the writings of popular writers and lecturers like Josiah Strong, the author of the 1885 best seller *Our Country: Its Possible Future and Its Present Crisis.* Such racialism led to new forms of genealogical interest because of the importance of establishing one's identity and the supposed Anglo-Saxon purity of one's blood.[3]

Simultaneously, new conceptions of heredity reinforced the American obsession with race and racial categories. The notion that heredity transmitted physical and genetic dispositions, not only moral and historical exemplars, transformed the old pride in ancestry, which most antebellum Americans had experienced as a moral imperative and a constraint rather than a means of personal status and vanity. The United States in the late nineteenth century thus provided fertile ground for genealogy to develop along hereditarian lines and then into its later by-product, eugenics.

In his April 1878 address before the New York Genealogical and Biographical Society, the Reverend Samuel Osgood alerted his audience to the "rising sense of the principle of inheritance, or the law of heredity." Osgood emphasized that this growing recognition had a "scientific principle." Science, he argued, had taken "a sober and conservative turn in favor of what it calls the law of heredity." Many Americans were "now ready to find the whole of themselves in their ancestry, or, at least, to ascribe to each generation but a little part in shaping itself." Now that it was recognized that each age was "the product of its predecessor," Osgood's generation corrected "the frenzy of its acquisitiveness by serious thought of its dependence upon the men and events that were before." This view resulted in the growth of genealogy in the United States. According to Osgood, Americans were interested in their ancestors because they believed that they were connected to them "by a more vital power of heredity than that which makes wills and transmits houses and lands." Osgood concluded that "the science of heredity" underlay the "careful study of the genealogy of this generation."[4]

The new intellectual climate in American genealogy originated in Charles Darwin's *On the Origin of Species,* Arthur de Gobineau's *On the Inequality of Human Races,* and especially works by Darwin's cousin Francis Galton. While Darwinism generated lasting controversies and Gobineau's book provided a rationale for racism, Galton's work on "hereditary genius" was widely read and commented on in the United States. As a reviewer in *Appleton's Journal of Literature* pointed out, Galton's hereditarianism disproved the notion that "ability [was] irrespective of descent" and caused a cultural revolution in a country that presented itself as the land of the common man.[5]

As Samuel Osgood's 1878 address suggested, genealogists did not fail to read Galton. Only four months after the publication of the Englishman's article on the hereditary talent of English judges in the March 1869 issue of *Macmillan's Magazine,* the exacting genealogist William H. Whitmore wrote an essay titled "Hereditary Ability," in which he used the example of Massachusetts judges between the late seventeenth century and the American Revolution to test Galton's hypothesis that heredity mattered. Members of the New York Genealogical and Biographical Society heard of Galton's ideas in February 1871 when its president Henry R. Stiles mentioned the Englishman's name in his anniversary address in connection with what he called "philosophical genealogy."[6]

Within a few years heredity became an obsession, as well as a new rationale for genealogy. Its relation to biology and natural science now stood above its obvious connection with history. As George Brown Goode suggested, hereditarianism made genealogy "more reputable" in the eyes of "those sternly practical men who represent the working side of science." Genealogy continued to interest historians and clergymen, but it now fascinated medical doctors, natural scientists, and biologists, many of whom practiced and advocated genealogy. The natural philosopher, mathematician, and meteorologist Elias Loomis of Yale published several genealogical works in the 1870s, showing "how from a single man, established in Connecticut in 1639," had descended "an army of sturdy men" who took part in the American Revolution and the economic, political, and intellectual development of the country. His family history therefore had "a value with reference to questions of General History and Political Philosophy." Genealogy "aids science in investigations into the theory of heredity," another genealogist noted in 1893. The Harvard geologist Nathaniel Southgate Shaler, an Anglo-Saxonist who thought that "a man is what his ancestral experience has made him," read a paper titled "Genealogy from the Point of View of Natural Science" at a meeting of the New England Historic Genealogical Society in 1891. Genealogy attracted the likes of Shaler, George Brown Goode, the inventor Alexander Graham Bell, the natural scientist and Stanford University chancellor David Starr Jordan, the biologist and leading eugenicist Charles B. Davenport, and many other men of science. Goode, for instance, published his nearly 600-page family genealogy, *Virginia Cousins,* in 1887 and continued to work on a projected second edition until his death in 1896.[7]

Bell's scientific research on inherited deafness used genealogy extensively during the 1880s. Bell painstakingly explored the pedigree of a New England family with several deaf children, the Lovejoys. He spent time in the Library of Congress and made a discovery that sent him in the summer of 1885 on a genealogical trip to northern New England. Two years later Bell went to Moncton, New Brunswick, and Halifax, Nova Scotia, in search of missing Lovejoy links, while his research assistant, Annie Pratt, interviewed a

96-year-old woman who had "a clear memory and a vast fund of genealogical information." Bell also traveled several times to the island of Martha's Vineyard to explore the genealogical dynamics of deafness in a small insular community, Squibnocket. There he copied "valuable material" for his research in the old town records. While he was in Nova Scotia, he investigated his wife's pedigree with delight; the following year he used his trip to England to research his own ancestry.[8]

By the 1890s hereditarianism was solidly entrenched in the United States. It was controversial, however, and the debate between heredity and environment lasted well into the twentieth century. Critics derided heredity as "the scientific shibboleth of our time" and pointed out that it could be misleading. "Sir John Jones boasts loudly of his lineage because he knows the names of his little line of Jones ancestors for, say, ten generations back," explained Henry Smith Williams. But what he really knew of "that boasted tenth generation" was "that *one* member was named Jones"; he ignored completely "the 1,023 other individuals who make up the remainder of the phalanx."[9]

Despite this type of criticism, the language of heredity strongly influenced American genealogists of the late nineteenth and early twentieth centuries. When the historian Herbert Baxter Adams completed his family genealogy in 1880, he rejoiced that "both lines" seemed "to have been satisfactorily traced to their English origin" and proudly pointed to one "Lord Ap Adams of England, Baron of the Realm from 1296 to 1307," from whom he thought he was descended. James Kendall Hosmer, the author of an essay titled "Anglo-Saxon Freedom," boasted of his Saxon ancestors and of the fact that his "stock had been fixed in America since 1635."[10] John Fiske, the period's most popular history lecturer and a fervent evolutionist who had published essays on Darwinism, was all too happy to report to his mother that he had traced the Fiske family, "how they came to Connecticut, where they lived in Massachusetts, and in England, and how they were doughty Puritans." Fiske had "worked back 12 generations from Bezaleel, going back into the fourteenth century"; he had *proved every step,* discovered that "the great John Locke's grandmother was Elizabeth Fiske, of our family," found the Fiske coat of arms, and altogether "nailed the Fiske genealogy." In England in 1880, Fiske and his wife visited "the home of [his] Fiske ancestors at Laxfield" in Suffolk and were moved to see their house. Twenty years later, when the aging Fiske was invited to deliver an address at the unveiling of a statue of Alfred the Great in Winchester, he hastened to accept the honor, proudly commenting: "We New Englanders are the offspring of Alfred's England. It curiously happened, that I am myself a lineal descendant of Alfred."[11]

"Genealogy bears out heredity law," the *New York Times* explained in 1910 in an article about the genealogist Henry Whittemore, the author of genealogies of the families of Russell Sage and Jay Gould and a firm believer in the laws of heredity. In 1913 the biologist Frederick Adams Woods imitated Galton's example by studying the Hall of Fame and claiming that American genius was hereditary. Senator Henry Cabot Lodge of Massachusetts, a fierce proponent of immigration restriction, explained in 1913 that "definition of a man's birth and ancestry" was now indispensable since "the waves of democracy" submerged "the old and narrow lines within which the few stood apart." Lodge referred to Darwin, Galton, Mendel, and the triumph of "the modern biologists" to argue that "a man's origin has become a recognized part of his biographer's task." In his case, he proudly traced his father's English maternal ancestors and boasted of his mother's Cabot and Higginson family, especially his famous great-grandfather Senator George Cabot and his ancestor Francis Higginson, "the first minister of the first church of Salem in 1630."[12]

Many Americans who had previously maintained discretion about their actual or imagined descent from royal or noble blood now publicized it, relying on the notion of heredity to legitimize their claims to social superiority. Charles H. Browning, a genealogist who specialized in royal lineage in the late 1870s, made his living off the new fashion. He asked hundreds of individuals to send him their "descent from any royal family," compiled the pedigrees he received, and published the results in *Americans of Royal Descent,* a best-selling book that went through several editions between 1883 and 1920. To Browning's many correspondents, descent from royalty meant not only social status but also the assurance of a valuable hereditary stock. In 1900 Browning published a volume of "pedigrees showing the lineal descent from kings" of chosen members of the Colonial Dames of America. The feminist writer and reformer Charlotte Perkins Gilman, who fully adhered to the racialized tenets of Anglo-Saxonism, explained in her autobiography that in her young age she had delighted in searching Browning's book in the library, looking for her "extremely remote connection with English royalty," of which she was markedly proud. Others saw to it that their pedigree would appear in the British author Arthur Meredyth Burke's *Prominent Families of the United States* (1908), a book published in London and based on information provided by the individuals. Typically, each entry first listed a living person and then traced his descent, indicated his residence, and described his coat of arms when available.[13]

Lacking royal ancestors, some emphasized other lofty origins. "The Chappells," the author of a family genealogy explained in 1900, were "entitled to the proud distinction of being recognized as one of the oldest families in the United States." Roberdeau Buchanan underlined the fact that his Scottish Cunyngham ancestors wore "the old Saxon title of nobility" of thane and maintained "a high social position," while his first Roberdeau ancestor was a French Huguenot "gentleman" and the father of the Revolutionary War general Daniel Roberdeau.[14]

❧   ❧   ❧

The rise of the eugenic movement after the rediscovery of Gregor Mendel's laws of heredity in 1900 reinforced the connection between hereditarianism and genealogy. Eugenics, a term coined by Francis Galton in 1883, offered an evolutionary solution to the nature/nurture debate between hereditarians and environmentalists by developing "the science of the improvement of the human race by better breeding." It reassured those who were afraid of race decline or "suicide," a popular notion in the early 1900s, that there could be a better future ahead. As the sociologist Edward A. Ross explained in 1901, "race suicide" happened when a superior race ceased to expand and lost its "strong sense of its superiority." For Ross, such superiority could not be maintained "without *pride of blood* and an uncompromising attitude toward the lower races." Eugenics would help ensure that superiority, and genealogy would help eugenicists achieve their goal.[15]

Not all genealogists were eugenicists at the time, but most eugenicists were interested in genealogy, the key to "better breeding."

Genealogically minded eugenicists could be found among the members of the Committee on Eugenics formed in 1906 within the American Breeders' Association. The committee's goal was to focus on human heredity and "to emphasize the value of superior blood and the menace to society of inferior blood."[16] Besides the chairman David Starr Jordan, members included Alexander Graham Bell, the sociologist Charles Henderson, and Charles B. Davenport, who served as secretary to the committee. Many practiced genealogy personally, like Bell, or had genealogists in their family, like Davenport, whose father had published two family genealogies, was a corresponding member of the New England Historic Genealogical Association, and traced the Davenports back to a companion of William the Conqueror. In 1929 David Starr Jordan coauthored *Your Family Tree,* an essay on "scientific aspects of genealogy," which contained a plea for eugenic genealogy and numerous illustrious family trees, including his own, meant to illustrate the virtues of "superior blood."[17]

The eugenicists' project actually envisioned a new, different use for genealogy. Paul Popenoe, the editor of the eugenic *Journal of Heredity,* regretted in 1915 that genealogists had "sentimental purposes" and "historical or legal motives." Genealogy's scientific value would be much greater if it were "a means to a far greater end." Genealogists had to abandon what he saw as inadequate methods and focus on questions and materials "of real genetic value." Although the critical information about an ancestor was "the facts of his character, physical and mental," genealogists seldom mentioned them because they were not interested in experimental science. Popenoe called for change. The future of genealogy lay in genetics because genealogy could provide the means for learning more about the laws of heredity. Genealogists had "to learn to think like biologists" and to allow genealogy to "become the study of heredity, rather than the study of lineage." It would contribute to the advancement of genetics and possibly throw light on such scientific problems as the inheritance of longevity and disease, the determination of sex, the posterity of genius, and much more. For a eugenicist like Popenoe, genealogy should help define the factors that produced superior or inferior individuals, with major consequences for all. It would provide individuals with a thorough knowledge of their potential mates' genetic history and help them "marry wisely" and promote race betterment as good breeders should—by choosing or excluding a potential mate on what was considered a scientific basis, not randomly. It would also help identify those families that were considered bad breeders, or "dysgenic," and endangered the future of the country. In effect, therefore, genealogy could become "a splendid servant of the whole race" by offering the genetic information essential to improving humankind.[18]

The eugenicists' project for genealogy received institutional recognition and a definite echo among genealogists. At least three institutions were created in the United States "for the sole purpose of analyzing genealogies from a biological or statistical point of view." One was Alexander Graham Bell's Genealogical Record Office, which the inventor opened in Washington, D.C., in 1914. Another was the Eugenics Record Office (ERO), established as early as 1910 by Charles B. Davenport at Cold Spring Harbor, Long Island. Davenport persuaded Mary Williamson Harriman, the widow of the railroad magnate Edward H. Harriman, to sponsor his project. Until its closing on 31 December 1939, it served as the unofficial center for American eugenics. During the 1920s a California businessman, Ezra S. Gosney, created a third and similar institution in Pasadena, the Human Betterment Foundation, which he entrusted to Paul Popenoe. In turn, this process of institutionalization contributed to solidifying a genealogy-based conception of race and a race-based practice of genealogy.[19]

Within a few years of its creation, ERO researchers and field workers began to accumulate family case histories and pedigree charts. They also attempted to gain converts to the new science of eugenic genealogy. The ERO published *The Family-History Book* in 1912 and *How to Make a Eugenical Family Study* in 1915, two volumes of the ERO Bulletin whose recommendations were followed by thousands of Americans. Charles B. Davenport, Paul Popenoe, and ERO superintendent Harry H. Laughlin ceaselessly preached the new eugenic creed in various writings and lectures. "The study of genealogy in connection with eugenics bids fair to follow many a problem of the future," the genealogist Eben Putnam claimed in 1918 in the *Journal of Heredity*. "Forewarned is forearmed."[20]

Three years earlier the 1915 San Francisco Panama-Pacific International Exposition had provided a large forum for eugenic genealogy. The exposition hosted both the Second National Conference on Race Betterment and the International Congress of Genealogy. The Race Betterment Week and the related exhibit were a large success, as was the genealogical congress, the first of its kind. The idea of a genealogical congress during the Panama-Pacific Exposition was first proposed in the fall of 1912 by Boutwell Dunlap, a former diplomat who served as recording secretary of the California Genealogical Society. Dunlap suggested inviting "all genealogical, historical, family and eugenic societies and organizations" to meet during the exposition. The genealogy and eugenics conferences were kept separate, but the project's proponents made sure that the International Congress of Genealogy would meet just before the meeting of the American Genetic Association and the Second National Conference on Race Betterment. The eugenics *Journal of Heredity* advertised the congress and reported on it afterward. As Colvin B. Brown, one of the directors of the Panama-Pacific Exposition, explained to the delegates, genealogists embodied the spirit of the exposition because they represented "a forward movement in race betterment" and "for the uplift of the race." Not surprisingly, the relation between genealogy and eugenics was made a central theme of discussion during the congress, and Paul Popenoe was invited to give a plenary address on the topic.[21]

Eugenicists continued to push for eugenic genealogy throughout the 1920s and 1930s. Many genealogists were influenced by eugenic rhetoric and routinely used eugenic vocabulary in their writings. The American Eugenics Society, which was organized in 1923 to bring together the local groups and societies that had mushroomed in the United States, had a Committee on Biological Genealogy, chaired successively by the zoologist Vernon L. Kellogg, who served as permanent secretary to the National Research Council, the anthropologist Clark D. Wissler, Charles B. Davenport, and the geographer Ellsworth Huntington of Yale University. In 1935 Huntington, by then president of the American Eugenics Society, coauthored a study of the Huntington family that had been approved and supervised by the Committee on Biological Genealogy of the American Eugenics Society and proposed to demonstrate the value of good breeding to the nation. Eugenic projects using genealogy developed in various American states, targeting rural areas and their supposedly degenerate population. Arthur E. Estabrook and Ivan E. McDougle's 1926 study *Mongrel Virginians: The Win Tribe* focused on several poor families of the Blue Ridge Mountains. In Vermont the Eugenics Survey of Vermont initiated by zoology professor Henry F. Perkins collected family histories and drew pedigree charts of what he called "dysgenic" families, which were often of French Canadian or Abenaki origin. In Virginia, Vermont, and several other states, such genealogical studies of "dysgenic" families resulted in the forced but legal sterilization of thousands of individuals.[22]

The development of eugenic genealogy illustrates well the extent to which the meaning of genealogy in the postbellum decades became saturated with race. A good example of this long-term trend took place during the 1920 presidential campaign between James Middleton Cox and Warren Gamaliel Harding, both of Ohio. In the summer of 1920 the *New York Times* published their genealogies. This may have been a traditional means of introducing presidential contenders to the public; after all, the newspaper had published Grover Cleveland's genealogy at the time of his election in 1884. It may also have been prompted by rumors about Harding's ancestry that had been circulating since the Republican Convention in Chicago in June.[23]

During the summer circulars explaining that Harding had a black grandmother were distributed throughout the country. The Ohio Republican and Democratic committees traded barbs and charges in the newspapers as the presidential campaign turned into a racialized genealogical battlefield. A Wooster, Ohio, college professor, William Estabrook Chancellor, was accused of being the author of the circulars. For his defense, Chancellor collected sworn depositions about Harding's ancestry, with local men swearing that Harding's father was black, that his mixed ancestry was common knowledge in his birthplace, and that he had never denied having black ancestors. By late October Chancellor was fired from his academic position at the College of Wooster for writing "malicious propaganda circulars." The *Dayton Journal,* owned by the former Republican governor of Ohio, Myron T. Herrick, published the results of a lengthy investigation of the incident, which the *New York Times* reprinted the next day on its first page. The *Journal's* investigation included an "authoritative genealogy" of Harding that traced him back to various European ancestors (Dutch, English, German, and Scotch-Irish)—making him "in 1920 as American as they come"—as well as testimonies from respected Ohio Democrats. The *Times* also published the results of a second investigation by the genealogist Charles A. Hanna and an editorial denouncing "an odious attack" on Harding.[24]

As this brouhaha suggests, the language, practice, and meaning of American genealogy had become fully racialized by the interwar period. No longer was the pursuit of ancestors an intellectual and affective pastime of voracious antiquarians. The quest for family trees was now fully part of American racial politics. To substantiate an individual's claim to social and racial respectability, lineages were called on to testify to purity of blood and antiquity of roots.

✻   ✻   ✻

Genealogy validated racial claims on an individual basis, but it also served to reinforce collective affirmations of American national identity and superiority. During the decades after the Civil War, American nationalism became more powerful, visible, and debated. The war had left open the questions of who constituted the nation and whether it was to be based on inclusion or exclusion. The half century of debates that followed produced a version of American nationalism that was more vocal, exclusive, and genealogically minded than ever. At its core was a conception of the nation "as a living organism, not a contractual relationship."[25]

In this new racially inflected construction, those who were included in the nation were part of a large family bound by quasikinship ties; individuals who did not share these ties could not hope to be fully included in the nation. The definition of membership became racial. According to the period's social Darwinist wisdom, white Americans constituted a race and a nation that was the result of a long history of racial conflicts in which the more civilized races triumphed over the weaker ones. The idea that Germanic peoples had successfully invaded Britain in the fifth century, defeated Britons and Celts, and created the Anglo-Saxon race that became the English and then the American race and nation provided a convenient ideological basis for defining true Americans at the expense of outsiders of all stripes. John W. Burgess argued at the time that the United States "must be regarded as a Teutonic national state." Genealogical knowledge, in turn, ensured restriction of national membership to those who could prove lineal descent from Anglo-Saxon ascendants. In Stuart McConnell's words, "The nation was re-envisioned as a kind of extended family, held together by the blood of kinship." In this way, genealogy aided the process of reconciliation between white Southerners and white Northerners by underscoring their American racial unity and their shared lineage and ancestry at the expense of African Americans. A commonality of ancestors served to define the present boundaries of the nation.[26]

Although pride of ancestry was nothing new in the United States, it had been mostly local and regional during the antebellum era. In contrast, many late nineteenth-century Americans established a racial link between ancestral pride and a newfound sense of national superiority. As David Starr Jordan explained in 1894, "Good blood as well as free schools and free environment are essential to making a nation."[27] Men like John Fiske and Josiah Strong ceaselessly praised Americans as the proudest representatives of the Anglo-Saxon (or, as Fiske preferred to put it, the English) race by virtue of their pedigree. In an influential essay Fiske envisioned that they would rule over the world and predicted that soon "four-fifths of the human race" would "trace its pedigree to English forefathers, as four-fifths of the white people in the United States" did at the time. Strong likewise devoted an entire chapter of *Our Country* to extolling the virtues of Anglo-Saxons as representatives of liberty and Christianity. Like Fiske, he was convinced that they would "outnumber all the other civilized races of the world." Since most Americans were Anglo-Saxon, the United States could look ahead safely to "the final competition of races" until "it has Anglo-Saxonized mankind." America was patriotic, nationalist, Anglo-Saxon, and the strongest of the fit.[28]

Many Americans experienced this new genealogical nationalism through hereditary societies, which experienced tremendous growth in the years after the nation's and the Constitution's centennials (1876 and 1889). These societies embodied the institutional conflation of race, nationalism, and genealogy. As a Wisconsin genealogist recognized in 1894, "The origin of several societies" lay in the growing "feeling" in the United States "that the descendants of the first settlers have reason to be proud of their ancestry." Dozens of such organizations were created, particularly during the 1890s. There were almost fifty of them by 1895 and seventy by 1900. Ad hoc books and journals catering to the needs of their members soon appeared. Membership was restricted on the basis of ancestry. Applicants had to prove their pedigree, thus giving genealogy a boost and enormous social importance. These organizations were so successful that "by 1900 no man, woman, or child whose lineage went back a century in this country needed to deny himself the company of his genealogical peers."[29]

Unlike the myriads of preexisting fraternal societies like the Odd Fellows, Red Men, and Knights of Pythias, the new societies linked race, patriotism, and heredity in their appeal to descendants of white Anglo-Saxon colonists. The movement started slowly in the late 1870s, perhaps because sectional reconciliation still lay a long way ahead. The first organization, the Society of Sons of Revolutionary Sires, was founded in California in 1876. Another, New York–based society, the Sons of the Revolution (SR), developed in the early 1880s and grew slowly, having in 1890 only three branches in New York, Pennsylvania, and the District of Columbia. One member of the Sons, William Osborne McDowell, broke with the organization in 1889 and created a rival society, the National Society of the Sons of the American Revolution (SAR). Stung by the challenge, the SR soon formed its own General Society. By the late 1890s the SR was present in twenty-nine states, the SAR in thirty-five. According to the SAR's constitution, membership was reserved to those "descended from an ancestor" who had fought for American independence. From some 3,503 members in 1892, the SAR grew to over 10,000 ten years later, 14,000 in the mid-1910s, and some 20,000 around 1930.[30]

The SAR's 1890 constitution reserved membership to men aged 21 or older and thereby excluded women from its ranks. Indignation about this policy combined with a tradition of women's patriotic organizations that went back at least to the Woman's Relief Corps (founded in 1883 as a national organization) to stimulate the creation of women's patriotic societies. "Were there no mothers of the Revolution?" asked Mary Smith Lockwood in the *Washington Post* in July 1890. A few weeks later McDowell, always willing to support another patriotic project, seconded Lockwood's position and called for the creation of a society to be called Daughters of the American Revolution (DAR); a new organization bearing that name was founded in Washington by a small group of women. Internal strife soon led one of them, Flora Adams Darling, to secede and set up her own Daughters of the Revolution (DR). By 1900 there were some 30,000 DAR and 6,000 DR members in hundreds of chapters throughout the country. As they spread the gospel of racial patriotism, these organizations diffused the practice of genealogy in parts of the country where it had heretofore been infrequent. Turn-of-the-century patriotic societies nationalized genealogy.[31]

To be sure, for the DAR, the SAR, and the members of other patriotic-hereditary societies, genealogy was a means, not an end. Applicants filled out forms listing ancestors over four to six generations and describing the selected ancestor's actions during the Revolution. Their genealogical efforts aimed at proving an essential but limited blood line. Many applicants were not interested in genealogical research and were all too happy to hire professional genealogists to do the work, but others demonstrated a personal interest in establishing their pedigree beyond the extent needed for admission and became genealogists. Thus Theodore M. Banta's wish to join the Holland Society of New York (founded in 1885) led him to write his family genealogy despite the fact that "at the start he had but little idea of the amount of work involved, nor of the numbers represented in the family." A wish to become a member of the Colonial Dames led Elizabeth S. Rogers of Philadelphia to trace her pedigree and then to write a book that would serve as "record of my ancestory" [sic].[32]

For those who succeeded in being admitted to the SAR, the DAR, and other patriotic-hereditary organizations, the importance of genealogical interest and practice varied widely. Many organizations operated mostly as social clubs. Among the DAR, on the other hand, although genealogy was never central to the organization, it played an important role when the women of the DAR embarked on patriotic crusades and civic mobilization. In the case of the Ann Arbor (later Sarah Caswell Angell) Chapter of the DAR, organized in 1896, members busied themselves with patriotic activities, particularly during the Spanish-American War in 1898, and they undertook to locate and mark the graves of Revolutionary War soldiers. Genealogy did not seem a priority during the chapter's first years: in 1903 its historian explained that her work had been limited to "reporting the meetings to the daily papers as *none of the members had furnished her material for writing a family history.*"[33]

Although not central, genealogy was part of the DAR's spectrum of activities. "The Records of American family life have been enriched by the tireless energy of devoted workers," the DAR's president general noted in 1930. "Pillar-like, these families uphold our national integrity." The DAR Library in Constitution Hall in Washington, D.C., was meant to become "a great genealogical library, the greatest in this country," as DAR chapters from all around the country compiled and sent genealogical records to develop its collections. One of the early tasks undertaken by the organization was to establish lineage books, meaning rolls of membership tracing each member to her revolutionary ancestor(s). The first volume, originally published in 1895 and revised in 1908, covered the society's 818 charter members. Six were actual daughters of revolutionary soldiers; a few were granddaughters; most were great-granddaughters and great-great-granddaughters. Not only did each entry connect the member to the revolutionary past, but it also served to bring this past to life. In the words of the editor of the

1908 edition, "The American Revolution has become of living, breathing personal interest and not a mere abstraction."[34]

Because of their gender and their role in developing the cult of the revolutionary past in a context of racial exclusiveness, the DAR helped reconfigure the genealogical paradigm that had dominated the United States during the antebellum period. Most women had practiced genealogy privately and inside the family circle during the first half of the nineteenth century. During the 1890s and the early part of the twentieth century, the DAR's visibility and influence in the public sphere transformed the culture of genealogy. Women became legitimate actors in the public quest for family trees and gave that quest a new political and racial dimension. On the one hand, they emphasized race, white supremacy, and Anglo-Saxonism with an urgency that had been absent before 1860. "This country is fundamentally Anglo-Saxon," the DAR's president general declared in the early 1920s. The DAR stood for "the purity of our Caucasian blood" and "the perpetuity of our Anglo-Saxon traditions of liberty, law, and the security and gradual elevation of the white man's standard of living," said another president general in 1911.[35] On the other hand, despite their emphasis on race, heredity, and birth, most members retained at least some of the antebellum interest in history and moral worth. The DAR emphasized birth over deeds but constantly insisted that birth alone was not enough, not surprisingly, perhaps, given the need for its members to insert themselves into a revolutionary tradition. Their attempts at managing the American past for their own purpose were legitimate in their view because they represented the true heirs of American identity. Facing her audience at the thirtieth Continental Congress in 1921, the president general exclaimed, "*You* stand for America."[36]

In the context of turn-of-the-century American racial national-ism, the DAR was a patriotic as much as a hereditary organization. Not all societies that sprang to life during the 1890s could make the same claim. Some operated as exclusive and hereditary social clubs with no evident patriotic activity. Others, like the Colonial Dames, also proclaimed their patriotism but had a harder time demonstrating it because of their reference to the colonial rather than to the revolutionary period. In the midst of this wealth of new societies, the DAR displayed a remarkable ability to embody a ra-cial and nationalist vision of patriotism that built on its genealogi-cal self-consciousness.

*   *   *

By the late 1880s the new racialized and nationalist genealogy be-gan to reach beyond white Americans of British descent and con-cern descendants of other immigrant groups and even some Afri-can Americans. One observer noted at the time that there was no reason why only the descendants of Puritans should practice gene-alogy, and he called for "a roll-call of the descendants of the Puri-tans, of the Huguenots, of the countrymen of Luther, of Gustavus Adolphus, of Saint Patrick,—of all who value good government."[37]

This enumeration deliberately forgot the migrants and groups who were settling in the United States in great numbers at the time, perhaps because, in the commentator's mind, they did not value what he called "good government," perhaps also because he was aware that it took a while for immigrants to begin to practice genealogy in their host country. Save for a few individuals, the Ital-ians, Greeks, and eastern European Jews who constituted the larg-est share of yearly arrivals to the United States did not launch genealogical investigations at the time. Very different was the case of Americans of German, Huguenot, Scotch, Swedish, Irish, and even German Jewish origin, who all used genealogy to attempt to counterbalance what they perceived as the undue weight of Anglo-Saxonism in the United States. Their notion of genealogy was fully as racialized as that of the proponents of Anglo-Saxonism, but they defended the idea that genealogy helped demonstrate that the founding groups of the United States were more diverse than the Anglo-Saxonists claimed.[38]

Americans of Scotch-Irish origin organized in the Scotch-Irish Congress in 1889. "In large part we have a common ancestry," they telegraphed the Sons of the American Revolution in 1890. They insisted on their specific contribution to the colonial and national history of the United States, but also on their connections to other Protestant groups. "About one fifth of our whole population has Scotch-Irish blood in their veins," the Reverend John S. MacIntosh explained in 1891. "If we add the associated and affiliated Hollander and Huguenot, you get more than a fourth; add in the North German and Welsh, our British cousins, and you widen the sweep of our race-kinships. What a magnificent arch it is—finest European stocks." However, the Scotch-Irish Congress was not very successful in developing a genealogical program. One member lamented in 1896 that meetings offered only "eloquent words of self-praise, based on glittering generalities." In contrast, "the New Englander does the same," but "back of his feast and eloquence is the most thorough research in his pedigree."[39]

Unlike the Scotch-Irish, descendants of Huguenots used genealogy successfully to affirm their contribution to and place in American history. "More noble blood never settled American soil than that which circulated through the veins of the Huguenots," one genealogist boasted in the early twentieth century. During the 1870s Charles W. Baird and Edward F. De Lancey published several contributions on Huguenot genealogy in the *New York Biographical and Genealogical Record*. In 1875 hundreds of descendants of Jacques and Louis Du Bois met for a family reunion at New Paltz, New York. Others published family genealogies in growing numbers.[40] The celebration of the bicentennial of the revocation of the Edict of Nantes, in 1885, saw both the publication of Charles W. Baird's pathbreaking *History of the Huguenot Emigration to America* and the founding of two organizations in New York and Charleston, the Huguenot Society of America (1883) and the Huguenot Society of South Carolina (1885). Other similar societies followed in the early twentieth century in Pennsylvania, New Jersey, Washington, D.C., and Virginia, and a Federation of Huguenot Societies was created in 1931. All these organizations used genealogy as a means to stimulate a sense of ancestral pride and consciousness of belonging to a "Huguenot race."[41]

The Huguenot Society of South Carolina not only held social functions and regular meetings where papers of diverse interest and originality were read but also encouraged its members to collect Huguenot memorabilia and artifacts and research Huguenot genealogy. Its *Transactions,* published beginning in 1889, included genealogical notes and pedigrees of major South Carolina Huguenot families like the Legarés, Hugers, Gaillards, Prioleaus, Marions, Ravenels, and Manigaults. In 1906 the society's president, Robert Wilson, summarized the gains made during the previous two decades. Although very little had been known about the South Carolina Huguenots at the time of the society's creation, now "scarcely a family among their descendants has failed to find their names available for any Society demanding honorable service for eligibility."[42]

By the 1880s and 1890s many descendants of South Carolina Huguenot families were practicing genealogists. Eulogies of the former Confederate general Wilmot Gibbes de Saussure insisted on his connoisseur interest in genealogy. Eliza C. K. Fludd of Charleston, who in the 1840s had compiled family chronicles that included genealogical material about her ancestor Solomon Legaré and his descendants, decided in 1886 to commit them to print at the request of family members who wanted to own a copy. Elsewhere in the United States, many other genealogists researched Huguenot ancestors in the first decades of the twentieth century.[43]

The language used by genealogically minded descendants of Huguenots was very similar to that adopted by patriotic hereditary societies such as the DAR. Although they emphasized racial pride, they always connected it to moral obligations. President Daniel Ravenel explained in 1889, "Pride of birth and ancestry" found "its only justification in lives of high endeavor and noble action, in earnest and loyal services to State and Church and Humanity." This became a favorite theme in presidential addresses at the society's annual meetings. Robert Wilson, one of Ravenel's successors, repeatedly insisted that the society's goal was not "the exploiting of individual claims to distinguished ancestry" but "a sacred and noble obligation" to preserve memories of Huguenot ancestry. "We are not here to flaunt ourselves in the plumes of a noble ancestry," he emphasized in 1911; his comment suggests that not all society members may have shared their president's concerns.[44]

The obvious tension between collective moral obligation and individual social pride was not limited to Huguenots. Descendants of Dutch migrants to New Netherland who joined the Holland Society in New York (created in 1885) and founders of the American-Irish Historical Society (AIHS, 1897) who openly challenged what

they called the "Anglo-Saxon fetish" shared similar feelings. Criticizing those who divided themselves "into classes and races" and
assumed "superiority for the so-called 'Anglo-Saxon race' over all
the other races of men created by Almighty God," the AIHS's president in 1899 called on society members to resist the idea that "all
the other peoples, including the Irish, are inferiors in race." To the
contrary, many individuals who decided to join the AIHS emphasized pride "in their Irish lineage" and the feeling that "they represented the best blood of the island." Like the descendants of the
Huguenots and the Dutch, the Irish constantly adopted the vocabulary of race and lineage, insisting on the necessity of better learning "the history of the stock as a whole" and celebrating "a race so
prolific, so inwrought with the old stock of the land."[45]

German American Jews also adopted a celebratory stance. The
first Jewish local histories usually included biographies and genealogies of esteemed community representatives. Beginning in the
1890s, members of the American Jewish Historical Society (AJHS)
set up for themselves the goal of documenting the contribution of
Jews to American society. Although genealogy was never the main
focus of the AJHS, Cyrus Adler and his associates made room for
family histories of important American Jews of the past in the annual meetings of the society and the pages of its *Publications*. To
write "the genealogy of these men and the record of their achievements" became a useful strategy to fight anti-Semitism. The twelve
volumes of the *Jewish Encyclopedia* published between 1901 and 1906
also contained dozens of biographies, genealogies, and family trees
of American Jewish families.[46]

As in the past, elite Jewish American families continued to collect genealogical information. Much of it remained private. In 1901
Joseph Jacobs explained that "the desks and bureaus of the Jewish

Daughters of the Revolution" hid family history treasures because there was "nothing more secretive than a family with an ancient record." At least some American Jews, however, published the results of their genealogical research in book form, and many more, like Judge Mayer Sulzberger of Philadelphia (whose family tree and genealogy were included in the *Jewish Encyclopedia*), gathered information assiduously.[47]

Likewise, some African Americans partook in the late nineteenth-century genealogical mania. In their small number, as in their motivations, they differed from the many former slaves or descendants of slaves who demonstrated their genealogical consciousness as they searched for missing relatives during Reconstruction and well into the 1890s. To "glory in lineal ancestors," as one black journalist wrote in the 1870s, and to "trace up linealogy," as another put it a quarter of a century later, were favorite activities among blood-conscious, well-to-do African-Americans who skillfully connected knowledge of ancestry, respectability, and pride in success. Some created hereditary societies based on lineage, like the Society of the Sons of New York (1884), the Society of the Daughters of New York (1886), and the Society of the Descendants of Early New England Negroes founded in the 1920s in Boston by the black teacher and clubwoman Florida Ruffin Ridley. Most gathered genealogical data about their family without committing them to print. There were exceptions, however, like Daniel Alexander Payne Murray, the assistant librarian of Congress and a historian, bibliographer, and genealogist who embarked on an unfinished "Historical and Biographical Encyclopedia of the Colored Race" during the 1900s. Murray was convinced of what he called "the power of blood inheritance," and he researched his Maryland family genealogy extensively. He and others played a pioneering role in black historical organizations.[48]

Like whites, most African American elites relied on genealogy as much to exclude as to include. If "knowledge of family history was counted as highly important," as W. E. B. Du Bois explained of New England black elites, it was because it allowed them to insist on social and racial differences among African Americans and to fight the idea, common among whites in the racial context of the period, that all blacks were indistinguishable from one another. Those who dealt "heavily in family trees" insisted that their lineage made them different. On the one hand, they associated ancestral pride with their or their ancestors' status in slavery and freedom—whether they had been free persons of color, privileged slaves, or vocal opponents of the slave system. On the other hand, many also acknowledged white ancestors they considered as significant as glorious African and Indian forebears, whether real or imagined. Black New Yorkers with Dutch names, for instance, celebrated their Dutch and Indian ancestors. One explained in 1899 to a journalist "that his great-grandparents were Manhattan Indians, that his grandmother was a queen, that she married a Holland Dutchman of great wealth, etc. ad nauseam." For black elites who prized "well-ancestored people," in Langston Hughes's words, genealogy served to confirm status and reinforce social networks.[49]

In contrast, Native Americans did not resort to genealogy to celebrate their social status. Nevertheless, by the early twentieth century the dominant Euro-American language of race began to influence and transform Native American notions of ancestry. Until then, these notions were derived from each group's kinship system, which could vary considerably—between matrilineal and patrilineal systems, for instance—but was central to Native American culture. Kinship's defining feature was often the web of significant social interactions that existed among kin rather than biological connectedness. Native American genealogical consciousness was strong, and many Indians knew their ancestors and could trace their genealogy, but their relationship to ancestry conformed to rules and patterns of their own, not to the Euro-American kinship system.[50]

After the end of the Indian wars, the Dawes Act (1887), which authorized allotment of land to individual Indians, and the weight of the language of race in American culture and public policy influenced Native American notions of ancestry. In order to receive land, Indians had to prove tribal membership and ancestry, and they had to conform to Euro-American genealogical standards to do so. For example, the Cherokees in Oklahoma, the Anishinaabeg on the White Earth Reservation (Minnesota), and the Mississippi Choctaws borrowed the American language of race and blood, which they had never used before, to prove citizenship in their respective nations because the required emphasis on blood quantum—and the racial categories of "full-bloods" and "half-bloods" imposed by the federal government—meant eligibility for land allotment. Although traditional conceptions of the relationship to ancestry remained alive in early twentieth-century Native American cultures—as anthropological studies revealed during the 1920s and 1930s—, the new notions that conformed to the dominant Euro-American racialized genealogical model began to gain ground, suggesting significant changes in Native American visions of kin and identity.[51]

*　　*　　*

The conflation of race, heredity, and nationalism transformed the meaning and practice of genealogy in the decades after the Civil War. During a period of cultural and psychological unease about collective and individual identities, the search for roots was infused with the notion of white American superiority. Moreover, the racial and nationalist meanings of family trees that became predominant served to transform genealogy's nature in yet another way. Their success made the quest for pedigrees more popular and more accessible than ever in the United States. As demand grew, so did supply, and this growth redefined the nature of the genealogical market and business.

❧ 5 ❧

PEDIGREES AND THE MARKET

We are becoming the most genealogical nation on the face of the earth," the *New York Times* observed in 1879, adding that this interest extended beyond elite families to "our great middle class." Fueled by racial and nationalist considerations, late nineteenth- and early twentieth-century Americans turned to genealogy in increasing numbers. They demanded more products and services in order to satisfy their quest for roots. Some wished to learn how to become a genealogist. Others were willing to hire somebody else to draw their pedigree. Many hoped to know who their ancestors really were. Not a few wanted ancestors who fit their ideas of the family past, and they were willing to pay for this. Within a few decades their demands transformed the genealogical marketplace.[1]

Genealogy became an industry, saturated with race, nationalism, and conspicuous consumption. In order to match demand, numerous individuals and firms entered the genealogical market, offering products and services on a commercial basis to their clients. Not only were pedigrees bought and sold on a regular basis, but the numbers of genealogical societies, journals, and paraphernalia reached unprecedented heights. Moreover, many unscrupulous genealogists took advantage of the lack of market regulation to develop fraudulent practices on a new scale.

In reaction against the rise of pecuniary genealogy, there were attempts to regulate and professionalize the practice. Other Americans elected to pursue their interest in family trees fully outside the market, either for religious reasons, like the Mormons, or because of the moral and family values they attached to genealogy. At the time, however, these opponents of pecuniary genealogy were a minority. Their efforts to emphasize a scientific, moral, and religious dimension of genealogy were consistently overshadowed by the powerful coalition of racist, patriotic, and business rationales.

❖   ❖   ❖

Until the last decades of the nineteenth century demand was scarce, and the market for pedigrees remained limited. Most genealogical works were published as subscription books. With the exception of Horatio Gates Somerby, there were no professional genealogists. The economy of genealogy was largely based on giving and receiving rather than selling and buying. For two decades after its creation in 1847, the *New England Historical and Genealogical Register* faced almost overwhelming economic difficulties, barely surviving severe crises during the 1850s and early 1860s. The Albany publishing house of Joel Munsell, the only one of its kind in the United States, fared little better. It was common wisdom that there was no money to be made in genealogy.[2]

Within a decade or two after the Civil War this situation changed as the United States experienced the rapid growth of a national market for the new racial and exclusive genealogy. In the context of the nation's centennial, of the creation of numerous patriotic organizations, and of a postwar reconstruction based on racial solidarity between former enemies at the expense of African Americans, many upper- and middle-class Americans bought and sold artifacts or information related to family trees. "Ribbon and coronets" could be purchased "at market rates," a magazine sarcastically noted in 1877.[3] Numerous actors entered the new genealogical scene. Countless enthusiasts, professional pedigree researchers and recorders, book and journal publishers and authors, and makers of genealogical and heraldic artifacts partook in the growth of an economy of genealogy that was fully commercialized by the late nineteenth century and kept on growing during the first decades of the twentieth century.

"So general is the desire of our people to know whatever is known of their family history," Thomas Amory remarked in 1872, "that an adept is sure of lucrative employment." During the antebellum era most genealogy enthusiasts searched their pedigree themselves and did not pay for it. By the 1870s the context had changed. Americans with no inclination for the difficulties of research but with a desire to own a pedigree chose to hire a professional genealogist, both in Britain and the United States. As a result, many British genealogists began to work for American clients, and some Americans followed in Horatio Gates Somerby's antebellum steps and settled in Britain to work for American patrons.[4]

Somerby himself was active until his death in 1872. His two most important successors were Joseph L. Chester during the 1870s and Henry F. Waters for the next two decades. Born in 1821 in modest circumstances, Chester tried his hand at many trades during the 1840s and 1850s. He was a teacher, a clerk in a mercantile house, an amateur poet who published a volume in 1843 *(Greenwood Cemetery and Other Poems)*, a temperance lecturer, a musical editor for *Godey's Lady's Book*, an editor for the *Philadelphia Enquirer* and the *Daily Sun*, a member of Philadelphia's City Council, and an assistant clerk in the U.S. House of Representatives in Washington, D.C. In 1858 he served as an aid to the governor of Pennsylvania, James Pollock, with the rank of colonel, a title that he used proudly during the rest of his life. His life took a turn when he went to England on business in the late 1850s. London suited him, and he decided to remain there, first as a journalist and then to cultivate his true vocation as a professional genealogist and historian. Waters, a graduate of Harvard College and a Civil War veteran, was a teacher, local historian, and amateur genealogist in Salem, Massachusetts, until he spent some time in England in the late 1870s and coauthored a volume prepared in London, *Gleanings from English Records about New England Families*, that earned him recognition. When John T. Hassam, a rich Boston lawyer and genealogist, suggested that the New England Historic Genealogical Society hire a permanent agent in England and provided initial funding, Waters agreed to serve in that capacity, settling in England and faithfully sending "genealogical gleanings" to his employers for the next seventeen years.[5]

Like Somerby during his lifetime, Chester and Waters enjoyed respect and recognition in Britain and in the United States. Chester, for instance, began his career as a genealogist by exploring and copying massive amounts of English archives, including wills preserved in the repository at Doctors' Commons, the matriculation register of Oxford University, and the registers of the Abbey of Westminster, which he published in 1876. His thorough research earned him rare access privileges in the collections of the British Museum and other repositories. One of the founders of the Harleian Society in 1869 and a profound Anglophile, Chester became a fellow of the Historical Society of Great Britain (later the Royal Historical Society) in 1870 and received an honorary degree from Oxford in 1881.[6]

As his reputation grew, numerous American enthusiasts hired him to search their ancestry. Typically they wrote to introduce themselves, describe what they were looking for, and ask for his terms. Chester replied and upon receipt of a retainer got to work on their behalf in London or in other parts of England. Some of his patrons were wealthy, like Eliphalet W. Blatchford, a Chicago businessman and philanthropist, and Edward E. Salisbury, who held the chair of Arabic and Sanskrit at Yale University. Others with fewer means explained that they would not like "to go to heavy expenses" and hoped that their investment would cover all the necessary investigations.[7]

Although many American pedigree hunters who needed transatlantic information resorted to the services of Somerby, Chester, Waters, and other lesser-known names in Britain, even more numerous were those who employed paid genealogists in the United States. Among the thousands of hopeful applicants to the new patriotic societies, most were not willing or simply not versed enough in genealogy to undertake to trace their pedigree. The ensuing rise of demand led many late nineteenth-century enthusiasts to embrace genealogical researching and writing as their main or secondary activity. "It almost deserves to rank as a profession," one genealogist explained in 1894. By 1900 dozens of genealogists for hire could be found throughout the country. In Washington, D.C., for instance, Anderson C. Quisenberry offered various services to his clients, ranging from research in the Library of Congress and in public records to advice on finding genealogical information in

England and preparing applications to patriotic-hereditary societies. William Armstrong Crozier of Pennsylvania similarly explained that he was particularly "conversant" with the demands of Americans "seeking to establish their Trans-Atlantic Pedigree." He was also routinely employed by hopeful candidates to gather the necessary documentation for applying to a hereditary society, sometimes with positive and other times with disappointing results. The development of the Daughters of the American Revolution and similar organizations also resulted in a growing number of professional women genealogists. Louise Tracy, a New Haven former schoolteacher, explained in 1895 that she started genealogical work by looking up "the data necessary for joining one of the revolutionary societies for several cousins and friends, as well as for myself," and then turned her interest into a profession. Other women, like Lucy Blacknall of Virginia, specialized in the painting of coats of arms.[8]

Clients sometimes asked their employees not only to provide them with genealogical materials but also to gather and publish their family tree. Some genealogists specialized in this full service. The Reverend Frederick Chapman, who had written a book about his genealogy in 1854, worked in the 1860s for Senator William Buckingham of Connecticut and published the results of his genealogical investigation in 1872. John Adams Vinton published the *Vinton Memorial* before he extended his reach to the Giles, Sampson, Symmes, Upton, and Richardson families. During the 1880s and 1890s the process went one step further. Following the example of publishing houses that developed the fashion of county and other local histories at the time of the nation's centennial, new genealogical firms like the American Genealogical Company of Philadelphia offered a large range of genealogical and heraldic services.[9]

✻   ✻   ✻

American genealogists understood that they needed more and better documentary resources. Until 1869 they could rely only on the New England Historic Genealogical Society (NEHGS), its library, and its quarterly *Register*. Over the next decades the society's officers worked assiduously at building up its resources, particularly its library. Between 1871 and 1885 the number of books in its collections grew from 7,600 to 20,200, while pamphlets went from almost 7,000 to almost 63,000. Donations of manuscripts became an important addition to the collections. At the same time, admission policies changed in a way that illustrated genealogy's new exclusivism. Until the 1880s anybody could apply, and few were turned down. By 1890 the society's leadership felt the need for a restrictive policy and decided to screen applicants "for character, interest, and financial backing." Although these changes were attuned to the atmosphere of the times, they stood in stark contrast with the NEHGS's original choice of admitting members because of their interest in genealogy, not their birth, wealth, or family connections. The new policy played a significant role in creating an image of the NEHGS as an exclusive organization that it kept well into the twentieth century. Meanwhile, the society decided to admit women members as long as they conformed to its new social and financial criteria. The proposal was approved in January 1897 by 451 out of 523 ballots. Within a year a new charter had been adopted by the legislature of Massachusetts, new bylaws had been written, and the first women members had been admitted. In 1900 the NEHGS reached almost 1,000 members. Its growth and redefinition illustrated the changing meaning of family trees in late nineteenth-century America.[10]

By then the NEHGS's de facto monopoly on genealogical research in the United States had come to a halt. Americans could join other organizations in various mid-Atlantic, southern, and western states. Together these organizations offered many new resources to the amateur of family trees. Eliphalet W. Blatchford, the Chicago businessman who had been a client of Colonel Chester, helped found the Newberry Library and turn it into a major resource for pedigree hunters. New genealogical societies were created in New York (1869), Pennsylvania (1892), Utah (1894), and California (1898). More often, existing historical societies supported both local history and genealogy. Virginia and South Carolina genealogists contributed to the *Virginia Magazine of History and Biography* (1893) and the *South Carolina Historical and Genealogical Magazine* (1900). Demand was so steady in Virginia for genealogical publications that another periodical, Lyon Gardiner Tyler's *William and Mary College Quarterly Historical Magazine,* also began a long and prestigious career in the 1890s.[11]

By the early twentieth century Americans read genealogy columns and articles in local historical journals in such diverse places as Hunterdon County, New Jersey; Columbus, Ohio; and Wilkes-Barre, Pennsylvania. Many of these journals and magazines included advertisements, sections of questions and answers, and information about ongoing genealogical searches that played important roles as intermediary and clearinghouse among participants. Readers of the *Maine Historical and Genealogical Recorder* in the mid-1880s benefited from "a Postal Interchange Club for mutual assistance in genealogical research," as did those of the *Virginia Magazine of History and Biography* and many other journals. They requested information from one another relative to genealogical problems and advertised their publications. In a significant way, these exchanges contributed to creating among participants a sense of belonging to a larger community of genealogists.[12]

These communities were local and regional, not national. The National Genealogical Society, created in Washington, D.C., in 1903, remained a local organization for many years, and its quarterly journal (1912) long did not reach far beyond the District of Columbia. All attempts to create a nationwide commercial genealogical magazine failed. *The Chronotype: An American Memorial of Persons and Events,* published in 1873–1874 by Albert Welles of the American College of Heraldry and Genealogical Registry in New York City, did not go beyond eight issues. During its brief lifetime it was severely criticized by serious genealogists like William H. Whitmore and Joseph L. Chester for publishing "the mere ravings of a would be genealogist, full of errors and contradictions." *The Genealogical Advertiser: A Quarterly Magazine of Family History* by Lucy Hall Greenlaw, one of the first women members of the NE-HGS and a professional genealogist, lasted only three years. Other trials were no more successful. Although the United States boasted a genealogical culture united at the national level by racism and nationalism, late nineteenth-century American genealogists organized on the basis of local, regional, and sectional identities.[13]

In contrast, there was a growing national market for new research tools, how-to manuals, and various genealogical paraphernalia. As the number of published genealogies held in the Library of Congress swelled from some 414 in 1869 to 3,795 in 1909 (over 60 percent of which had been published since 1890), genealogists used William H. Whitmore's *Handbook of American Genealogy* (1862), which went through four augmented editions by 1900. His only serious competitor before the 1910s was the work of the librarian of the State Historical Society of Wisconsin, Daniel S. Durrie, *Bibliographia Genealogica*

Americana, which also had five editions between 1868 and 1900. Both books were superseded by the successive editions of *American and English Genealogies in the Library of Congress* in 1910 and 1919.[14]

Blank family registers or records also became more popular than ever. Demand for advice on how to organize family records and pedigrees led Whitmore to publish his successful how-to book, *Ancestral Tablets* (1868), which went through several editions. Several publishers, including Currier and Ives, sold more or less ornate genealogical lithographs to the public. Some of these records were simple sheets; others were more sophisticated. "Bailey's Photo-Ancestral Record," invented in the mid-1890s by a New Haven firm, the Bureau of American Ancestry, allowed its owner to enter data "for 14 generations in all directions with notes, coats of arms, and photographs." According to the advertisement, it was "very popular among genealogists, the colonial societies, and old families." Some firms catered to a specific constituency. A chromolithographed "Afro-American Historical Family Record," printed in 1899 by the Historical Publishing Company of Augusta, Georgia, suggested racial pride and emphasized the role of black regiments during the Spanish-American War. Publishers also routinely offered to print individual family histories with a luxury binding and other ornaments. Others specialized in county and state subscription histories, which usually included a large biographical and genealogical section.[15]

Many of these resources played on personal vanity rather than on science. Devotees of family trees bought them everywhere in the United States, but New York City, which had been the core producer of such objects during the antebellum era, remained the heart of the American "manufacture of ancestors." The American College of Heraldry and Genealogical Registry, founded in 1860, was housed in the New York Society Library on University Place near Washington Square. Its president, Albert Welles, surrounded himself with a council of regents and a list of honorary members that included, among many others, Hamilton Fish, William Seward, Governor John Dix of New York, and the poet and journalist William Cullen Bryant. Welles saw himself as an American herald and his college as the American equivalent of the College of Arms in London. During the 1870s he organized various heraldic events in New York City, gave numerous addresses, and printed circulars celebrating his American College of Heraldry. "The time may not be so far distant when we shall grant and create 'coats-of-arms,'" he wrote in 1873.[16]

Although the American College of Heraldry quickly proved a failure and disappeared after its founder's death in the early 1880s, Welles had identified an important niche in the American market for genealogical paraphernalia. Late nineteenth-century authors understood that heraldry sold well, and they hastened to flood the country with such promising titles as *America Heraldica* and *A Primer of Heraldry for Americans,* which catered to a seemingly limitless market. Like Mortimer Delano, the author of a *Bibliography of American Heraldry* who called himself Delano de Lannoy and assumed without authorization the heraldic title of "pursuivant-of-arms," many offered "heraldic assistance, critical and practical," to their many clients.[17]

❖   ❖   ❖

As this commercial genealogical culture developed, fraud proliferated in the United States. Although it was neither new nor unexpected in an unregulated market where demand was pressing and supply hardly controlled, it reached new heights during those decades. In fact, genealogical fraud became a feature of American culture that was not limited to a circle of enthusiasts or specialists. By the late nineteenth century it became common for magazines to publish short stories and critical comments centered on that theme.[18]

Americans falsified pedigrees out of ignorance or a desire to aggrandize themselves by aggrandizing their ancestors. Accordingly, genealogical frauds were heavily concentrated in the grayest areas of American genealogy at the time, particularly English origins of early colonists. Many frauds thus took place in England. Despite his emphasis on research and the serious genealogical work he accomplished during the 1850s and 1860s, Horatio Gates Somerby was not averse to pleasing some of his clients by forging genealogical data for them. He thus invented a connection between the ancestors of the rich Bostonian David Sears and several sixteenth-century English gentlemen, including a naval hero, Admiral Sir John Hawkins. Somerby's imaginative conclusions found their way into an 1857 book funded by Sears and edited by a kinsman, and they were not challenged until the 1880s.[19]

One of his successors in London during the 1870s, Harriet Bainbridge (later known under her married name, De Salis), practiced a less sophisticated type of fraud for her American clients. De Salis, who began her career as a secretary for Joseph L. Chester in the 1860s, soon went into business for herself. Like Somerby, she was respected in New England at first and was even recommended to potential clients by officers of the NEHGS. Many trusted her. Stephen Whitney Phoenix, for instance, published a three-volume genealogy of the Whitney family of Connecticut based in large part on Harriet De Salis's statements. Soon, however, Chester discovered that she had confused, falsified, and forged data. She decided, for instance, that one George Eliot had died in 1548, seven years before his actual death, because she had mixed up the signing and the probing of his will. In the Whitney case, De Salis actually confessed to Chester that "the two wills were fabricated." By 1880 the scandal was such that De Salis abandoned genealogy entirely.[20]

As the demand for status among newly wealthy Americans accelerated, fraud increased. Bogus heraldry was its most visible aspect and a genre in itself. In the post–Civil War decades the use of fictitious heraldic devices became extremely frequent and visible in the United States. Critics lampooned the "modern democrats" who did not think heraldry "to be out of place in a republican commonwealth," but irony had little effect on the general thirst for coats of arms. As Thorstein Veblen would soon explain, pedigrees were now for sale on a much larger scale than ever before in the United States. Money bred exclusiveness and a sense of belonging to an imagined aristocracy.[21]

In the early twentieth century Somerby's most notorious successor was a genealogist named Gustave Anjou, who perpetrated dozens of falsifications with an unbridled imagination. Anjou was something of a fraud himself. Although he let people believe that he had been born in Paris and had earned a doctorate at Uppsala in Sweden before he migrated to the United States, he was actually born Gustav Ludvig Ljungberg in Stockholm in 1863. He never studied at Uppsala but served a six-month term of hard labor for forgery in 1886. After his marriage to Anna Maria Anjou in 1889, the couple moved to New York in 1890. By the early 1900s Ljungberg was listed under his wife's maiden name as Gustave Anjou in the pages of the *New York Biographical and Genealogical Record*. For over three decades he fabricated genealogies for American clients. His frauds were far less sophisticated than Somerby's or De Salis's inventions. As befit a charlatan operating on a relatively large scale, he very successfully tried to satisfy his clients' gullibility, particularly their wish for noble ancestry. He operated a mail-order business out of his home, distributing twenty-four-page catalogs that offered complete genealogies for a $250 fee. "Traffic in ancestors is put on a democratic basis by Staten Island dealer," the *New York Times* commented.[22]

The other great source of genealogical frauds was the claims relative to American, English, and Dutch estates. Compared with the 1840s and 1850s, the late nineteenth century saw a fantastic development of this type of fraud. Countless Americans, like those described by Mark Twain in his satirical novel *The American Claimant* (1892), dreamed of becoming heirs to an English fortune. Most were genealogically ignorant, in good faith, and gullible. Like Twain's putative heir to the earldom of Rossmore, they believed that they had been deprived of their rights to their titles and properties when their ancestors had departed for America, and that they should be reinstated. At a time when the country's economic growth on an increasingly continental and industrial basis produced new wealth at an impressive rate, the success of these fraudulent foreign estate schemes testified to the centrality of the search for riches in Gilded Age America. During the 1860s and 1870s *Harper's* regularly published advertisements for "next of kin"—supposedly forgotten heirs to English and other properties—inserted by various individuals and firms located in London and New York City. Some offered to search records for a fee; others only proposed to send prepaid lists of "names entitled to property." Their successful antebellum predecessor Columbus Smith of Vermont, never to be outdone in these matters, compiled and sold an *Index* for American claimants.[23]

Attempts at estate frauds included the revival of the old Jans Bogardus claim on Trinity Church property in New York City. Despite the 1847 judgment against claimants in New York's Court of Chancery, various individuals and associations reactivated the case in later decades. All their claims were dismissed by the courts. In one case, in 1913, the judgment resulted in the arrest of the claimant and his lawyer for mail fraud; a few years later a counsel was disbarred after a similar attempt. In the early 1920s the Jans Bogardus claim reappeared in Los Angeles. After an article in the *Los Angeles Herald* was picked up all over the country, an heir apparent, Thomas Bentley Wikoff of Indiana, published a book that told the Jans story and reignited interest and hope among alleged heirs.[24]

Aside from this celebrated case, there were literally dozens of lesser-known claims, often based on fictitious genealogical claims. Columbus Smith, for one, was active until the late 1860s on behalf of various hopeful American families, like the Jenningses and the Browns, organizing investigations in England and issuing reports on their claims. The Browns hoped to prove descent from Mark Anthony Browne, the last Viscount Montagu, who had died without issue in 1797, and the Jenningses from the rich William Jennings of London, who had died intestate in 1798. Smith's business regularly excited the furor of serious genealogists like William H. Whitmore, who attacked him relentlessly while denouncing the credulity of Smith's clients.[25]

After Smith retired in the early 1870s, he had numerous successors. On their advice, the Hyde Family Association looked in vain for a supposed estate in England in the late 1870s and early 1880s. Claimants to an Edwards estate started a long legal battle in the late 1870s that dragged into the 1890s. So numerous were estate claims that in 1885 one of the secretaries of the American legation in London prepared "a paper on the subject of unclaimed estates" that purported to "blight the hopes of hundreds of American 'claimants.'" American diplomats in the Netherlands issued a similar warning about Dutch estates, and the American press regularly exposed the fraudulent nature of estate claims and derided the quest for "great estates on the moon."[26]

The estate fever, however, did not abate. In 1893 a member of the Gibbs family reprinted Columbus Smith's forty-five-year-old report on the Gibbs property in a book devoted to his family history. In 1895 some Hyde heirs decided to revive their claims. "That curious disease, the English unclaimed-estate fever, is no sooner suppressed in one part of this country than it breaks out in another," a newspaper explained.[27] The most spectacular of all scams took place during the 1910s and 1920s when Oscar Hartzell of Iowa persuaded thousands of Americans to contribute to his efforts to recover the estate of Sir Francis Drake, whose only living heir he claimed to represent. Hartzell collected huge sums of money but was tried for mail fraud and convicted in the early 1930s. During the appeal trial, which Hartzell lost, Judge Gardner of the Eighth Circuit Court summed up the reasons for the remarkable increase in genealogical and heraldic frauds and scams in the late nineteenth- and early twentieth-century United States. "Despite the palpable fraud in the representations made," he wrote, "and the incredible nature of the representations of defendant and his agent, they seem to have fired the imagination and dulled the sense of reason of many honest people who relied on them."[28]

※   ※   ※

As early as the 1860s some Americans reacted to the growing commercialization of genealogy and the multiplication of frauds. Over
the next half century they defended their vision of a science of genealogy that emphasized erudition over imagination and proof
over spoof. The same decades witnessed the emergence of the first
generation of professional academic historians, many of whom
took pains to distinguish themselves from genealogists. Not only
did history and genealogy remain intertwined for the most part,
however, but also for scientific genealogists, as well as for historians,
realism triumphed over romanticism, accuracy became a leading
principle instead of narration, and subjective judgment mostly inspired diffidence. Both genealogy and history reflected the influence
of the natural sciences, the more so because they were evolutionary.

There was one significant difference between genealogy and history. In the latter case, partisans of science and professionalization
took control of the field, in large part because of the growing place
of history in American universities. Although opponents of professionalization were active and vocal well into the twentieth century,
they were marginalized.[29] Partisans of a scientific approach to genealogy, in contrast, remained a minority of all practitioners. Few were
professional genealogists, and not all professionals were partisans
of scientific methods. Few actually lived off genealogy. All were convinced, however, that genealogy was a science that should be ap-
proached positively, not romantically. In order to be established, any
genealogical linkage had to be proven.

Among the defenders of scientific genealogy were men like Chester,
Waters, and Whitmore, as well as George Ernest Bowman of Boston, Roger Cope of Pennsylvania, and Lyon Gardiner Tyler of Virginia. All were recognized by outsiders as professionals. They knew
and respected one another and established clear-cut distinctions

between themselves and those who did not share their scientific values and priorities. When Joseph L. Chester explained to William H. Whitmore in 1865 that he had decided to ask a retainer of £20 from any American who wished him to do research on his behalf, he hastened to add that Whitmore was entitled to a different treatment: "*We* stand on a different footing altogether." Throughout the 1860s and 1870s Chester and Whitmore exchanged information about various genealogical searches and frauds, sending each other their publications and agreeing on the importance of a scientific, critical, and positivist approach to genealogy.[30]

Reformers like Chester and Whitmore targeted both heraldry and genealogy. In heraldic matters Whitmore played a leading role. In 1865, at age 29, he was chosen to chair the Committee on Heraldry, which the NEHGS created at his initiative, and to co-edit the short-lived *Heraldic Journal* with the Boston Brahmin William Sumner Appleton. The following year Whitmore published his *Elements of Heraldry*. In his mind, the committee, the journal, and the *Elements* were all part of his desire to produce much-needed knowledge about armorial bearings. He hoped to counterbalance the trend that led Americans to assume arms with "a total disregard of all authority." *The Elements of Heraldry* was meant to change that. Whitmore believed that "familiarity with the science" would improve the quality of American heraldry. In 1868 Whitmore and the Committee on Heraldry even proposed congressional legislation to regulate its use.[31]

Despite Whitmore's efforts until his death in 1901, it must have been clear by then to everyone, including himself, that the battle for an American science of heraldry was lost. Coats of arms proliferated without justification throughout the late nineteenth century. In 1866

Whitmore remarked that those who wanted to assume arms only had to visit "the nearest seal-engraver," who would look at "some heraldic Encyclopedia" and provide them "with the arms of any family of the same name." Three decades later, that remained true.[32]

Efforts to promote genealogy as a science fared slightly better during the late nineteenth century as reformers defended the use of genealogical procedures, methods, and tools. Genealogy, they argued, should follow scientific rules lest it produce mistakes or fallacies. Genealogists could be enthusiasts, but they had to master their trade professionally. When Whitmore dedicated his *Handbook of American Genealogy* to the erudite John Ward Dean, the respected librarian of the NEHGS, he chose his words carefully. Dean was honored for his work "in promoting the advancement of the science of genealogy in New England."[33]

Advancing the "science of genealogy" meant distrusting tradition and relying exclusively on archival evidence. John Farmer and his friends had made the point repeatedly in earlier decades, but in the late nineteenth-century context of racialization, nationalism, and commercialization, it had to be reiterated ceaselessly. One famous early case involved the sensitive topic of George Washington's ancestry. In his best-selling *Life of George Washington* (1837), Jared Sparks had included a chapter on the genealogy of the Washington family that presented the widely held thesis that George Washington's emigrant ancestors John and Lawrence, who arrived in Virginia in the seventeenth century, were the sons of a Northamptonshire gentleman, Lawrence Washington. Many authors expatiated on George Washington's genteel ancestry. In 1860, for instance, Charles Sumner described the tombstones of Lawrence Washington and his daughter Elizabeth in Brington, Northamptonshire,

their coats of arms, and their satisfying proximity to the aristocratic family of Spencer. The same year, the rector of Brington's
parish published *The Washingtons,* a historical novel that told the
family history at length, including its genealogy. The book was
favorably reviewed in the *North American Review,* and the reviewer
insisted on "these noble elements of character which had distinguished the Washington family long before they culminated in
him who has made the name immortal."[34]

The consensus about George Washington's lineage soon disinte-
grated, however. Prompted by the publication of yet another article
on Washington's genealogy, Joseph L. Chester decided to search the
family pedigree, which was *"clearly all wrong."* At first he intended
to complete his work within a few months, but Washington's ancestry was more complicated than expected. "If you know what I
suffered over this pedigree you would not hurry me for my paper,"
he confided. In fact, it took Chester almost two years to complete
his task. The results were unexpected. "I can only yet *prove* the fal-
sity of the existing pedigree. I cannot give *Pater Patriae* an ancestor." Chester nonetheless published his findings in article and pamphlet form in London and Boston. He demonstrated that George
Washington's ancestors John and Lawrence were not the sons of
Lawrence Washington of Brington, whose two sons, also named
John and Lawrence, could be identified positively in English archives and never went to Virginia. Whitmore commented drily in
his book *American Genealogist,* "It seems, therefore, that the Washingtons are, like the great majority of families in this country, un-
able to prove an English pedigree." Chester had advanced the
science of genealogy by confronting a traditional interpretation
with archival evidence, thus exposing "the mistakes of our predecessors in a manner so thorough and convincing."[35]

Not all Americans were convinced by this provocative revision. In the early 1870s Chester's conclusions were disputed by authors trying to reaffirm Washington's traditional origins. "I hear that my Washington paper is recently making a stir in the U.S.," Chester mused. A series of articles published in Albert Welles's *Chronotype* in 1873 attacked Chester's interpretation frontally. Whitmore decided to answer on his friend's behalf and published a long rejoinder in the *American Historical Record* that read like a tutorial in proper genealogy. After summarizing the traditional interpretation and Chester's revision of Washington's pedigree, Whitmore took to task the *Chronotype*'s author, H. H. Clements, demanding that he "present his views with precision, and fortify his position by the careful citation of authorities"; he regretted that Clements had "no special facilities for investigating the doubtful points," quoted "from printed books solely," and wrote "in so loose a manner as to perplex any ordinary reader as to his meaning." Whitmore looked minutely at each of Clements's suggestions before he concluded that "his pretentious essay adds nothing to our previous knowledge." As well as refuting Clements's attacks on Chester, Whitmore's essay reiterated scientific genealogy's ground rules. "It seems hardly necessary for us," he wrote, for instance, "to add that coincidence of names alone is not satisfactory evidence." Chester, who had read the *Chronotype*'s articles with contempt ("a collection of greater *balderdash* I never saw put together") but had not bothered to answer, could only thank Whitmore for his public defense. "Your article is *crushing*, as far as Mr. Clements is concerned, who will thereafter I should think, sing small."[36]

The battle over Washington's pedigree was revived a few years later by Albert Welles. By then the president of the American College of Heraldry and Genealogical Registry was also the author of a book-length genealogy of the Washington family that generously linked the first American president to "Odin, the founder of Scandinavia." Welles attacked Chester again, only to have the white knight of scientific genealogy, William H. Whitmore, enter the fight and offer a scathing review of Welles's book.[37]

What was at stake in the quarrel over Washington's ancestors was the definition of genealogy as a science based on verifiable methodology. Chester's first genealogical publication was a book on John Rogers that disproved an ancient tradition in his own family that its members were descended from the great English religious reformer and martyr. Likewise, Samuel Pearce May believed in a scientific approach to genealogy when he started in the 1880s to revise the Sears genealogy established three decades earlier by Horatio Gates Somerby at the request of David Sears of Boston. What he found when he decided to check the facts much surprised him. There were "discrepancies in the pedigrees, seemingly irreconcilable." Submitting the Sears genealogy to a rigorous test allowed May to conclude that Somerby had fabricated Sears ancestors and had reached conclusions based on fictitious sources.[38]

In contrast, when Henry F. Waters looked into John Harvard's ancestry, he established who were the parents of the famous but then-mysterious benefactor of Harvard College, and he was able to trace the ancestry of Harvard's mother, Katherine Rogers, who came from Stratford-upon-Avon. When he heard about this, his friend James Kendall Hosmer suggested that Waters should speculate beyond the information offered by his sources and use "circumstantial evidence." Perhaps, Hosmer hinted, William Shakespeare knew Katherine Rogers, since his and her families were neighbors; perhaps there was a direct link between the Bard and John Harvard. Waters's reaction was typical of a scientific genealogist. Although he acknowledged Hosmer's "pleasant and picturesque specula-tions," he found them useless because they were not based on any "solid documentary fact." He concluded, "With might-have-beens, however glittering, I have nothing to do." To the contrary, he was known for basing his conclusions on serious, positive evidence and never establishing "a stepping-stone until he was sure of it."[39]

Meeting the burden of proof was decisive. The greatest risks a genealogist encountered were inference and pseudoconnections. When an article in a genealogical journal in 1871 about English peerage and lineage books as useful sources for American geneal-ogy included a reference to a companion of Richard I who was said to be an ancestor of the Lawrence family of New York, William Whitmore answered that the original article had no factual basis. The author had relied on tradition and hearsay and had not quoted any "parish record, will, or herald's visitation." Whitmore demanded proofs. In response, the Lawrence family questioned Whitmore's gentlemanliness and invoked family traditions against this "gene-alogical knight-errant." Their reaction underlined the gap between scientific genealogy and older ways of basing pedigrees on tradition and status.[40]

For scientific genealogists, tradition was the enemy. Chester ex-plained that he could "find a ready ancestor for every New England man," but he refused to work that way. "What I do, I intend doing *thoroughly*." By that, Chester meant that facts should be checked. "I will not jump at conclusions, or tolerate forced constructions. I never record a name or a date on any pedigree I have commenced," he wrote, "unless I have also the evidence that positively justifies it."[41]

Once research had been carried on with appropriate skills and documentary evidence had been carefully gathered, information had to be organized properly. Chester, Whitmore, Waters, and many others repeatedly insisted on the necessity for genealogists to "follow one of the well known and approved modes of arrangement." How-to books, like Whitmore's *Ancestral Tablets,* were meant to help enthusiasts succeed in this all-important task. Scientific genealogists insisted on rules of presentation of pedigrees and authorities, which journals like the *New England Historical and Genealogical Register* attempted to spread to their readers.[42]

Mastery of professional skills did not mean that genealogy should be reserved to professionals. Here genealogy and history began to diverge in the late nineteenth century. Professionalization of history took place within universities and organizations like the American Historical Association (established in 1884), with academic degrees (MA, PhD) validating training. The situation of genealogy was different. There was no attempt at that time to define a genealogist through his or her diplomas or education. As a consequence, whereas history and genealogy had developed in close proximity until the 1880s, some historians later began to contrast history and genealogy. J. Franklin Jameson, for instance, criticized state and local historical societies in 1897 for showing "too much concern for genealogy," and Dixon Ryan Fox sang a song familiar to many professional historians when he accused genealogy of growing out "of snobbishness and vanity."[43]

❧   ❧   ❧

The fact is that late nineteenth-century efforts to professionalize genealogy were seldom successful. For one William Whitmore, there were dozens of Albert Welleses. Whitmore's high standards were seldom met by others, who preferred to comment on the Bostonian's admittedly difficult temper. By the 1910s and 1920s it was clear that

the strategy adopted by late nineteenth-century reform-minded genealogists was a failure. Professional scholarly standards were seldom met; far too many pedigrees, books, and articles were based on
scant evidence, and countless Americans assumed glorious ancestors
at the expense of historical documentation. The success of so many
commercialized genealogical undertakings suggested that truth and
scholarship were not central to most Americans interested in pedigrees. The battle for regulation and professionalization seemed lost.

It took a new generation of genealogists and new strategies to
revive the fight for scholarly standards. Their assessment of American genealogy was harsh. "Conditions in the genealogical profession are unsatisfactory," Donald Lines Jacobus explained in 1930.
Anyone could become a professional genealogist. "No course of
training is required, no examinations as to fitness have to be passed."
Genealogy, Jacobus regretted, often appealed "to many who lack
the mentality for this kind of work, and who might be unsuccessful in other professions."[44]

Jacobus hoped to change this unacceptable situation. A preco-
cious genealogist (he published his first article in the *New England
Historical and Genealogical Register* in 1904 at age 17) and a Yale graduate, Jacobus served in France during World War I before living a
solitary and scholarly life in the large house he occupied with his
mother in New Haven, Connecticut, devoting all his time to genealogical pursuits. In 1922 he created a new periodical, the *New Haven
Genealogical Magazine,* which became *The American Genealogist* (soon
called *TAG* by many genealogists) in 1932. Contrary to other journals, *TAG* was linked neither to a genealogical organization nor to
a commercial undertaking. It was a scholarly endeavor from the
start. Jacobus was interested in science and believed in scientific
principles, which he saw at work in other disciplines. He devoted his

life to implementing them in genealogy and wrote much about the topic. His originality did not lie in his goal to establish scholarly standards for genealogy nor in his emphasis on research, methodology, and evidence. Chester, Whitmore, and many others had shared these goals but had never been in a position to have a wide and lasting impact on the field. They were too isolated and lacked institutional support. In contrast, Jacobus and his fellow genealogists could rely on *TAG* to promote their ideas.

What became known later as the "Jacobus school" of genealogy was, in fact, a "loosely knit group" of persons who shared the desire to improve the quality of American genealogy. Some of them, like Jacobus himself, the civil servant and lawyer George Andrews Moriarty, and Arthur Adams, the librarian of Trinity College in Hartford, Connecticut, were during the 1930s men in their fifties who had grown up seeing commercialization and fraud overcome the efforts of the Chester-Whitmore generation of scholarly minded genealogists. Younger men completed the group. John Insley Coddington was an instructor in history at Harvard during the early 1930s, Milton Rubincam a civil servant at the Commerce Department in Washington, D.C., and Meredith S. Colket an archivist at the National Archives.[45]

Together with a few others, they made *TAG* their flagship. Donald Lines Jacobus was not the first genealogist to state that every element of a pedigree had to be properly documented, but he was the first who was in a position to systematize the use of documentation in articles in *TAG*. Even in the *New England Historical and Genealogical Register* there had been articles with little or no documentation alongside more scholarly pieces in previous decades. Over time, *TAG* set the standards for others to follow.

By the late 1930s modernizers went one step further. They recognized that scholarly standards had little impact on the general

public. Attacking "many of the absurdities and atrocities committed in the name of genealogy" by "armchair dilettantes who con-
jured lines of descent from their own fervid imaginations," as John
Insley Coddington later put it, was certainly a duty and probably a
pleasure, but they understood that they needed to give scholarly
genealogy more professional visibility. Arthur Adams imagined
a society of fifty fellows chosen solely on the basis of the quality
and quantity of their genealogical publications. As Coddington
explained, Adams had the notion "that it was necessary to build a
core of professional genealogists who were reliable and who could
be used by the public with confidence." In December 1940 Adams,
Coddington, and Meredith Colket founded the American Society
of Genealogists (ASG) during the annual meeting of the American
Historical Association in New York City. It aimed at securing "recognition of genealogy as a serious scientific subject of research in
the historical and social fields of learning." Although the creation
of the ASG and the choice of the first fellows (who would thereafter
proudly add the acronym FASG to their name) did not result in immediate transformation of the everyday practice of genealogy, they
indicated how regulatory and professionalizing efforts had pro-
gressed since the 1860s. No longer did the science of genealogy
depend on brave, erudite, but lonesome knights, as in the time of
William H. Whitmore. *TAG* and the ASG finally offered a promising answer to the challenge of commercialization.[46]

❧   ❧   ❧

Although late nineteenth- and early twentieth-century genealogy
was thus dominated by mercantile concerns and efforts to regulate
the quest for pedigrees, there were alternatives to the prevailing

vision, albeit often of lesser visibility at the time than the dominant genealogical regime.

Beginning in 1865 and until the end of the nineteenth century,
African Americans offered the first challenge to the newly emerging
racial and mercantile American approach to genealogy. Their stub-
born efforts to reunite families separated and sold away during
slavery revealed their sense of the importance of kin as a social institution, their knowledge of their family connections, and the intensity of their genealogical longing. Some wrote to the Freedmen's
Bureau, providing information about their immediate as well as
their distant kin and asking for help in locating relatives often lost
from sight for decades. Others searched for their families in person
or ran advertisements about missing kin in black newspapers such
as the *Christian Recorder,* the voice of the African Methodist Episcopal Church, for decades after the end of the Civil War and requested
that ministers read these requests to their congregations. For all of
them, Reconstruction became a profoundly genealogical moment.
Whether sketchy or detailed, knowledge of kin served their need to
redefine their identity as free individuals and families in the post-
slavery world they were inventing.[47]

Some white Americans also perpetuated the middle-class, democratic character of antebellum genealogy. When Rutherford B.
Hayes, the future U.S. president, experienced "an attack of genealogical mania" in 1870, he began to request information from family members but reflected "how futile" it was "to trace one's descent
from a distinguished name in the past." Family associations and
reunions, which began to appear during the 1840s and 1850s in
limited numbers, experienced dramatic growth after the Civil War
and the 1876 centennial. The number of published accounts of
family reunions provides one indication of the phenomenon: 7 dur-

ing the 1850s and 1860s, 25 during the 1870s, 46 during the 1880s, 88 during the 1890s, and 108 during the first decade of the twentieth century. Contemporary newspaper accounts also draw attention to the rising number of family reunions throughout the country.[48]

Family reunions and associations boosted family pride, but they also emphasized collective kin identities and pointed to the democratic worth of familial relationships in an age of mercantile individualism. The whole process of organizing a family reunion served those purposes. It took time and energy for organizers to call together "the widely separated members" of a family. Months before the celebration date, they would send letters to family members near and far, publish press notices of the meeting, and set up various organizational committees. In the case of the Selden family, a "vigorous but ineffectual effort" to have a reunion failed in the summer of 1876 but succeeded the following year, bringing together over 100 Seldens who undertook to unravel, "as well as they could, their ties of relationship."[49] The promoter of the 1883 Dickinson family reunion began by sending informal letters to his relatives to test their interest and then created a committee that sent a formal call to hundreds of Dickinsons. Participants would not only display their pride in their ancestry but also "make more intimate acquaintance with each other" and "cultivate more fully those higher attributes of our nature which have their source in the love of kindred."[50]

Family reunions usually followed an identical scenario. The *Boston Herald* commented about one family reunion that it displayed "the usual feast of reason and flow of soul incident to such occasions."[51] By this it meant a formula that was reproduced from one family reunion to another. Family members would come to the meeting place from many areas of the United States, although New

England still dominated. They would elect the officers of the day, making sure that all sections would be represented. Festivities usually included songs, prayers, an address of welcome, at least one historical address on the family's history, poems, banquets for dozens or hundreds of persons, more speeches, photographs, reading of the letters of those who could not attend, a business meeting to organize a family association or elect its officers, more occasions to socialize, and in some cases preparation of the publication of an account of the family reunion.

Participants in these family reunions often expressed a different relation to genealogy and their ancestry than individual genealogists did. They seldom emphasized a scientific vision of family trees and usually preferred to expatiate on their "family traditions." Unlike many American amateur genealogists who used these traditions to invent a glorious past or ancestry, participants in family reunions usually emphasized kin values and generational continuities at the expense of individual glories. At the 1883 Dickinson family reunion, one orator mentioned a tradition that there was in the family "the blood of the Plantagenets," but he added jokingly that it had "doubtless become rather thin by this time." On the other hand, he insisted on "the blood of a sturdy, honest line of men and women . . . untitled and uncrowned" and celebrated "the great unnamed multitude" of "farmers, mechanics, tradesmen, who served well their day and generation."[52] Family reunions and associations, in other words, often preserved antebellum, middle-class genealogical values at a time when the new, dominant, racial, nationalist, and commercial genealogy was assailing them.

Another alternative to the dominant market-oriented quest for family trees developed out of Mormon Utah. When the president of the Church of Jesus Christ of Latter-Day Saints, Wilford Woodruff, stated in 1894 that the church wanted Mormons "from this time to trace their genealogies as far as they can, and to be sealed to their fathers and mothers," he provided a new impetus to an interest in genealogy that went back to the early days of Mormonism and had a doctrinal core. It started in 1836 when Joseph Smith had a vision in Kirtland, Ohio: following Malachi's prophecy, the prophet Elijah appeared to Smith and enjoined the new church to "turn the hearts of the fathers to their children, and the hearts of the children to their fathers" (Mal. 4:6). Mormons would seek for the dead and baptize them, thereby ensuring salvation of family members who had died without the possibility of accepting the restored gospel. In 1840 Smith announced the doctrine of baptism of the dead by proxy. Over the next five decades, as church members migrated to and settled in Utah, they baptized the dead and adopted other rituals (called ordinances) with a genealogical dimension, including "sealings," that is, the validation of eternal family bonds during a marriage ceremony performed by a church official.[53]

At the time, however, despite the genealogical dimension of Mormon religious doctrine, the church did not display any organized efforts related to family trees. Mormons involved themselves in genealogy on an individual basis. Wilford Woodruff began his family genealogy during a trip to England in the 1840s. Orson Pratt similarly began to gather material about his family tree in the 1850s. Benjamin Franklin Cummings launched a successful career as a journalist and genealogist in the late 1870s, visiting the New England Historic Genealogical Society and conducting research there. Franklin D. Richards, who served as church historian from 1889 until he died ten years later, accumulated a personal genealogical library that became the basis of the church's collections.[54]

Between the 1880s and the 1920s Mormon genealogical interest and institutional investment grew significantly. Wilford Woodruff's 1894 revelation and subsequent policy reinforced its religious basis and provided a new impetus. Until then, proxy baptisms had taken place at times through adoption into the family of a church official, a procedure that raised doctrinal questions about eternal families. Woodruff's new policy forbade such adoptions and encouraged the discovery of genealogical lines instead. Mormons also interpreted the growing interest "over genealogical matters" in the United States as "the hand of the Lord." The church-controlled *Deseret News* explained in 1885 that "thousands of men [were] labouring assiduously to prepare the way, though unconsciously, for the salvation of the dead." At the same time, these "unconscious" efforts underlined the need for the church to better organize its genealogical activities.[55]

Beginning in the 1880s, a growing number of Mormons served as genealogical missionaries, mostly traveling east to meet with distant relatives, copy family records, search old registers and cemeteries, and contact genealogical societies. Religious leaders recognized that the church should develop an organization to address genealogical issues. After considering creating a genealogical bureau within the church, in 1894 they incorporated the Genealogical Society of Utah, with Franklin D. Richards serving as its first president. The new society was to create a library, educate Mormons in genealogical matters, and acquire records of the dead to make baptisms possible. The beginnings were difficult. The Genealogical Society was originally located in Richards's office of church historian. By 1908 there were only 173 members, and the library's holdings reached the modest total of 800 volumes.[56]

Within a decade, however, genealogy occupied a far more important position within the church. Central in the process of change that took place at the time were Mormon women, especially Susa Young Gates. Gates, a daughter of Brigham Young, was a progressive, a writer, and a suffragist. She was active locally and nationally in many organizations, including the church's Relief Society, the Daughters of Utah Pioneers, the Young Ladies' Mutual Improvement Association, and the National Council of Women. Gates had also been a dedicated genealogist since the late 1870s. For her, genealogy was "temple work"; she worked on the Young family genealogy and served as stenographer of baptisms for the dead.[57]

By the early 1900s Gates was well aware of the contrast between the religious importance of genealogy for Mormons and the actual weakness of the resources offered by the church. When she was told that she could use the Genealogical Society's small library to research her family genealogy, she acknowledged in 1904 that she did not know that such a library existed. Her reaction was typical of the organizational impulse that was one of the defining traits of Progressivism. She explained later, "I felt that I must do something more, something to help all the members of the Church with their genealogy and temple work." At the time, she regretted, "there was practically no book of lessons in genealogy in existence," and there were "no classes in schools or printed instructions to enlighten" beginners. She had defined her road map.[58]

Within a few years, Gates and a group of other Mormon women determined to change the church's genealogical landscape. At first operating through the Daughters of Utah Pioneers, which she cofounded in 1901 and of which she became president in 1905, Gates developed a program of genealogical education, the first in the

United States. By late 1907 there were weekly genealogical classes, as well as special sessions for church members who came to Salt Lake City for the semiannual general conference. Gates also began to write genealogical columns in Utah newspapers.

As the program developed, church officials transferred its control from the Daughters of Utah Pioneers to the Women's Committee of the Genealogical Society in 1908 and to the Relief Society in 1912. Since the Relief Society was present in every ward and stake (the church's administrative divisions), this transfer ensured growth. By the mid-1910s about 700 ward organizations and some 30,000 Mormon women studied genealogy through church-sponsored programs. They could also read Susa Young Gates's *Lessons in Genealogy* (1912). Within a few years Gates and her associates had transformed the nature of genealogy within the church. Her organizational skills, personality, and authority helped spread genealogical interest among Mormon women, thousands of whom became genealogists.[59]

The Genealogical Society quickly followed in Susa Young Gates's steps. It created the *Utah Genealogical and Historical Magazine* in 1910 and developed its library, which grew from 800 books in 1908 to almost 20,000 in the late 1930s. By then it was the fifth-largest genealogical library in the country and the largest one west of the Mississippi River. Moreover, the society began to follow the example of the Relief Society and use the church's administrative organization. By 1920 it had 2,000 members and new headquarters in the church's administration building in Salt Lake City. It was strong enough to be entrusted again with responsibility for the church's genealogical programs.[60]

Organizational efforts continued throughout the 1920s and 1930s. The Genealogical Society created a Research Bureau, organized into a Research Department, an Instruction Department, and a Research Clearing House (later called the Church Genealogical Archives and then the Church Records Archives), to assist and supervise research carried on at the library. Thousands of new members joined the society, which moved again in 1934 into more spacious headquarters, capable of accommodating hundreds of researchers. In parallel, the society developed genealogical organizations at the local level. By the late 1930s it had built an impressive infrastructure. Each subdivision had its genealogical representative and local committee. The society supported regional genealogical conventions and classes, including night school and junior classes for children. Last, it tackled the problem of duplication of genealogical and temple work due to poor information and coordination. A clearinghouse, the Temple Index Bureau, was created in 1922. Five years later the transfer of data available from temple records onto about three million index cards was completed, and the bureau was in charge of clearing genealogical data before they could be used during church rituals.[61]

By the late 1930s the Church of Jesus Christ of Latter-day Saints had developed its religious vision of genealogy as a search for unbaptized ancestors into an enormous and efficient organization. To be sure, it was not completely isolated, and there were contacts between Mormon genealogists, like Benjamin Franklin Cummings and later Archibald Fowler Bennett, and non-Mormon genealogists. Indeed, Cummings and Bennett shared the views of genealogical reformers and modernizers who defended scientific and professional values. But Mormon genealogy differed from mainstream American genealogy because at the time it did not take part in the marketplace orientation that pervaded the United States. Genealogy had a unique and central place in the church for doctrinal reasons, and this unique place at the same time prevented any attempts at decentralization. Records and books remained in Salt Lake City, and members of the church were ordered to "confine their activities to their own lines" for religious reasons. Impressive though they were, the programs developed by the church were meant for the church and its higher goals.[62]

✤   ✤   ✤

From the Civil War to World War II, most Americans used genealogy to define identity in racial and nationalist terms. Ancestor worship served their belief in racial differences and hereditary virtues, as well as in the superiority of Anglo-Saxon blood above all others. It was an important tenet of the culture of race that dominated the United States at the time. Ancestor worship ran so high that genealogy developed as a commercial activity more than as a science. In comparison with the numbers of enthusiasts who valued social climbing and racial exclusion at the expense of truth, only a minority of Americans practiced genealogy for moral, religious, or scientific reasons. Pedigree, the sociologist Thorstein Veblen explained in 1917, "is a pecuniary attribute" that could be acquired "by well-advised expenditure" in order to serve "as a background of current gentility." Clearly the author of *The Theory of the Leisure Class* (1899) regarded genealogists in a very different light than did John Farmer and other antebellum antiquarians. "Gentlefolk of such syncopated pedigree," Veblen wryly added, "may have to walk circumspectly, of course."[63]

To be sure, partisans of a scientific definition of genealogy fought against the effects of commercialization, but they met with only limited success, perhaps because they did not question the racial and nationalist foundations of genealogy. It took decades in the middle of the twentieth century, Nazism, a world war, and the civil rights movement to lead to the discrediting of genealogy as it was practiced between the 1860s and the 1930s, and to the redefinition of family history and genealogical identities in democratic and multicultural terms.

❧ 6 ❧

EVERYBODY'S SEARCH FOR ROOTS

On 4 July 1977, *Newsweek*'s cover story was a special report titled "Everybody's Search for Roots." The magazine recognized the recent "phenomenal" success of "the quest for personal origins" and the fact that it had "turned ethnic, where once it was the sport of brahmins." Appropriately, the photograph on the cover represented an (Italian) immigrant family. The article described how "younger hyphenated Americans" now reclaimed "a heritage denied them" by their parents and "in the process" worked at "a redefinition of their Americanism." *Newsweek* also remarked that genealogy had become fully commercialized, with airlines advertising "ancestor hunting" trips and "local entrepreneurs . . . cashing in as well." *Newsweek*'s rival *Time* also published feature essays devoted to the topic and explained that Americans were now "frantically climbing family trees." By 1977 genealogy was a topic for popular magazines.[1]

As these and other observers perceptively noticed in the 1970s, genealogy not only had become extremely popular but also had attracted new practitioners for whom its meaning lay in stunning contrast with the situation of the first half of the twentieth century. A democratic interest in family history replaced the previously dominant elitist quest for ancient lineage that denoted racial and social superiority. Self-understanding superseded self-assertion. Ordinary Americans were legitimately looking for their ancestors, whether African American slaves from Georgia or immigrant maids from Finland.[2]

Behind this genealogical revolution apparently lay the success of Alex Haley's best seller *Roots,* which, in Maya Angelou's words, "burst upon the national consciousness" in the fall of 1976. *Roots* told the story of the author's black ancestors. It was not only a book, *Time* explained, but "a social phenomenon" and "a potentially important bench mark in U.S. race relations." The success of *Roots* signaled the emergence of a new cultural context and suggested that ideologies of racial and hereditary superiority had lost their legitimacy in the eyes of many Americans.[3]

Haley's book thus embodied a major transformation in the American culture of genealogy, but it did not cause it alone. As the historian Michael Kammen later argued, "The 'Roots phenomenon' did not strike as a bolt from the blue" but had "in fact roots of its own." Among these was the fact that the popular meaning of genealogy began to change long before *Roots.* Some analysts at the time recognized that new cultural and socioanthropological explanations were in order to account for the success of genealogy, now that racial motives were not dominant any more. Although they disagreed over such various and at times contradictory hypotheses as the need for firmer identities in a context of major social and cultural upheavals, the expression by children or grandchildren of immigrants of a demand for diversity, or a demand for more personalization in a society where technology and technological change reigned supreme, they understood that Americans had entered a new phase in the complex history of their relationship to genealogy—one that was and is defined by the newly democratic, pluralist, multiracial, and commercial nature of the quest for family trees.[4]

✽   ✽   ✽

As the emphasis on race- and pedigree-minded exclusiveness that had dominated earlier decades lost its intellectual legitimacy and social assertiveness during the 1950s and 1960s, American genealogists began to operate in a new cultural context. World War II and the emergence of the atomic age ushered in a widely felt sense of rupture between the past and the present and bred a new culture of anxiety, nostalgia, and concern with individual and collective memory. Concern about a nuclear future led to passionate interest in what came to be known as heritage. "The most striking feature of America today is change," the president of Colonial Williamsburg explained in 1957. "In a highly mobile, rapidly shifting society, we are in danger of losing our perspective, and of losing a refreshing contact with the well-springs of American tradition." In reaction, taking advantage of the country's economic prosperity and of the growing place of leisure in their lives, Americans visited Colonial Williamsburg in droves, read the newly founded magazine *American Heritage* (1947) by the thousands, encouraged historic preservation, bought Americana and other antiques, and looked for their ancestors in ever-growing numbers. Heritage now triumphed.[5]

Genealogists experienced these evolutions in a quiet but significant way. Until the 1930s the quest for social status and a racialized, imagined, Anglo-Saxon ancestry was their dominant motivation.

There were few national and state genealogical societies and al-most no local ones. Professional standards were an objective pur-sued by a small and select coterie around Donald Lines Jacobus, not by the large majority of genealogists who mostly wanted to as-sert their claim to distinguished forebears. In the three decades after World War II, the sense of loss of the past experienced by many Americans and the democratization of tradition stimulated change. In 1976 a newspaper noticed the "formation of numerous small groups of genealogists in local chapters throughout the coun-try," a process it dated from the mid-1960s. In fact, it went back to the early 1950s. A growing number of middle-class Americans be-came interested in genealogy and called for local organizations and resources. As a result, state genealogical societies emerged in vari-ous southern, midwestern, and western states during the 1950s: Ten-nessee (1952), Louisiana (1953), Oklahoma (1955), Alabama and Idaho (1958), and Ohio (1959). The 1960s and early 1970s saw even more growth. State societies were formed in New Mexico, Texas, and Vir-ginia in 1960, in Arkansas in 1963, in Georgia and Kansas in 1964, and in Arizona, Iowa, and Oregon in 1965. Illinois and Connecticut followed suit in 1968, Minnesota in 1969, South Carolina in 1970, Vermont in 1971, Michigan in 1972, Kentucky in 1973, North Caro-lina in 1974, and Rhode Island in 1975. By the time of the publication of *Roots,* thousands of Americans had joined these new organiza-tions during the preceding two decades.[6]

Local genealogists created these societies because they felt iso-lated and needed exchanges, tools, and programs adapted to each situation. In Richland County, Ohio, a small group of amateurs met in 1955 to share their interest; at the time of its incorporation four years later, the Ohio Genealogical Society numbered 52 mem-bers, who grew to 82 by 1962 and 452 by 1969. In Michigan, organized genealogy had been limited before World War II to the Detroit Society for Genealogical Research (1936) and its *Magazine,* which began publication in 1937. During the 1950s local genealogists created new organizations in the southwestern part of the state: the Western Michigan Genealogical Society (1954) and the Kalamazoo Valley Genealogical Society (1958). Other local societies emerged in the southern, central, and western parts of Michigan during the 1960s. Genealogists also started journals and bulletins. In Michigan, for instance, at least four such journals, with names like *Michigana, Michigan Heritage, Family Trails,* and the *Pastfinder,* appeared between the mid-1950s and the early 1970s. All around the country, similar local and statewide periodicals were launched during the 1950s and 1960s. By 1975, aside from the *New England Historical and Genealogical Register,* which served as a national but also as a regional and state journal in New England, statewide genealogical periodicals existed in twenty-nine states.[7]

The postwar geographic extension of institutionalized genealogy involved a process of democratization. The success of the *Genealogical Helper,* the first popular magazine in the field, created in 1947, testified to the existence of a widening audience. Thousands of middle-class Americans began to look for their family history, causing observers to comment on the evolving nature of genealogy. In 1955, for instance, the historian and archivist Lester J. Cappon delivered an inspired address at the annual dinner of the National Genealogical Society. Criticizing the distance he perceived between historians and genealogists, he argued that its origins were to be found not only in the process of academic specialization that had taken place at the end of the nineteenth century but also in what he called the "chauvinism" of that period, which had transformed genealogy from "handmaid of history" into "the indentured servant of neo-patriotism." In contrast, Cappon emphasized the fact that "in spite of its deference to 'first families,'" American genealogy had in 1955 "a strong 'democratic' strain which in itself" had "popularized interest quite uncritically in the family tree."[8]

Signs of the widening audience and changing meaning of genealogy could be found around the country, particularly in genealogical societies and programs, archival repositories, and public libraries. Membership in the Washington, D.C.–based National Genealogical Society grew from 395 in 1948 to about 700 in 1953. New members joined the New England Historic Genealogical Society during the 1950s, 1960s, and early 1970s. The 3,000 mark was reached in the early 1960s, and by 1974 there were over 4,000 members. In 1957 the National Genealogical Society published a book titled *General Aids to Genealogical Research* that collected and reprinted articles previously published in the society's journal. Their broad scope, ranging from Pennsylvania German genealogical materials to ordinary settlers before 1840 in an Illinois county, suggested a widening definition of American genealogical interests.[9]

Public librarians and archivists now extended a warmer welcome to genealogists. Until the 1950s they often did not take amateurs of family trees seriously, if only because pedigree hunters thumbed through books and indexes instead of reading them cover to cover and were known on occasion to celebrate vocally in the reading room the discovery of a newly found ancestor. Not much had changed since the American Library Association had reported in 1926 that "as a general custom" public libraries found it "inadvisable to devote any considerable amount of time to genealogical work or to specialize in genealogical departments and collection." A 1950 memorandum, typical of that time, at the Enoch Pratt Free Library in Baltimore exhibited little enthusiasm for genealogical research.

Large libraries with significant genealogical collections—like the Newberry Library in Chicago, the Detroit Public Library, the New York Public Library, and the Library of Congress—were an exception in the early 1950s.[10]

During the 1950s and 1960s this situation changed. More numerous and younger genealogical patrons began to use public libraries and archives, expecting to find helpful collections and materials there. Public libraries, state archives, and the National Archives reconsidered their policies and began to value their new visitors and cater to their needs. The archivist of the United States acknowledged that the "most numerous single class of searchers were genealogists" and appointed the archivist and genealogist Meredith B. Colket Jr., a fellow of the American Society of Genealogists, "to give full-time to the task of facilitating such research."[11] Some librarians embarked on major development programs. The Fort Wayne, Indiana, public library had acquired many secondhand local history and genealogy books since the late 1930s. In the early 1960s the head librarian, Fred J. Reynolds, increased the library's focus on genealogy by adding "collections and services specifically tailored for genealogists." When book-conservation problems endangered the genealogical collection at the Newberry Library in the mid-1960s, Reynolds persuaded the Newberry to let him make two copies of a large proportion of its genealogical holdings. He returned the originals and one copy to Chicago and kept the second. At least 15,000 and perhaps as many as 30,000 books were thus added to the Fort Wayne Public Library. By the late 1960s Reynolds had succeeded in turning his library's genealogical department into a remarkable resource with a national scope. His notion that genealogy was "worthy of pursuit" was shared by many librarians during the 1960s. In Baltimore the Enoch Pratt Free Library merged with

the Peabody Institute Library in 1966, bringing 20,000 genealogical volumes to the new entity. As a consequence, the Pratt's previous attitude of indifference and even hostility toward genealogists
soon changed.[12]

Professional genealogists welcomed the growing curiosity of
Americans about their family history and attempted to improve
the quality of genealogical research and to implement Donald
Lines Jacobus's program by developing standards, training, and certification. In the absence of an academic curriculum, many fellows
of the American Society of Genealogists (ASG) took a leading role
in the process during the postwar decades. They contributed to
Genealogical Research: Methods and Sources, a project directed by Milton Rubincam under the auspices of the society. Published in 1960,
it became the standard reference work in the field. They also partook in the establishment of the Board of Certification of Genealogists, a joint initiative of the ASG and the National Genealogical
Society in 1964. Successful applicants could become certified genealogists (CGs), certified American lineage specialists (CALSs), or
genealogical record specialists (GRSs), adding the appropriate ini-
tialisms to their signatures and advertisements. As it helped establish standards in the world of genealogy, the certification process
also helped clients distinguish between professional genealogists
and potential quacks. Fellows of the ASG also developed training
programs. One of them, Meredith Colket, was instrumental in
creating the National Institute for Genealogical Research in 1950.
Every summer the institute offered a three-week workshop in part-
nership with American University, the American Society of Genealogists, and the National Archives. The Library of Congress and
other institutions, like the Maryland Hall of Records, later joined
too. Arguably the first of its kind, the institute's program trained

hundreds of ordinary genealogists during the 1950s and 1960s. In 1972 it became the National Institute on Genealogical Research, conducted by the National Archives. At the suggestion of other fellows of the ASG, the Genealogical Society of Pennsylvania began to offer classes during the 1950s, and the New England Historic Genealogical Society followed suit a few years later. Americans could also attend the Institute of Genealogy founded in the mid-1960s at Howard College, now Samford University in Birmingham, Alabama.[13]

Another sign of the rising American interest in genealogy was the changing role of the Mormon Church and its genealogical programs. Until the 1960s the church's genealogical resources were used almost exclusively by church members. As they had done since the late nineteenth century, Mormon missionaries gathered genealogical materials all over the world and brought them back to Utah, but a 1955 survey showed that over 99 percent of the patrons of the Family History Library were church members. In later years, however, there were two significant changes. One was technological. In 1938 the church developed a massive microfilming program that eased record gathering and made it possible to collect larger volumes of potentially reproducible genealogical sources. The total number of microfilm rolls available grew from about 2,000 in 1945 to about 50,000 in 1950, 270,000 in 1960, 660,000 in 1970, and 880,000 in 1975. By the early 1960s the church also began to develop computer use.[14]

The second change was political. In 1964 the Church of Jesus Christ of Latter-Day Saints reversed its earlier stance and decided to open branch libraries (seventy-five by 1968) and develop genealogical seminars, conferences, and various outreach programs. The creation of a nationwide network of Mormon libraries and the fact that new technologies eased the reproduction and dissemination of genealogical materials resulted in the increased relative importance of Mormon resources for American genealogists. Not only did Salt Lake City's Family History Library receive more patrons every day (from 300 in the early 1960s to 600 at the end of the decade to 2,000 by the mid-1970s), but also a rising proportion of visitors were not church members. Branch libraries received sets of copies of the original microfilm rolls and were able to cater to the demands of tens of thousands of genealogy amateurs who would not necessarily have traveled to Utah. Genealogists who were not members of the Mormon Church could also attend the genealogical seminars, which the church-controlled Genealogical Society of Utah began to organize in the mid-1960s. In August 1969 the organization in Salt Lake City of the World Conference on Records, attended by thousands of visitors, provided the church with a forum to present its resources and publicize its interest in preserving genealogical materials.[15]

❖   ❖   ❖

The broadening and relative democratization of genealogy was a tentative and incomplete phenomenon during the 1950s and 1960s. Undoubtedly it was partly successful. There were hundreds of genealogical organizations in parts of the country where there had been none. There were new training programs, certification processes, and textbooks to help potential genealogists learn the tools of the trade. However, these transformations remained limited in large part to white Americans and dominated by descendants of immigrants from Britain. In the politically and culturally tense context of the Cold War and the civil rights movement, a sizable proportion of genealogists kept a traditional perspective on family trees, emphasizing the importance of lineage, race, and patriotism. A history of the National Genealogical Society explained in 1953, "The membership of the Society has necessarily consisted of persons of superior culture and intellectual character, since these qualities are essential and ingrained in serious and competent genealogists." Like their late nineteenth- and early twentieth-century predecessors, these pedigree hunters were highly selective in their choice of ancestors in order to emphasize social prestige.[16]

Some of the Americans who attempted to retrace their family tree in Britain during the 1950s and 1960s were in search of what one British genealogist called "snob value." According to a newspaper report in 1960, others were delighted to discover a link "with a British family that boasts a crest and coats of arms" and hastened "to have these 'armorial bearings' inscribed on writing paper, Christmas cards, wooden plaques or even cuff links." A few years later another newspaper noticed that "the cherished desire to boast of a distinguished pedigree" was still strong enough among Americans that "some disreputable genealogists" were always on hand to "go back to Adam himself" if needed.[17]

Other signs pointed to the survival of what one sociologist called "the hereditary network" in American genealogy. Conservative organizations like the Daughters of the American Revolution remained true to their traditional visions of lineage and exclusiveness while defending patriotism and fighting communism in every possible way at the height of the Cold War. In 1966 an American College of Heraldry and Arms was established in Baltimore. Although it lasted only four years, it had its moment of fame when it granted arms to Presidents Johnson and Nixon and Governor Spiro Agnew. Johnson, for one, apparently liked his coat of arms so much that he is said to have "ordered an extra set." Following this college's demise, the creation in 1972 of another organization, the American College of Heraldry, which is still active today, testified to the lasting interest in heraldry among Americans.[18]

Another indication was the founding of several programs of "first families" and "pioneers" in different states. Such organizations had appeared in the late nineteenth and early twentieth centuries to reinforce a sense of belonging to a particular and exclusive community of ancestry among their members. At that time the phenomenon remained limited to parts of the South and the West. During the 1960s the idea of organizing the descendants of the "first families" was revived in Ohio in 1964 and in Mississippi in 1967. There were also similar endeavors at the local level, like the Society of the Founders of the City of New Orleans, instituted in 1963. Membership in these and other programs was reserved to those who could prove that they were descended from a local resident before a given date—in the case of Mississippi and Ohio, before statehood in 1817 and 1821, respectively.[19]

❧   ❧   ❧

By the 1970s the emergence and increasing acceptance of diversity, itself a joint product of the civil rights movement and the new interest in white ethnicity, helped transform the practice of American family history in much greater depth. Many Americans who had not previously done so now turned to genealogy in order to reconsider and redefine their individual and family identity in new terms. A number of books explored the ethnic dimension of American society and genealogical memory and insisted on the democratic effect of diversity. Richard Gambino's *Blood of My Blood* (1974),

Michael Arlen's *Passage to Ararat* (1976), and Irwing Howe's *World of Our Fathers* (1976) explored the Sicilian, Armenian, and eastern European Jewish roots of their respective authors. More important than any of these for the future of American genealogy was Alex Haley's *Roots*, published, like Arlen's and Howe's books, in 1976.[20]

Born in 1921, Haley grew up in a middle-class African American family, living on the campuses of the southern black colleges where his father taught. In 1938, after spending two years in college, he enlisted for three years in the Coast Guard, where he served during World War II in the South Pacific. He began to write, and when peace returned, he remained in the Coast Guard as a writer in the Public Relations Office and later as the Coast Guard's chief journalist. He retired in 1959, moved to New York City, and became a full-time writer, publishing stories in the *Reader's Digest* and *Playboy* and working with Malcolm X on his autobiography, which came out in 1965 soon after Malcolm X was assassinated. By that time Haley had become interested in the history of his own family.

At first he projected a book on his family experience in post–Civil War Tennessee, but he then decided to write about the African ancestor he had been told about as a child by his grandmother, aunts, and cousins. Haley started doing research in American libraries and archives. Within a year or two he had traced his ancestor back to Gambia, where he went in 1966. In the village of Juffure he met a griot who told him the story of a man who had been captured by British slave traders in 1767, and whom Haley identified as his ancestor, Kunta Kinte. Between 1966 and 1976 Haley worked on his book, publishing advance parts in magazines and newspapers and speaking about his project in various venues. In June 1968, for instance, he described his project to hundreds of listeners gathered on the Washington Mall at an event organized under the auspices of the Poor People's University. Between 1969 and 1972 he addressed as many as 500 campus audiences about his research. His book went through several titles—Haley called it "Kebarro" in 1968 and "Before This Anger" in 1971 before settling on "Roots" in 1972. From the beginning, Haley expected the book to be translated into many languages and made into a motion picture. He knew that his articles and his speaking engagements stimulated interest about black genealogy before his book was even published. As he explained in 1972, "This isn't the story of a family, it's the saga of a people." Many African Americans who listened to him and read his writings in those years displayed a "burgeoning interest in genealogy"—searching for genealogical material in family Bibles and legal records and interviewing elderly relatives. On university campuses like Rutgers, Carleton, and Berkeley, professors like the writer Toni Cade Bambara and the historians Kenneth Goode and Kirk Jeffrey encouraged their African American undergraduate students to trace their family history and thus celebrate their heritage and black culture.[21]

When *Roots* was published in 1976, the "burgeoning interest" turned into a major cultural phenomenon. The book told the story of Haley's African "furthest-back person," Kunta Kinte, and how he was captured in Gambia, how he survived the middle passage, how he lived and revolted in his owner's plantation, and how he fathered a daughter in 1790. Haley went on narrating the story of Kinte's descendants in slavery and freedom down to his maternal grandmother, the person who had told him about "the African" when he was a child. Apart from the book's last chapter, which described Haley's genealogical quest, *Roots* was a narrative devoid of the technical apparatus of history and genealogy. In Haley's view, however, the book was not fictional. "Every statement in *Roots*," he explained, "is accurate in terms of authenticity—the descriptions of the culture and terrain are based in valid material. The beginning is a re-creation, using novelistic techniques, but as it moves forward more is known and it is more factually based." *Roots,* Haley suggested, was both fiction and fact; it was what he proposed to call "faction."[22]

In any case, it was an instant success. The publisher, Doubleday, anticipating large sales, printed a first run of 250,000 copies and then kept on reprinting. Within a year, over 1.5 million copies of *Roots* had found their way into American households. Most reviews were raves. James Baldwin's moving "How One Black Man Came to Be an American," which made the cover page of the *New York Times'* book section, called *Roots* "an act of faith and courage" and "an act of love." In January 1977 the ABC network showed a twelve-hour television series based on *Roots.* Filming had started in early 1976, months before the book came out. Producers had been uneasy about the project because it was a saga covering over a century of history in twelve hours, because it displayed female nudity, and because there was "the possibility that the unsparingly accurate depiction of slavery would prove repugnant to home viewers," as the *New York Times* explained. ABC, however, knew how to build its audience's expectations. Advance articles described how actors wept during filming. The network carefully announced that it was taking an "unprecedented approach," broadcasting *Roots* on eight consecutive nights. As a result, the television adaptation, starring Le Var Burton as Kunta Kinte, was a huge popular success, indeed, the largest audience in the history of television at the time. Several cities, including Los Angeles and New York City, proclaimed "Roots Week." Alex Haley became a national celebrity, "a folk hero."[23]

Haley hoped that after reading *Roots,* many African Americans would be "more concerned with their African background," and that "whites too may become more interested in their genealogy." He was not disappointed. A few weeks after the book came out, the *New York Times* reported that "interest by Blacks in genealogy is gaining." Thousands of African Americans began searching "for the long-lost past." Within months parents in various parts of the United States named their newborns after Kunta Kinte and his daughter Kizzy, African Americans planned genealogical tours to Africa and displayed more interest in black genealogy, and Americans of all origins began to reexamine their family histories and origins. Publishers hastened to put books with similar themes on the market. High schools and colleges offered classes on *Roots*. An African American travel agency in Atlanta launched a special tour called "Roots," which included a visit to Juffure. Boatloads of black visitors arrived in the small Gambian village, individuals as well as groups like a delegation of the National Association of Negro Business and Professional Clubs.[24]

The success of *Roots* underscored the fact that the civil rights movement had not satisfied black America's demands about identity, the past, Africa, and slavery. Now a search for cultural affirmation followed the decline of militancy. As for whites, Haley's book stimulated descendants of migrants of non-British origins to explore their own roots in turn. In March 1977 Senator John Glenn of Ohio and several other senators sponsored a resolution paying tribute to Haley "for the impact of his epic work *Roots*."[25]

To be sure, *Roots* also met with criticism. The critic Christopher Lehmann-Haupt, for instance, had little sympathy for Haley's "novelized history." "It all reads like fiction," he regretted, "and very conventional fiction at that." A better literary strategy, in his view, would have been to write the book as an autobiographical quest, based on the last chapter, which he found the most illuminating.

Others challenged Haley's literary originality. At least three lawsuits were filed against him for plagiarism. One, in particular, was damning. In 1967 Harold Courlander, a noted writer, folklorist, and anthropologist, had written a novel, *The African*, that told a story very similar to that contained in the Gambian moment of *Roots*. So much evidence of plagiarism was presented during a five-week trial in 1978 before the U.S. District Court of the Southern District of New York that Haley weakly explained that he had been a victim of unscrupulous research assistants and settled the matter out of court.[26]

Journalists, historians, and genealogists also took Haley to task. The historian Willie Lee Rose noted that "the real Juffure of two hundred years ago" was nothing "like the pastoral village Haley describes." Rose regretted that "history seems entirely suspended in the African section" of *Roots*. As for Kunta Kinte's experience in slavery, Rose listed many anachronisms, "too numerous," she said, which chipped "away at the verisimilitude of central matters in which it is important to have full faith." In April 1977 the British reporter Mark Ottaway raised serious doubts about Haley's research in a much-commented-on piece in the *Sunday Times* of London. Ottaway disputed Haley's description of Juffure and the griot Fofana's account of Kunta Kinte's capture and pointed to many factual errors. A few years later the historian Donald R. Wright, a specialist on Africa, followed up on Ottaway's leads. Using his own work and experience as an Africanist, he retraced Haley's steps in Juffure, only to find that "Fofana was not a true *griot*" and not a very knowledgeable informant. In particular, Wright discovered that local oral tradition had not preserved information about individuals living there before the nineteenth century. The only apparent exception was Fofana's account of Kunta Kinte. It was therefore suspect. As Wright explained, the griot had provided Haley with the exact story the African American writer was looking for, as he had made abundantly clear to all he met on arriving in Gambia.[27]

As for the American side of Haley's story, the distinguished genealogist Elizabeth Shown Mills, a fellow of the American Society of Genealogists, and her historian husband Gary B. Mills were no less critical. Submitting *Roots* to a demanding historical and genealogical test, they found that the results "exceeded the most dire projections" they had imagined. Haley's reliance on oral tradition and his lack of professionalism disqualified his findings. He had invented sources when he could not find what he wanted and had neglected other records that contradicted his narrative. The book was marred by "a number of such genealogical errors, each of such magnitude that even alone it could not be overlooked."[28]

All these and other criticisms were true but missed the book's point and the meaning of its extraordinary public reception. Flawed as it was from the point of view of professional historians and genealogists, marred by plagiarism, half-truths, and outright inventions, *Roots* inspired its readers. Alex Haley had a point when he insisted that "the book's theme" was "universal in terms of lineage, heritage, and the common concern with oral history." As James Baldwin had predicted, many African Americans felt an intimate connection with Haley's family saga. So did white Americans. One critic noted at the time that *Roots* made "an inestimable contribution to racial understanding in this country." Members of the history prize committee of the National Book Awards understood this when they awarded Haley "a special citation of merit," recognizing that his book "does not accommodate itself to the category of history, but transcends that and other categories."[29]

Roots inaugurated and symbolized an important disjunction between history and heritage in American culture. Heritage aimed at providing faith, not truth or critical reappraisal. It emphasized an individual's intimate connection and proximity to the past. It connected a person to a group at a time of growth of a new language of group identity. American reading and television audiences were ready to identify with Kunta Kinte, the imaginary hero, and Alex Haley, the imaginative writer, because they came to embody the ethnoracial diversity many Americans were looking for at the time. Genealogy had become family history. Americans were not looking for a narrow, exclusive status any longer. Rather, they wanted to link their lives broadly to those of relatives in previous generations in order to connect with the past and to make the past part of the present. They emphasized identity, not pedigree. Every American family was now entitled to its history and its sense of a collective ancestry. *Roots* convinced Americans that whatever their condition, they could legitimately expect to know who their ancestors were.[30]

✣   ✣   ✣

Since the 1970s interest in genealogy has increased exponentially in the United States. In 1977 a poll found that 29 percent of Americans were "very interested" in family history, a proportion that reached 45 percent in 1995, 60 percent in 2000, and 73 percent in 2005. Millions of Americans are now searching for their ancestors.[31]

Particularly striking is the post-*Roots* development of genealogy among African Americans. Before the book's publication, there had been few black genealogists, and they worked in relative isolation. Paul Sluby, for instance, then a member of the Metropolitan Police Department in Washington, D.C., explained in 1974 how he had started his family history fifteen years earlier and had slowly worked his way through the past while training himself as a genealogist. He could rely only on his own energy since there was no organization or network to help him at the time. Other black genealogists insisted that the country's racial context had long prevented African Americans from searching their family tree. "Up until 10 years ago," the historian and genealogist Elizabeth Clark-Lewis noted in 1977, "it was not easy for blacks to seek their past." Many places were "off-limits."[32]

In the new multicultural context symbolized by the success of *Roots,* many African American men and women began to research their family past, making new demands on archives and archivists. Soon realizing that they would need an organization to channel their genealogical energy and help them in their research, a small group of black genealogists founded the Afro-American Historical and Genealogical Society (AAHGS) in Washington, D.C., in 1977. Its first president, who served from 1977 to 1981, was James Dent Walker, who had risen in the National Archives to the positions of supervisor of military records and director of local history and genealogical programs and was said to have helped Alex Haley's first steps in the archives in the mid-1960s. Walker was an active and respected genealogist, the author in 1977 of *Black Genealogy: How to Begin,* one of the first two books aimed at African American genealogists and a great success. By 1980 the AAHGS was publishing its own *Journal,* and by the end of that decade it began to charter local and regional chapters—twenty-four were active throughout the country in 2004.[33]

Along with the AAHGS, African Americans began to join other local and national genealogical organizations in ever-growing numbers. Popular black magazines like *Ebony* regularly published articles on the subject. Spurred by a vogue of black family reunions since the late 1970s, amateurs joined support groups and genealogical workshops. Soon they discovered that contrary to common wisdom, searching for black ancestors was difficult but not impossible. Because many African American families preserved family traditions faithfully, interviewing elderly relatives pointed many new genealogists in the right direction for available late nineteenth- and twentieth-century sources. During the 1980s availability of these materials grew impressively, in large part as a result of the genealogists' new demands.[34]

The advent of the Internet in the 1990s transformed the nature of African American genealogical research by making more records readily available and providing genealogists with the type of data that white Anglo-Americans had used since the mid-nineteenth century. To be sure, African American genealogy had specific difficulties. Although reaching back to the 1860s was usually relatively easy and not vastly different for an African American and an Anglo-American, things became quite different for the period before 1860—the era of slavery. This was usually where black genealogists of the 1970s and 1980s hit a wall, although many pored over plantation correspondence and slave records in order to identify their ancestors. Their methods were correct, but the resources available to them were still too scarce to follow the paper trail of slavery. The Internet made a major difference by opening enormous databases of digitized records to the public and facilitating the circulation of information. Not unlike the advent of cell phones in countries where traditional telephone technology had never existed, the Internet helped black genealogists bridge a huge gap and partly overcome record fragmentation. As a result, some were able to trace their ancestry during the era of slavery.[35]

Descendants of white immigrants of the nineteenth and twentieth centuries were no less involved in genealogy than African Americans. Unlike lineage-minded ethnic genealogists of the past, the new amateurs were interested in family history and heritage rather than social and racial distinction. Jewish genealogy provides an example. Late nineteenth-century German American Jews had displayed an interest in genealogy that revealed nationalist and racial pride. Jewish American genealogy was slowly transformed in the decades after World War II. In 1949 Rabbi Malcolm Stern was appointed genealogist of the American Jewish Archives, created two years earlier by Jacob Rader Marcus in Cincinnati. Stern professionalized research in American Jewish genealogy during the 1950s and 1960s, publishing in 1960 an important study of Jewish families that had settled in America before 1840, *Americans of Jewish Descent*, which went through two new editions in 1977 and 1988.[36]

The most influential specialist in Jewish American genealogy, Stern was elected a fellow of the American Society of Genealogists in 1965 and served as the society's president from 1976 to 1979. The Jewish Genealogical Society of New York, which he helped found in 1977 and presided over from 1979 to 1984, attracted not only German American Jews but also descendants of eastern European Jews who had migrated to the United States in the late nineteenth and early twentieth centuries. Arthur Kurzweil, the author of one of the first how-to books of Jewish genealogy, *From Generation to Generation* (1980), described his genealogical quest as a "spiritual pilgrimage" in a world that was no more—the shtetl in the Polish town of Dobromil. When he unexpectedly happened on a book and pictures about Dobromil in the New York Public Library one day in 1970, Kurzweil felt the need to research his family's past. A few years later he joined Stern and others, particularly Neil Rosenstein and Steve

Siegel, in founding the Jewish Genealogical Society and a genealogical journal, *Toledot* (meaning "generation" in Hebrew). *Toledot*
lasted only five years (1977–1982), but in 1985 it was succeeded by
Avotaynu, still active today under the direction of Gary Mokotoff.[37]

Since the late 1970s thousands of American Jews have begun to
reconstruct their family trees because doing so has helped them
locate themselves and their families in a Jewish European past and
space that had been forever destroyed in the Holocaust. After the
fall of the Berlin Wall in 1989, they were able to travel to eastern
Europe more easily and found there many intact civil records that
provided valuable information about their family ancestors. Many
also have built on their genealogical quest and the connection to
the past it provided to strengthen their Jewish religious identity.
They have turned to the dozens of books, encyclopedias, and data-
base resources that have appeared over the past thirty years, joined
Jewish American genealogical societies, and traveled to Europe in
search of their roots.[38]

Members of other groups have been no less interested in genealogy
than African Americans and American Jews. By the 1980s and 1990s
descendants of many late nineteenth- and early twentieth-century
eastern and southern European immigrants researched their roots
and formed their own genealogical organizations. Americans with
Asian and Latin American ancestors soon joined them—the His-
panic Genealogical Society of New York was founded in 1993. A
survey of 1,500 Americans in the mid-1990s showed that a third
had investigated their family history in the previous year because
family history allowed them a personal connection to the past.
It was, in fact, the only connection to the past they felt in their
lives. It helped them locate their individual identity in a larger context while constructing a past that had to be personal and inti-

mate. For Americans of every origin, family history was about self-understanding and identity.[39]

*   *   *

The new culture of family history and heritage has had two major consequences over the past three decades. First, genealogy has become a billion-dollar industry and a significant component of the American economy of culture. *Roots,* the computer revolution, and the Internet together have given a major impetus to the size and dynamics of the family history market.

This impressive growth has contrasted with the modest transformations of the genealogy business during the 1950s and 1960s. At that time, market contours were not much different from what they had been since the mid-nineteenth century. An expanding supply of genealogy-related products, such as books, family trees, and heraldic objects, and services answered the demand, but both remained limited in size. Genealogical entrepreneurs could make a living and even a profit, but not a fortune. Jules Chodak, for instance, before World War II was a book collector and dealer interested in Americana. During the 1950s he decided to bet on the slowly developing family history market and began to republish out-of-print genealogical titles. He changed the name of his Baltimore-based firm to the Genealogical Publishing Company in 1959. By the time of his death in 1968, half of his firm's revenues came from genealogical publications. His son and successor Barry Chodak pursued his father's course and built the Genealogical Publishing Company into a leading American publisher of family history reference books, out-of-print classics, and original works. Many other firms, like the American Research Bureau in Los

Angeles (founded in 1935), catered to the age-old and profitable business of determining and locating missing and unknown heirs.

The steady growth of these and many other family history firms during the 1950s and 1960s did not mean that the frauds and temptations of earlier periods had vanished. Numerous organizations played on people's credulity, ignorance, and vanity, publishing fraudulent and complaisant genealogical compilations posing as authentic family histories. Ever mindful of professional genealogical standards, the American Society of Genealogists apparently forced one such firm out of business, the Media Research Bureau of Washington, D.C., but there were always others, like Beatrice Bailey, Inc., and Halbert Heritage, Inc.[40]

Market growth since the 1970s has taken place in two phases. Before the growth of the Internet came the commercial effects of the new interest in genealogy, symbolized by the success of *Roots,* and of technological change in the preservation, reproduction, and transfer of information. Not only did genealogy firms enlarge their market niche of reference and how-to books, but they also produced and sold compact discs containing genealogical databases. Computers soon attracted genealogists. In 1982 a computer terminal link that allowed Virginia Mormons to access the church's archives in Utah was set up in Newport News. The following year the Fifth Annual Genealogy Conference in Hartford, Connecticut, included a session on the use of computers in genealogy. "Computers are becoming quite common in genealogical research," the president of the Connecticut Genealogical Society declared on that occasion. Developers created such programs as Roots, Family Roots, Personal Ancestral Files, and Family Tree Maker to serve the needs of the owners of the new personal computers. At the same time, the growth of computer networks, however uncertain, announced the future. One observer noted in 1988, "The real pay-off in computer genealogy has just begun: it's beginning to rain information."[41]

With the advent of the Internet, a second phase of market growth built on these impressive transformations. The family history market has grown tremendously since the early 1990s. Never has the collection and transfer of genealogical information been as easy as in this digital age. The Internet made it possible for tens of millions of Americans to research their family tree from their homes, collaborate, and exchange information. Not surprisingly, genealogy consistently ranks among digital Americans' favorite hobbies. The genealogy sphere exploded as a result, recently undergoing major transformations that would have seemed ludicrous two decades ago. Amateurs now benefit from remarkable Internet resources such as Cyndi Howells's list of genealogy sites and Dick Eastman's online newsletter.[42]

The ever-growing demand for genealogical information stimulated the emergence of concurrent service providers and then a classic process of concentration. The story of the largest genealogy firm in the United States, Ancestry.com, is one example. It was the result of two entrepreneurial undertakings that merged in the late 1990s. One was a small genealogical firm, Ancestry, Inc., owned by John Sittner, who began publishing a genealogy newsletter in 1984 and ten years later turned it into *Ancestry Magazine*. The other was Infobases, an electronic publishing company founded in 1990 by two young Mormon entrepreneurs, Paul Allen and Daniel Taggart. In 1997 the parent company of Infobases, Western Standard Publishing, bought Ancestry, Inc., from Sittner. Within months Allen and Taggart bought Western Standard Publishing's interest in Ancestry, Inc., and created Ancestry.com.

Ancestry.com went through a series of phases and transformations frequent in corporate America but until then unknown in the world of genealogy. It adopted three different corporate names (one of them twice) in twelve years: Ancestry.com in 1997, MyFamily .com in 1999, the Generations Network in 2006, and finally Ancestry.com again in 2009. It raised millions of dollars from venture capitalists and other investors. It experienced major personnel turnover, including the departure of its founders. It bought and sold competitors and other firms. In 2003, for instance, it acquired Genealogy.com from its owner, A&E Television Networks. Most important, it grew tremendously over time to become the world's largest Internet genealogy provider. Thanks to the extraordinary range of information contained in its databases, the company provides access to billions of records from thousands of sources. It runs a series of family history websites, such as Ancestry.com, MyFamily.com, RootsWeb.com, and others. It also produces the leading genealogy software, Family Tree Maker. As Ancestry.com extended outside the United States to England and Germany, not to mention its many individual subscribers throughout the world, its revenues kept on growing. In the fall of 2009 the company went public and began trading on the NASDAQ. The number of subscribers to Ancestry.com continued to grow in recent years, reaching two million in July 2012. With its ten billion available records and 2011 revenues approaching $400 million, Ancestry.com is now an empire in American family history.[43]

❊   ❊   ❊

The second major transformation of the past three decades relates to the return of genetics to genealogy. At first the growth of multicultural genealogy represented a shift away from the previous era of racial genealogy. By the late 1970s genealogy was for everyone. Members of each ethnic and racial component of American society could legitimately research and emphasize their genealogical identity. This tended to reinforce the boundaries of a given group and the idea that one could have a clearly defined genealogical identity within this group. Groups were multiple but discrete units. The only remaining dimension of the era of racial genealogy was that multicultural genealogists tended to emphasize their connection with one particular group to which they felt related—in effect displaying the same kind of desire for and temptation toward genealogical purity that racial genealogists had emphasized in the early twentieth century, though now within a global context of diversity.[44]

Since the 1980s two evolutions have challenged and transformed this situation. One resulted from the pursuit of genealogical undertakings by Americans who previously had seldom researched their ancestries, like African Americans, and by others who had made highly selective choices about their family history in the past. Many African Americans, including celebrated figures like Alex Haley, Henry Louis Gates Jr., Alice Walker, and Michelle Obama, came to recognize that they also had white and sometimes Native American ancestors, although they chose to define their origin as African and their identity as African American. Some white Americans, like Edward Ball, the descendant of a South Carolina planter dynasty, found "slaves in the family." Genealogical identities that had been hardened by decades of racial categorization suddenly became more flexible—at least for some. Genealogical research helped them undermine rigid group categories and emphasize individual situations, uncertain and dramatic as they sometimes were.[45]

Despite the magnitude of change since the 1950s, this evolution has not come easily in contemporary American culture, as is shown by the debate over the children of Thomas Jefferson and Sally Hemings. Until the late 1990s there was, on the one side, a corpus of oral traditions and contemporary historical evidence that suggested that Hemings and Jefferson had children together; on the other side, there was a 200-year-old ideological resistance to acknowledging this situation for racial reasons. As Annette Gordon-Reed powerfully argues, this was "an American controversy." Gordon-Reed's book on the subject, written much like a legal brief, came out in 1997. It did not bring forward new evidence but challenged the ways in which old evidence had been discarded on racial grounds and convinced many readers that there had always been a racial bias and a double standard against the idea of Hemings-Jefferson children.[46]

In November 1998 the journal *Nature* reported the results of DNA tests on male descendants of the Jefferson and Hemings families that suggested that Thomas Jefferson fathered Hemings's youngest son Eston. Although Gordon-Reed wryly commented that historians need not have waited for DNA tests to know that, the new evidence caused an extraordinary reaction throughout the country. In hundreds of articles, in radio and television shows, including Oprah Winfrey's, and soon in television films and documentaries, commentators debated the findings and its implications for American conceptions of race. Not everyone accepted the conclusions of the *Nature* article. In 2002 members of the Monticello Association, which maintains Thomas Jefferson's burial place there, decided to uphold their longtime policy of restricting membership in their association to descendants of Martha and Maria Jefferson only. The Thomas Jefferson Heritage Society was created in 1999 "to stand always in opposition to those who would seek to undermine the integrity of Thomas Jefferson" and to denounce what they called "the Jefferson-Hemings Myth."[47]

A majority of observers, however, including the Monticello Foundation, which runs Jefferson's estate in Charlottesville, accepted the very high probability that Jefferson was the father of several of Sally Hemings's children. What to make of this general acceptance of a situation that remained unmentionable a few decades ago is not easily decided. When Annette Gordon-Reed published her new book in 2008, *The Hemingses of Monticello: An American Family,* it stirred no polemics and instead received both the National Book Award and the Pulitzer Prize for History. Analysts of the contemporary cultural scene hesitate to ascribe this radical change to Americans' growing understanding of multicultural and racial diversity or to the triumph of forms of cultural relativism that emphasize avoidance of conflicts at all costs. In fact, both may be simultaneously true. For the history of genealogy, at least, the Jefferson-Hemings affair strongly contributed to disseminating among a large public the notion that group boundaries are more flexible than was previously assumed and that individual family histories tell far more complex stories than we sometimes want to know.[48]

The use of DNA in the Jefferson-Hemings affair drew public attention to a second major evolution of the past three decades. DNA tests provide a new form of certification and evidence that is often deemed more scientific than the traditional search for roots. They also signal the return of biological reasoning that had largely faded away since the mid-twentieth-century demise of racialized genealogy. Until about 2000 DNA tests were reserved for legal cases and scientific research by geneticists and molecular evolutionary biologists. Their use in the Jefferson-Hemings case created enormous publicity about DNA and its possible commercialization and use. Within a few years many commercial firms entered this new market, bringing down the price of testing. How-to books taught genealogists to use genetic tests for their specific purposes. New companies created DNA genealogical databases for their individual users. Some catered to African Americans, like African Ancestry Inc., founded by Rick Kittles of the National Human Genome Center at Howard University, and AfricanDNA, created by Henry Louis Gates Jr. of Harvard University. Gates, an academic figure of international stature, has played a central role in the popular success of DNA technology over the past ten years through his DNA-based PBS specials, *African American Lives* (2006 and 2008), *Finding Oprah's Roots* (2007), and *Faces of America* (2010), and their companion books.[49]

Tests examine chromosomal markers, either on the Y chromosome or on mitochondrial DNA. When markers match, it means that two individuals most likely have a common ancestor. Within a family or namesake association, DNA tests help in identifying clusters of descendants, linking them to the genealogical knowledge already accumulated. They can reveal unexpected genealogical relations that had escaped attention, or they can confirm family traditions. For African American genealogists who could not find clues about their ancestors in available documentary resources, DNA offered helpful hints and broad new directions of inquiry. The talk-show host Oprah Winfrey thus learned in 2006 that she had no Zulu ancestry, as family tradition claimed, but that many in her family were Kpelle people from what is now Liberia. The New York City writer Pearl Duncan knew from family tradition that her father's ancestors came from present-day Ghana. A comparison of her father's DNA and that of New Yorkers who knew they were descended from Akwapim people in Ghana revealed that all shared an unusual genetic mutation present with high frequency in Ghana. The actor Isaiah Washington was told that his maternal ancestors were Mende people from Sierra Leone, while Henry Louis Gates Jr. discovered French and Irish origins next to his African ancestry. Such discoveries also took place among white families: descendants of the Rose family of Virginia and Tennessee discovered, much to their surprise, that they had a family connection to a Rose family of New England. Edward Ball's exploration of his family history through DNA revealed the presence of African and Native American ancestors.[50]

The benefits of DNA-related genealogy are obvious, particularly for genealogists who know little or nothing of their family's ancestry. DNA information provides a direction for further research, as well as a modicum of knowledge that in many cases helps the genealogists in their quest for identity. Moreover, DNA tests provide a picture of ancestral genetic complexity, illustrated by the evidence they frequently offer of ancestors of different origins. In a world where racial, national, and social boundaries are quite high, they can remind us that "we are all multiracial, related to each other only to a greater or lesser extent."[51]

But DNA-based genealogy is not without its risks, threats, and drawbacks, which geneticists, social scientists, and genealogists have debated over the past decade. The amount of information provided by the tests is restricted and at times contradictory. Both Y-chromosome and mitochondrial DNA testing provide information about one ancestor in the father's line (for Y-chromosome testing) or in the mother's line (for mitochondrial DNA): that is, one of two parents, one of four grandparents, one of eight great-grandparents, and so on. The use of DNA also represents a major transformation in genealogical practice. As one British genealogist argued, "What DNA represents is a shift in the nature of authority—a shift away from the authority of the book to the authority of the test, away from the library to the lab." DNA testing creates a new form of belief, a type of certification that, to the general public at least, seems more certain because it is based on biology rather than historical genealogy. Although test results are actually probabilistic estimates, they create genetic claims to identity that appear to be legitimate. When the tests are contradictory, they produce a disorientation that is reinforced by the scientific nature of the procedure. Thus tests for Ron Nixon placed his ancestors among Mende people in Liberia, Songhai in Mali, and others in West and East Africa—creating confusion and indeterminacy rather than certainty. The consequences are troubling for the individuals concerned because of the authoritative weight of science in these types of pronouncements. Under certain conditions, therefore, DNA genealogy either reinforces genetic essentialism in American culture or produces greater uncertainty.[52]

In the last analysis, the question is not whether genealogists should adopt or refuse DNA technology. It is here to stay, and with it genetic genealogy, now multicultural instead of being limited to whites of Anglo-American parentage, as in the late nineteenth and early twentieth centuries. However, DNA technology raises major issues for seekers of family trees. In the present context of multicultural diversification and democratization of genealogy, the return of genetic perspectives is not without its ironies and tensions. In order to minimize the risks and take advantage of new horizons opened by the use of DNA technology in genealogical research, family historians need to appraise the real possibilities and limits of these new tools in their search for a usable genealogical past.

✳   ✳   ✳

The popular success of such television programs as *African-American Lives, Finding Oprah's Roots, Faces of America,* and *Who Do You Think You Are?,* as well as family history's importance and visibility on the Internet, testifies to genealogy's weight and significance in contemporary American culture. What was once an exclusive, class- and race-based cultural activity and means for self-assertion has become over the past few decades a democratic and multicultural pursuit. Not only does the new electronic media culture abundantly reflect this transformation, but traditional avenues for family history have also fully grasped its meanings and implications. The oldest genealogical society in the United States, the New England Historic Genealogical Society—once a New England Brahmin preserve and now a vibrant organization proud of its 25,000 members worldwide—made the point clear when it invited Annette Gordon-Reed and Henry Louis Gates Jr. to be the special guests of its 2010 Annual Dinner and honored them on the occasion. The new interest in genealogy was fueled by, and fueled in turn, a widespread interest in questions of identity and heritage, now potentially extended to all groups and individuals in the United States.

This process of multicultural democratization has also been a process of commercialization. Genealogy has become big business, with millions of potential and actual customers. Alongside products, customers, and a market have come new organizational and economic developments, symbolized by companies like Ancestry

.com. Financial aspects are now an important part of the new American genealogy, and they become more important every day. Not surprisingly, this development comes with both rewards and risks. Resources that fifty years ago were unknown, unimaginable, or reserved to a precious few are now easily available to everyone for a relatively modest price. At the same time, the spectacular development of genealogy as a service sector should not conceal the fact that genealogy now is fully and more than ever before in the market, and that market rules and demands come first and scientific knowledge only second. Since market developments in the past seldom brought good news for the quality of genealogical research, it is legitimate to wonder how scientific ambitions, values, and knowledge will be preserved. After all, the commercialization of family trees in the late nineteenth and early twentieth centuries led directly to the development of professional genealogy as we know it today, including the prestigious American Society of Genealogists and its distinguished fellows. Whether this type of professional regulation will suffice in the era of the Internet or whether new forms of scientific validation and control are necessary remains an open question.

Finally, over the past half century genealogy's place and meanings in debates over race and racial issues have changed no less dramatically. First came a break with the racialized vision of genealogy that had dominated the era between the Civil War and World War II; later, genealogists embraced DNA testing and returned to a mode of biological reasoning that had temporarily disappeared. As we have seen, the new genetic perspectives provide some answers to the questions raised by family historians, but they also raise new issues and suggest new dangers. Charges of essentialism versus claims of scientificity, tensions between genetics and culture, "collision of DNA, race, and history," and questions about the relationship between technology and the politics of identity—genealogy is part of a contentious debate, more intense than any involving the quest for ancestors since the era of triumphant eugenics in the early twentieth century. Separated by a century, these two debates share an emphasis on the importance of genealogy for their purposes. In common, they also focus on questions of identity as they relate to individuals, groups, and concepts of race. Their tenets differ, however, as well as their context: unlike in the 1910s, genetic genealogy in the 2010s does not explicitly aim at demonstrating the superiority of one individual or group over another. It hopes to provide solid evidence of an individual's genetic patrimony. But this is precisely where contentious questions begin: how solid is the evidence, how meaningful is it for the individual in question, and how dangerous is this return to a genetic vision of society? The geneticization of genealogy raises even more issues than its commercialization, and they are not likely to be resolved any time soon.[53]

The fact that genealogy's democratization, commercialization, and geneticization are relevant and contentious issues in contemporary American culture should not surprise us. Over the past four centuries, family trees have always said more about the genealogists than about their ancestors. For Americans, genealogy has been a quest of discovery of who they were, or who they thought they were, or who they wanted to be. They have relied on genealogy to reinforce otherwise-weak identities within the larger society, to locate themselves in historical time, and to include and exclude others. Genealogy has filled many of their needs—social, economic, moral, political, racial, religious, and familial—depending on time, place, and the individuals concerned. Family trees, in other words, have always contributed to the fabric of America. This suggests that more than ever, now that they grow everywhere, they will continue to offer important insight into American culture.

ABBREVIATIONS

NOTES

ACKNOWLEDGMENTS

INDEX

ABBREVIATIONS

AAAPSS   *Annals of the American Academy of Political and Social Science*

AFP   Appleton Family Papers, Massachusetts Historical Society

AHR   *American Historical Review*

CCP   Chester Collection, Pedigrees, College of Arms, London

CSP   Columbus Smith Papers, 1835–1911, Stewart-Swift Research Center, Henry Sheldon Museum, Middlebury, Vt.

HBP   Henry Bond Papers, New England Historic Genealogical Society

HGSP   Henry Gates Somerby Papers, New England Historic Genealogical Society

HSM Stewart-Swift Research Center, Henry Sheldon Museum of Vermont History, Middlebury, Vt.

HSP Historical Society of Pennsylvania

JFP John Farmer Papers, New Hampshire Historical Society

JSP James Savage Papers, Massachusetts Historical Society

LCP Library Company of Philadelphia

LSC Lemuel Shattuck Collection, Massachusetts Historical Society

MHS Massachusetts Historical Society

NAR *North American Review*

NEHGR *New England Historical and Genealogical Register*

NEHGS New England Historic Genealogical Society

NEQ *New England Quarterly*

NYGBR *New York Genealogical and Biographical Record*

NYPL New York Public Library

NYT *New York Times*

PAJHS *Publications of the American Jewish Historical Society*

PMHB *Pennsylvania Magazine of History and Biography*

RQ *Renaissance Quarterly*

TAG *The American Genealogist*

THSSC	*Transactions of the Huguenot Society of South Carolina*
VG	*Virginia Genealogist*
VHS	Virginia Historical Society
VMHB	*Virginia Magazine of History and Biography*
WMQ	*William and Mary Quarterly*
WP	*Washington Post*

NOTES

PROLOGUE

1. See, for instance, Rachel L. Swarns and Jodi Kantor, "First Lady's Roots Reveal Slavery's Tangled History," *NYT*, 8 October 2009; "Room for Debate: One Family's Roots, a Nation's History," http:// roomfordebate.blogs.nytimes.com/2009/10/08/one-familys-roots -a-nations-history/; Sheryl Gay Stolberg, "Obama Has Ties to Slavery Not by His Father but His Mother," *NYT*, 30 July 2012; Ancestry .com, www.ancestry.com/obama.
2. James T. Kloppenberg, *Reading Obama: Dreams, Hope, and the American Political Tradition* (Princeton: Princeton University Press, 2011), 8; Barack Obama, *Dreams from My Father: A Story of Race and Inheritance*, 2nd ed. (1995; reprint, New York: Three Rivers Press, 2004), xvii.

I. LINEAGE AND FAMILY IN COLONIAL AMERICA

1. "Letter from Rev. John Walrond of Ottery, Eng., to Rev. William Waldron, Minister of Boston, and Brother of Secretary Waldron," *NEHGR* 1, 1 (January 1847): 66; John Farmer, *A Genealogical Register*

of the First Settlers of New England (Lancaster, Mass.: Carter, Andrews & Co., 1829), 300-301.

2. "Letter from Rev. John Walrond," 66.

3. Léopold Génicot, *Les généalogies* (Turnhout: Brepols, 1975), 14-15, 19-20; Georges Duby, *The Chivalrous Society* (London: Arnold, 1977), 134-148, 149-157; Constance B. Bouchard, "The Origins of the French Nobility: A Reassessment," *American Historical Review* 86, 3 (June 1981): 508, 514; Francis Ingledew, "The Book of Troy and the Genealogical Construction of History: The Case of Geoffrey of Monmouth's *Historia Regum Britanniae*," *Speculum* 69, 3 (July 1994): 676.

4. Ingledew, "Book of Troy," 675-676, 683-684; Marian Rothstein, "Etymology, Genealogy, and the Immutability of Origins," *RQ* 43, 2 (Summer 1990): 332-347; Bouchard, "Origins of the French Nobility," 512; Jean-Marie Moeglin, *Les ancêtres du prince: Propagande politique et naissance d'une histoire nationale en Bavière au Moyen Âge (1180– 1500)* (Geneva: Droz, 1985), viii-ix, 65-70.

5. Christiane Klapisch-Zuber, *La maison et le nom: Stratégies et rituels dans l'Italie de la Renaissance* (Paris: Éditions de l'École des hautes études en sciences sociales, 1990), 19-20, 37-39; Stanley Chojnacki, "Kinship Ties and Young Patricians in Fifteenth-Century Venice," *RQ* 38, 2 (Summer 1985): 241-242.

6. Albert A. Sicroff, *Les controverses des statuts de "pureté de sang" en Espagne du XVe au XVIIe siècle* (Paris: Didier, 1960); María Elena Martínez, *Genealogical Fictions: Limpieza di Sangre, Religion, and Gender in Colonial Mexico* (Stanford, Calif.: Stanford University Press, 2008); Anthony Richard Wagner, *The Records and Collections of the College of Arms* (London: Burkes Peerage, 1952), 15-22; Wagner, *Heralds of England: A History of the Office and College of Arms* (London: Her Majesty's Stationery Office, 1967); Wagner, *English Genealogy* (Chichester: Phillimore, 1983); Janet Verasanso, "The Staffordshire Heraldic Visitations: Their Nature and Function," *Midland History* 26 (2001):

128–143; Jean Meyer, *La noblesse bretonne au XVIIIe siècle*, 2 vols. (Paris: S.E.V.P.E.N., 1966), 1:1–27, 49–51, 53; Michel Nassiet, *Parenté, noblesse et États dynastiques, XVe–XVIe siècles* (Paris: Éditions de l'École des hautes études en sciences sociales, 2000), 13–14, 31, 41–42; Guillaume Aubert, "'The Blood of France': Race and Purity of Blood in the French Atlantic World," *WMQ* 61, 3 (July 2004): 439–478.

7. Kathleen Ashley, "Creating Family Identity in Books of Hours," *Journal of Medieval and Early Modern Studies* 32, 1 (Winter 2002): 145–165; André Burguière, "La mémoire familiale du bourgeois gentilhomme: Généalogies domestiques en France aux XVIIe et XVIIIe siècles," *Annales: Économies sociétés civilisations* 46, 4 (July–August 1991): 771–788; Pierre Monnet, "La ville et le nom: Le livre des Melem, une source pour l'histoire privée des élites francfortoises à la fin du Moyen Âge," *Journal des Savants*, July–December 1999, 490–539.

8. André Burguière, "L'État monarchique et la famille (XVIe–XVIIIe siècles)," *Annales: Histoire sciences sociales* 56, 2 (March–April 2001): 326–328; Burguière, "Mémoire familiale," 771–788; Monnet, "Ville et le nom," 538.

9. Roberto Bizzocchi, *Genealogie incredibili: Scritti di storia nell' Europa moderna* (Bologna: Il Mulino, 1995); Steven Shapin, *A Social History of Truth: Civility and Science in Seventeenth-Century England* (Chicago: University of Chicago Press, 1994).

10. Burguière, "Mémoire familiale," 773–775; Wagner, *Records and Collections of the College of Arms*, 8–12; Wagner, *English Genealogy*, 354–355, 361–369; Michael Maclagan, "Genealogy and Heraldry in the Sixteenth and Seventeenth Centuries," in *English Historical Scholarship in the Sixteenth and Seventeenth Centuries*, ed. Levi Fox (London: Oxford University Press, 1956), 31–48; Charles Lancaster, "Learned, Judicious and Laborious Gentlemen: Collectors of Genealogies and Gentry Histories in Later Seventeenth-Century England," *Limina: A Journal of Historical and Cultural Studies* 5 (1999): 76.

11. Peter Laslett, "The Gentry of Kent in 1640," *Cambridge Historical Journal* 9, 2 (1948): 155-157; Maclagan, "Genealogy and Heraldry," 31, 43-48; Wagner, *English Genealogy*, 369-375; Lancaster, "Learned, Judicious and Laborious Gentlemen," 76-92; J. F. R. Day, "Primers of Honor: Heraldry, Heraldry Books, and English Renaissance Literature," *Sixteenth Century Journal* 21, 1 (Spring 1990): 93-103; Brian Patton, "Preserving Property: History, Genealogy, and Inheritance in 'Upon Appelton House,'" *RQ* 49, 4 (Winter 1996): 824-839.

12. Day, "Primers of Honor," 97; Lancaster, "Learned, Judicious and Laborious Gentlemen," 76-92; Wagner, *English Genealogy*, 377-378.

13. J. Horace Round, *Family Origins and Other Studies,* ed. William Page (London: Woburn, 1930), 170-171, cited in Wagner, *English Genealogy*, 358; Lawrence Stone, *The Crisis of the Aristocracy, 1558–1641* (London: Oxford University Press, 1967), 37-61.

14. "Browne Family Letters," *NEHGR* 25, 4 (October 1871): 352-355; "A New Clue to the Lee Ancestry. Letter of Lancelot Lee of Coton, England, to Thomas Lee, of Stratford, Va.," *VMHB* 6, 3 (January 1899): 257-260; Cazenove Gardner Lee and Dorothy Mills Parker, *Lee Chronicle: Studies of the Early Generations of the Lees of Virginia* (New York: Vantage Press, 1997), 343-346.

15. Elizabeth A. Crowell and Norman Vardney Mackie III, "The Funerary Monuments and Burial Patterns of Colonial Tidewater Virginia, 1607-1776," *Markers* 7 (1990): 129.

16. Alice P. Kenney, "Neglected Heritage: Hudson River Valley Dutch Material Culture," *Winterthur Portfolio* 20, 1 (1985): 68, 69; Waldron Phoenix Belknap, "Notes on the Duyckinck Family," in *American Colonial Painting: Materials for a History* (Cambridge, Mass.: Harvard University Press, 1959), 63-128; Arnold J. F. Van Laer, ed., *Minutes of the Court of Rensselaerswyck, 1648–1652* (Albany: University of the State of New York, 1922), 207; I. N. Phelps Stokes, *The Iconography of Manhattan Island, 1498–1909*, 6 vols. (New York: R. H. Dodd, 1915), 4:956; Berthold Fernow and E. B. O'Callaghan, *The Records of New*

Amsterdam from 1653 to 1674 anno Domini, 7 vols. (New York: Pub. under the authority of the city by the Knickerbocker press, 1897), 2:183; "Fac-similes of Signatures and Seals," *Collections of the Massachusetts Historical Society,* 4th ser. (Boston: The Society, 1863-1865), 6:587 sq. [unpag.] and 7:635 sq. [unpag.]; Louisa Dresser, "Portraits in Boston, 1630-1720," *Archives of American Art Journal* 6, 3-4 (July-October 1966): 19-20.

17. Bible Records, 1670-1791, Carter Family Papers, VHS; Ronald Hoffman and Sally D. Mason, *Princes of Ireland, Planters of Maryland: A Carroll Saga, 1500–1782* (Chapel Hill: University of North Carolina Press, 2000), xxiv-xxv.

18. Norman H. Dawes, "Titles as Symbols of Prestige in Seventeenth-Century New England," *WMQ* 6, 1 (January 1949): 69-83; Crowell and Mackie, "Funerary Monuments," 113; Frederick B. Tolles, *Meeting House and Counting House: The Quaker Merchants of Colonial Philadelphia, 1682–1763* (Chapel Hill: University of North Carolina Press, 1948), 131; William Nelson, "Nelson Letter Book," *William and Mary College Quarterly Historical Magazine* 7, 1 (July 1898): 30.

19. William Johnson, *The Papers of Sir William Johnson,* 14 vols. (Albany: University of the State of New York, 1921-1965), 1:266; 2:343-350; 3:x; 4:8, 12, 31.

20. Bernard Bailyn, *The New England Merchants in the Seventeenth Century* (Cambridge, Mass.: Harvard University Press, 1955), 139-140, 192-197; Donald R. Friary, "The Use of Heraldry as a Status Symbol in Colonial Boston, 1675 to 1725," seminar paper, University of Pennsylvania, 3 May 1963, Henry N. Flynt Library, Deerfield, Mass.; Lillian B. Miller, "The Puritan Portrait: Its Function in Old and New England," in *Seventeenth-Century New England: A Conference,* ed. Colonial Society of Massachusetts (Boston: The Society, 1984), 156-163, 172-178; Roy C. Strong, *The English Icon: Elizabethan and Jacobean Portraiture* (London and New York: Paul Mellon Foundation for British Art and Pantheon Books, 1969), 29; Charles Knowles Bolton, *The Founders: Portraits of Persons Born Abroad Who Came to the*

Colonies in North America before the Year 1701, 3 vols. (Boston: Boston Athenaeum, 1919).

21. Richard Beale Davis, ed., *William Fitzhugh and His Chesapeake World, 1676–1701: The Fitzhugh Letters and Other Documents* (Chapel Hill: University of North Carolina Press, 1963), 192–195, 215–217; Bernard Bailyn, "Politics and Social Structure in Virginia," in *Seventeenth-Century America: Essays in Colonial History,* ed. James Morton Smith (Chapel Hill: University of North Carolina Press, 1959), 99–100; Martin H. Quitt, "Immigrant Origins of the Virginia Gentry: A Study of Cultural Transmission and Innovation," *WMQ* 45, 4 (October 1988): 632, 651.

22. John Weever, *Ancient Funerall Monuments within the United Monarchie of Great Britaine and Ireland* (London: Printed by Tho Harper, 1631), 10, quoted by Crowell and Mackie, "Funerary Monuments," 115.

23. Phyllis W. Francis, "Some Lineal Descendants of Captain Adam Thorowgood (1602–1640), Lynnhaven Parish, Princess Anne County, Virginia," *VG* 16, 1 (January–March 1972): 119–123.

24. Theodore Chase and Laurel K. Gabel, *Gravestone Chronicles,* 2 vols. (Boston: NEHGS, 1997), 2:518–520, 530, 534, 538, 550; Henry R. Stiles, "Notes on the Graveyards of Long Island," *NYGBR* 2, 1 (January 1871): 31.

25. Samuel Sewall, *The Diary of Samuel Sewall,* ed. M. Halsey Thomas, 2 vols. (New York: Farrar, Straus and Giroux, 1973), 1:140, 387, 499, 509; 2:655, 745, 794, 827, 866, 945, 997, 1016, 1037, 1045; Chase and Gabel, *Gravestone Chronicles,* 2:507, 593–594.

26. Thomas Coffin Amory, "Seals from the Jeffries Collection of Manuscripts," *NEHGR* 31, 1 (January 1877): 57, 59, 61, 64, 65, 66.

27. Davis, *William Fitzhugh,* 244, 246.

28. Patricia E. Kane, "Artistry in Boston Silver of the Colonial Period," in *Colonial Massachusetts Silversmiths and Jewelers,* ed. Patricia E. Kane (Hanover, N.H.: University Press of New England, 1997), 48, 49–53, 60, 70; Gerald W. R. Ward, "The Democratization of Precious Metal:

A Note on the Ownership of Silver in Salem, 1660-1820," *Essex Institute Historical Collections* 126, 3 (1990): 187; Esther Singleton, *Social New York under the Georges, 1714-1776: Houses, Streets, and Country Homes, with Chapters on Fashions, Furniture, China, Plate, and Manners* (New York: D. Appleton, 1902), 136-137, 144; Alice P. Kenney, *The Gansevoorts of Albany: Dutch Patricians in the Upper Hudson Valley* (Syracuse, N.Y.: Syracuse University Press, 1969), 40-42 and illustrations 5 and 7.

29. Kane, "Artistry in Boston Silver," 68-102.

30. "Command from the Council of Virginia to the College of Heralds to record the names and orders of rank of a colonial aristocracy, 1609," Harley MS 6067, fol. 6, British Library; Alexander Brown, *The Genesis of the United States: A Narrative of the Movement in England, 1605-1616, Which Resulted in the Plantation of North America by Englishmen,* 2 vols. (Boston: Houghton, Mifflin and Company, 1890), 1:308-309; Joseph I. Waring, "The Carolina Herald," *South Carolina Historical Magazine* 72, 3 (July 1971): 160-163.

31. Rita Susswein Gottesman, *The Arts and Crafts in New York, 1726-1776: Advertisements and News Items from New York City Newspapers,* Collections of the New-York Historical Society, vol. 69 (New York: Printed for the New-York Historical Society, 1938), 8, 9, 12, 13-14, 34, 65, 304.

32. Chase and Gabel, *Gravestone Chronicles,* 92.

33. Alfred Coxe Prime, *The Arts and Crafts in Philadelphia, Maryland, and South Carolina, 1721-1785: Gleanings from Newspapers* (Topsfield, Mass.: Walpole Society, 1929), 10, 19, 26-27, 293.

34. Gottesman, *Arts and Crafts in New York,* 65; Davis, *William Fitzhugh,* 192-193; Bailyn, "Politics and Social Structure in Virginia," 216.

35. John Guillim, *A Display of Heraldrie,* 6th ed. (London: Printed by T. W. for R. and J. Bonwicke and R. Wilkin and J. Walthoe and T. Ward, 1724); Chase and Gabel, *Gravestone Chronicles,* 2:540, 577; Harold Bowditch, "The Gore Roll of Arms," in *Genealogies of Rhode Island Families,* 2 vols. (Baltimore: Genealogical Publishing Company,

NOTES TO PAGES 26-28

1983), 2:707-808; D. Brenton Simons, "The Gore Roll: New England's Roll of Arms," *New England Ancestors* 4, 5-6 (2003): 2-25.

36. John Spencer Bassett, ed., *The Writings of "Colonel William Byrd of Westover in Virginia Esqr."* (New York: Doubleday, Page & Co., 1901), 413; James Raven, *London Booksellers and American Customers: Transatlantic Literary Community and the Charleston Library Society, 1748–1811* (Columbia: University of South Carolina Press, 2002), 360, 363 (I am indebted to Bertrand Van Ruymbeke for this reference); E. Millicent Somerby, ed., *Catalogue of the Library of Thomas Jefferson*, 5 vols. (Washington, D.C.: Library of Congress, 1952), 1:183-184.

37. "Miscellaneous documents relating to Edmund Andros," MS C 4900, NEHGS; Bassett, *Writings of "Colonel William Byrd,"* 444; Quitt, "Immigrant Origins of the Virginia Gentry," 649-651; Marion Tinling, ed., *The Correspondence of the Three William Byrds of Westover, Virginia, 1684–1776*, 2 vols. (Charlottesville: University Press of Virginia, 1977); Pierre Marambaud, *William Byrd of Westover, 1674–1744* (Charlottesville: University Press of Virginia, 1971); Kenneth A. Lockridge, *The Diary and Life of William Byrd II of Virginia, 1674–1744* (Chapel Hill: University of North Carolina Press, 1987).

38. Thomas Jefferson to Thomas Adams, February 20, 1771, in *The Works of Thomas Jefferson*, ed. Paul Leicester Ford, 12 vols. (New York: G. P. Putnam's Sons, 1904), 2:5.

39. See the cases of Enge of Boston (1742), Corbin of Virginia (1765), Sparhawk of Philadelphia (1765), and Mortimer of Virginia (1765), Waiting Book, vol. 6, 1741-1767, 10, 464, 480, 493, MS, College of Arms, London.

40. John W. Jordan, "Franklin as a Genealogist," *PMHB* 23, 1 (1899): 5-6; Notes on the Franklin Family, with a genealogical chart, 1 bound vol., Benjamin Franklin Papers, 1747-1794, HSP.

41. Henry Laurens to Messieurs and Madame Laurence, 25 February 1774, in *The Papers of Henry Laurens*, ed. Philip M. Hamer, George C. Rogers Jr., David R. Chesnutt, and C. James Taylor, 16 vols. (Columbia: University of South Carolina Press, 1968-2003), 9:309-311; Ber-

trand Van Ruymbeke, "Cavalier et Puritain: L'ancêtre huguenot au prisme de l'histoire américaine," *Diasporas: Histoire et sociétés* 5 (2005): 12–21.

42. Harry Lee to William Lee, December 8, 1771, folder a 13; Genealogical Notes by William Lee, September 1771, folder a 20, both in Edmund Jennings Lee Papers, VHS.

43. David Cressy, "Kinship and Kin Interaction in Early Modern England," *Past and Present* 113, 1 (1986): 38–69; Cressy, *Coming Over: Migration and Communication between England and New England in the Seventeenth Century* (Cambridge: Cambridge University Press, 1987).

44. Ira Berlin and Leslie S. Rowland, eds., *Families and Freedom: A Documentary History of African-American Kinship in the Civil War Era* (New York: New Press, 1997), 10; Helen Tunnicliff Catterall, ed., *Judicial Cases Concerning American Slavery and the Negro,* 5 vols. (Washington, D.C.: Carnegie Institution of Washington, 1926–1937), 4:53; Robert E. Desrochers Jr., " 'Not Fade Away': The Narrative of Venture Smith, an African American in the Early Republic," *Journal of American History* 84, 1 (June 1997): 52; Negro Mary v. Vestry of William and Mary's Parish, 3 H. & McH. 501 (October 1796).

45. Catterall, *Judicial Cases,* 4:49, 50, 51, 53–55; William and Mary Butler v. Boarman, 1 H. & McH. 371 (September 1790); Butler v. Craig, 2 H. & McH. 214 (June 1791); Mahoney v. Ashton, 4 H. & McH. 63 (October 1797) and 214 (June 1802); Toogood v. Scott, 2 H. & McH. 26 (May 1783); Rawlings v. Boston, 3 H. & McH. 139 (May 1793); Philip D. Morgan, *Slave Counterpoint: Black Culture in the Eighteenth-Century Chesapeake and Lowcountry* (Chapel Hill: University of North Carolina Press, 1998), 523; Lorena S. Walsh, "Rural African Americans in the Constitutional Era in Maryland, 1776–1810," *Maryland Historical Magazine* 84, 4 (1989): 334–335; Ira Berlin and Ronald Hoffman, eds., *Slavery and Freedom in the Age of the American Revolution* (Charlottesville: University Press of Virginia, 1983), 190–191; Eric Robert Papenfuse, "From Recompense to Revolution: *Mahoney v. Ashton* and the

Transfiguration of American Culture," *Slavery and Abolition* 15, 3 (December 1994): 38-62.

46. Hoffman and Mason, *Princes of Ireland, Planters of Maryland,* 252; Cheryll Ann Cody, "There Was No 'Absalom' on the Ball Plantations: Slave-Naming Practices in the South Carolina Low Country, 1720-1865," *American Historical Review* 92, 3 (1987): 573-579, 595.

47. Family record, Daniel Dunbar Papers, NEHGS.

48. Abigail Langley Granbery Hargroves, Commonplace Book, 1694-1818, VHS; Christine Rose, "The Turpin Notebook," *VG* 31, 1 (January–March 1987): 3-10; David Allen Lambert, transc., "Burial Records from the Account Book of Thomas Clap of Dorchester, Massachusetts, 1762-1797," *NEHGR* 158 (July 2004): 280-286; Paul Heinegg, comp., *Free African Americans of North Carolina and Virginia* (Baltimore: Clearfield, 1997), 125; Harriette Merrifield Forbes, *New England Diaries, 1602–1800: A Descriptive Catalogue of Diaries, Orderly Books and Sea Journals,* 2 vols. ([Topsfield, Mass.]: Privately printed, 1923), 2:322.

49. William Stoughton, *New-England's True Interest: Not to Lie* (Cambridge, Mass.: Printed by S. J. and M. J., 1670), 8, 9, 25, 33.

50. Cotton Mather, *Magnalia Christi Americana; or, The Ecclesiastical History of New-England* [1702], 2 vols. (Hartford, Conn.: Silas Andrus and Son, 1855), 1:17, 18.

51. J. O. B. [Joseph O. Brown], "Nestell," *NYGBR* 8, 1 (January 1877): 44; William Bose Marye, "Records of the Marye and Staige Families of Virginia," *TAG* 10 (1933-1934): 141. See, for instance, the Bibles of the Stille (Swedish), Ortigen (German), and Duché (French) families in the collections of the Library Company of Philadelphia.

52. Bible Records, 1670-1791, Carter Family Papers, VHS; Robert W. Robins, "Throckmorton Prayer Book, Gloucester County," *VG* 9, 2 (April–June 1965): 65-66; Edward F. De Lancey, "Original Family Records of Loockermans, Bayard, Van Cortlandt, Van Rensselaer, and Schuyler," *NYGBR* 5, 2 (April 1874): 69, 72-76; Corinne P. Earnest and Russell D. Earnest, *To the Latest Posterity: Pennsylvania-*

German Family Registers in the Fraktur Tradition (University Park: Pennsylvania State University Press, 2004), 96–97.

53. Gloria Seaman Allen, *Family Record: Genealogical Watercolors and Needlework* (Washington, D.C.: DAR Museum, 1989), 2; Laurel Thatcher Ulrich, "Furniture as Social History: Gender, Property, and Memory in the Decorative Arts," in *American Furniture*, ed. Luke Beckerdite (Hanover, N.H.: University Press of New England, 1993), 53–66; Ulrich, *The Age of Homespun: Objects and Stories in the Creation of an American Myth* (New York: Knopf, 2001), 108–141.

54. Commonplace Book of Reverend Seaborn Cotton, 1650–1752, NEHGS; John Langdon Sibley, "Rev. Joseph Baxter of Medfield," *NEHGR* 20, 2 (April 1866): 157; Commonplace Book of Samuel Brown, ca. 1700–1812, NEHGS; Kenneth A. Lockridge, *On the Sources of Patriarchal Rage: The Commonplace Books of William Byrd and Thomas Jefferson and the Gendering of Power in the Eighteenth Century* (New York: New York University Press, 1992), 1.

55. Abigail Langley Granbery Hargroves, Commonplace Book, 1694–1818, VHS; Commonplace Book of Reverend Seaborn Cotton, 1650–1752, NEHGS; Josiah Chapin Genealogy, 1658–1760, MHS; Commonplace Book of Samuel Brown, ca. 1700–1812, NEHGS; Anne R. Greenhalgh, "Beverley Family Bible, Essex Co., Va," *VG* 16, 2 (April–June 1972): 130–133.

56. "Brief Memoirs and Notices of Prince's Subscribers," *NEHGR* 7, 1 (1853): 72.

57. "Autobiography of Major-General Daniel Denison," *NEHGR* 46, 2 (April 1892): 127, 131, 132; Cressy, *Coming Over*, 290–291.

58. Homer W. Brainard, "The Reverend Henry Smith of Weathersfield," *TAG* 10 (1933–1934): 7–8; [Samuel Sewall], "Letter of the First Chief-Justice Sewall to His Son, Samuel Sewall, Esq., of Brookline, Giving an Account of His Family," *NEHGR* 1, 2 (April 1847): 111–113; Sewall, *Diary*, xxix–xxxiii, 196, 209; Cressy, *Coming Over*, 290.

59. Josiah Cotton, Memoirs, 1726–1756, 3, 4, 14, 34, 36, 67, 94, 160–166, 167–168, MHS.

60. Donald Lines Jacobus, "The Leonard Family of Taunton, Massachusetts," *TAG* 10 (1933-1934): 163; Hilda Justice, *Life and Ancestry of Warner Mifflin, Friend—Philanthropist—Patriot* (Philadelphia: Ferris & Leach, 1905), 34-37; "Memoirs of the Bolling Family by Robert Bolling of Buckingham Continued by Blair Bolling of Richmond, Va. 1838," section 9, folder 61, Bolling Family Papers, VHS; Robert Bolling, *Memoirs of the Bolling Family* (Chellowe, Buckingham County, Va.: R. Bolling, 1803); Robert Bolling, *A Memoir of a Portion of the Bolling Family in England and Virginia* (Richmond, Va.: W. H. Wade & Co., 1868).

61. Memo[randum] of the Jaquelin and Ambler Family now in Virginia, NEHGS.

62. Bible Records, box 1, folder 1, Hosea Starr Ballou Papers, NEHGS; Adin Ballou, *An Elaborate History and Genealogy of the Ballous in America* (Providence, R.I.: Press of E. L. Freeman & Son, 1888), 124-125.

63. Roger Clap, *Memoirs of Capt. Roger Clap Relating Some of God's Remarkable Providences to Him, in Bringing Him into New-England* (Boston: Printed by B. Green, 1731).

64. *A Genealogy of the Family of Mr. Samuel Stebbins and Mrs. Hannah Stebbins, His Wife, From the Year 1707, to the Year 1771, With their Names, Time of their Births, Marriages and Deaths of those who are deceased* (Hartford: Printed by Ebenezer Watson, for the Use of Descendants now living, 1771), v.

2. THE RISE OF AMERICAN GENEALOGY

1. Leverett Saltonstall to Anna Saltonstall, 30 December 1815, in *The Saltonstall Papers, 1607–1815*, ed. Robert Earle Moody, 2 vols. (Boston: Massachusetts Historical Society, 1974), 2:594; Leverett Saltonstall to Anna Saltonstall, 2 February 1816, in *The Papers of Leverett Saltonstall, 1816–1845*, ed. Robert Earle Moody, 5 vols. (Boston: Massachusetts Historical Society, 1978), 1:7-8.

2. "American Genealogies," *NAR* 82, 171 (April 1856): 470; "Peerages and Genealogies," *NAR* 97, 200 (July 1863): 37.

3. Bernard Bailyn, *The Ideological Origins of the American Revolution* (Cambridge, Mass.: Harvard University Press, 1967), 302; Gordon S. Wood, *The Creation of the American Republic, 1776–1787* (New York: Norton, 1972), 70–71.

4. *Proceedings of the Pennsylvania Society of the Cincinnati* (Philadelphia: Printed by John Steele, 1785), 3, 4-5, 10.

5. Cassius [Aedanus Burke], *Considerations on the Society or Order of Cincinnati: Lately Instituted by the Major Generals, Brigadier-Generals, and Officers of the American Army; Proving That It Creates a Race of Hereditary Patricians, or Nobility.* (Charleston: Timothy, 1783), 16, 3, 4; Wallace Evan Davies, "The Society of the Cincinnati in New England, 1783-1800," *WMQ* 5, 1 (January 1948): 11, 12; Davies, *Patriotism on Parade: The Story of Veterans' and Hereditary Organizations in America, 1783–1900* (Cambridge, Mass.: Harvard University Press, 1955), 10. On Burke, see John C. Meleney, *The Public Life of Aedanus Burke: Revolutionary Republican in Post-revolutionary South Carolina* (Columbia: University of South Carolina Press, 1989).

6. George Washington to Hannah Fairfax Washington, 24 March and 9 April 1792, in *The Papers of George Washington: Presidential Series,* ed. Philander D. Chase, 12 vols. (Charlottesville: University Press of Virginia, 2002), 10:152-153, 240-242; Sir Isaac Heard to Washington, 7 December 1791, ibid., 9:258-260; Washington to Sir Isaac Heard, 2 May 1792, ibid., 10:332-338; Thomas Jefferson to Washington, 16 April 1784, in Thomas Jefferson, *Writings* (New York: Library of America, 1984), 791. On Jefferson's fluctuations, see Jefferson to Thomas Adams, 20 February 1771, in *The Papers of Thomas Jefferson,* ed. Julian P. Boyd, 36 vols. (Princeton: Princeton University Press, 1950–), 1:62; Jefferson to James Madison, 6 September 1789, in *The Works of Thomas Jefferson,* ed. Paul Leicester Ford, 12 vols. (New York: G. P. Putnam's Sons, 1904-1905), 6:4.

7. Michael G. Kammen, *A Season of Youth: The American Revolution and the Historical Imagination* (New York: Knopf, 1978), 36; Jefferson,

Writings, 3; Thomas Hamilton, *Men and Manners in America,* 2 vols. (Philadelphia: Carey, Lea & Blanchard, 1833), 1:35.

8. "American Genealogies," 469.

9. Michael G. Kammen, *Mystic Chords of Memory: The Transformation of Tradition in American Culture* (New York: Knopf, 1991), 41–48; Ralph Waldo Emerson, "Nature," in *The Complete Works of Ralph Waldo Emerson,* 12 vols. (Boston: Houghton Mifflin Company, 1903), 1:3; Ralph H. Orth and Alfred R. Ferguson, eds., *The Journals and Miscellaneous Notebooks of Ralph Waldo Emerson,* vol. 13, *1852–1855* (Cambridge, Mass.: Harvard University Press, 1977), 443.

10. Peter Chardon Brooks to Lemuel Shattuck, 9 August 1838, box 1, folder 1833–1839, LSC.

11. John Demos, *Past, Present, and Personal: The Family and the Life Course in American History* (New York: Oxford University Press, 1986); Steven Mintz and Susan Kellogg, *Domestic Revolutions: A Social History of American Family Life* (New York: Free Press, 1988).

12. Joseph Sharpless, *Family Record Containing the Settlement and Genealogy to the Present Time of the Sharples Family in North America* (Philadelphia: Published and sold by the author, 1816), 3; Jedediah Herrick, *A Genealogical Register of the Name and Family of Herrick* (Bangor, Maine: S. S. Smith, Printer, 1846), 3.

13. Georgia Brady Barnhill, " 'Keep Sacred the Memory of Your Ancestors': Family Registers and Memorial Prints," in *The Art of Family: Genealogical Artifacts in New England,* ed. D. Brenton Simons and Peter Benes (Boston: NEHGS, 2002), 60; Jon Butler, *Awash in a Sea of Faith: Christianizing the American People* (Cambridge, Mass.: Harvard University Press, 1990), 277–278; Paul C. Gutjahr, *An American Bible: A History of the Good Book in the United States, 1777–1880* (Stanford, Calif.: Stanford University Press, 1999).

14. Simons and Benes, *Art of Family;* Corinne P. Earnest and Russell D. Earnest, *To the Latest Posterity: Pennsylvania-German Family Registers*

in the Fraktur Tradition (University Park: Pennsylvania State University Press, 2004).

15. James Ball to Burgess Ball, 11 September 1789, section 2, folder 2, Ball Family Papers, VHS; Terry Bradshaw O'Neill, ed., "The Memoirs of John Moore, Esq.," *NYGBR* 136, 1 (January 2005): 21, 22; John Howard Redfield, *Genealogical History of the Redfield Family in the United States* (Albany, N.Y.: Munsell & Rowland, 1860), iii; Elias Warner Leavenworth and William Leavenworth, *A Genealogy of the Leavenworth Family in the United States* (Syracuse, N.Y.: S. G. Hitchcock & Co., 1873), 3.

16. Family Record, Loyal Case (1825), Case Family Papers, HSM; Daniel Webster to Cyrus Perkins, 17 April 1829, in *The Papers of Daniel Webster,* ser. 1, *Correspondence,* ed. Charles M. Wiltse, vol. 2, *1825–1829* (Hanover, N.H.: University Press of New England, 1976), 409; [Autobiography], in *The Papers of Daniel Webster,* ser. 1, *Correspondence,* ed. Wiltse, vol. 1, *1798–1824* (Hanover, N.H.: University Press of New England, 1974), 3; Anthony Charles Cazenove, Memoir, 1775–1843, VHS.

17. Jonathan Roberts, Memoirs, MS, 2 vols., 1:3, HSP; O'Neill, "Memoirs of John Moore, Esq.," 21, 22; Charles H. Stubbs, *Historic-Genealogy of the Kirk Family* (Lancaster, Pa.: Wylie & Griest, 1872), 217; Elizabeth Tucker Coalter Bryan, Diary, 1853, VHS.

18. Frederick Douglass, *My Bondage and My Freedom* (New York: Miller, Orton, & Mulligan, 1855), 34; Herbert G. Gutman, *The Black Family in Slavery and Freedom, 1750–1925* (New York: Pantheon Books, 1976), 93–95; Ira Berlin and Leslie S. Rowland, eds., *Families and Freedom: A Documentary History of African-American Kinship in the Civil War Era* (New York: New Press, 1997), 10, 17–20; Helen Tunnicliff Catterall, ed., *Judicial Cases Concerning American Slavery and the Negro,* 5 vols. (Washington, D.C.: Carnegie Institution of Washington, 1926–1937), 4:61, 80; Shorter v. Boswell, 2 H. & J. 359 (December 1808); Burke v. Negro Joe, 6 G. & J. 136 (June 1834); Ariela J. Gross, *What*

Blood Won't Tell: A History of Race on Trial in America (Cambridge, Mass.: Harvard University Press, 2008).

19. Jotham Sewall, *A Memoir of Rev. Jotham Sewall of Chesterville, Maine* (Boston: Tappan & Whittemore, 1853), iii, 9, 10; Thomas Coffin Amory to [Samuel Amory?], 10 April 1849, box 3, folder Papers 1848-1849, Thomas Coffin Amory Papers, MHS; Alexander Gunn, *Memoirs of the Rev. John H. Livingston* (New York: W. A. Mercer, Printer, 1829), 14; William Whiting, "Address before the Historic Genealogical Society," *NEHGR* 7, 2 (April 1853): 107.

20. James Thacher, "Biographical Sketches of the Thacher Family, from Their First Settlement in New England," *New England Magazine* 7, no. 1 (July 1834): 1-2, 14; John Farmer, *A Family Register of the Descendants of Edward Farmer in the Line of the Youngest Branch of His Family* (Concord, N.H.: Printed by George Hough for John Farmer, 1813); Aaron Lummus, *The Life of Aaron Lummus* (Portland, Maine: Printed by Francis Douglas for the author, 1816); Wheeler Martin, *The Genealogy of the Family of Martins* (Providence, R.I.: Hugh H. Brown printer, 1816); Sharpless, *Family Record.*

21. [William Shattuck] to Lemuel Shattuck, 19 February (quote) and 28 May 1853, box 4, folder Correspondence n.d., LSC; William Bullard to Abner Morse, 26 November 1855, box 2, folder Mr. Morse's Correspondence, October 1855-July 1856, LSC; Jonathan Brown Bright to Henry Bond, 9 December 1857, box 8, folder 12, HBP.

22. Linda K. Kerber, *Women of the Republic: Intellect and Ideology in Revolutionary America* (Chapel Hill: University of North Carolina Press, 1980), xiv; Peter Benes, "Family Representations and Remembrances: Decorated New England Family Registers, 1770 to 1850," in Simons and Benes, *Art of Family,* 14, 16, 24.

23. Benes, "Family Representations and Remembrances," 14-28, 41. On the history of the tree as a genealogical symbol, see Christiane Klapisch-Zuber, *L'ombre des ancêtres: Essai sur l'imaginaire médiéval de la parenté* (Paris: Fayard, 2000).

24. Anna Saltonstall to Leverett Saltonstall, 12 February 1816, in Moody, *Papers of Leverett Saltonstall, 1816–1845,* 1:11; Mary Ann Dickerson Album (1822–1858), LCP; Sarah Thompson, Commonplace Book, 1782–1849, HSP; Sarah Robinson, *Genealogical History of the Families of Robinsons, Saffords, Harwoods, and Clarks* (Bennington, Vt., 1837), iv.

25. Phyllis Cole, *Mary Moody Emerson and the Origins of Transcendentalism: A Family History* (New York: Oxford University Press, 1998); John Kelly to John Farmer, 12 January 1827, box 2, folder 15, JFP; William H. Gilman and Alfred R. Ferguson, eds., *The Journals and Miscellaneous Notebooks of Ralph Waldo Emerson,* vol. 2, *1822–1826* (Cambridge, Mass.: Harvard University Press, 1961), 316; William H. Gilman and Alfred R. Ferguson, eds., *The Journals and Miscellaneous Notebooks of Ralph Waldo Emerson,* vol. 3, *1826–1832* (Cambridge, Mass.: Harvard University Press, 1963), 349–358.

26. Ray Allen Billington and Martin Ridge, *Westward Expansion: A History of the American Frontier,* 6th ed. (Albuquerque: University of New Mexico Press, 2001); Bernard Bailyn, *The Peopling of British North America: An Introduction* (New York: Knopf, 1986); Bailyn, *Voyagers to the West: A Passage in the Peopling of America on the Eve of the Revolution* (New York: Knopf, 1986); Joyce Oldham Appleby, *Inheriting the Revolution: The First Generation of Americans* (Cambridge, Mass.: Harvard University Press, 2000).

27. Elinor Kinsman to Lemuel Shattuck, 15 July 1840, box 1, folder Various genealogies Hildreth-Longby, LSC.

28. Ulysses S. Grant, *Memoirs and Selected Letters: Personal Memoirs of U. S. Grant, Selected Letters, 1839–1865* (New York: Library of America, 1990), 20; Abraham Lincoln to Solomon Lincoln, 6 March 1848, to David Lincoln, 2 April 1848, and to Jesse Lincoln, 1 April 1854, in Abraham Lincoln, *Speeches and Writings, 1832–1858* (New York: Library of America, 1989), 177–178, 180–181, 209–211.

29. Sylvanus Adams to Sanford Adams, 19 March 1853, MA-6, Dwight Manufacturing Company Papers, Special Collections, Baker Library,

Graduate School of Business Administration, Harvard University, Cambridge, Mass.

30. Sarah J. Purcell, *Sealed with Blood: War, Sacrifice, and Memory in Revolutionary America* (Philadelphia: University of Pennsylvania Press, 2002); John Resch, *Suffering Soldiers: Revolutionary War Veterans, Moral Sentiment, and Political Culture in the Early Republic* (Amherst: University of Massachusetts Press, 1999); Jerry A. O'Callaghan, "The War Veteran and the Public Lands," *Agricultural History* 28, 4 (1954): 163-168; James W. Oberly, *Sixty Million Acres: Veterans and the Public Lands before the Civil War* (Kent, Ohio: Kent State University Press, 1990).

31. John Frederick Dorman, comp., *Virginia Revolutionary Pension Applications,* 51 vols. (Washington, D.C.: J. F. Dorman, 1958), 2:47-48; Thomas Green Ledger, VHS.

32. Wesley Frank Craven, *The Legend of the Founding Fathers* (New York: New York University Press, 1956), 62; David Ramsay, *The History of the American Revolution,* 2 vols. (Philadelphia: Printed and sold by R. Aitken & Son, 1789); Mercy Otis Warren, *History of the Rise, Progress, and Termination of the American Revolution: Interspersed with Biographical, Political, and Moral Observations,* 2 vols. (Boston: Printed by Manning and Loring, for E. Larkin, 1805); Kammen, *Season of Youth,* 41-43; David J. Russo, *Keepers of Our Past: Local Historical Writing in the United States, 1820s–1930s* (Westport, Conn.: Greenwood Press, 1988).

33. David D. Hall, "Reassessing the Local History of New England. Part One: The Rise and Fall of a Great Tradition," in *New England: A Bibliography of Its History,* ed. Roger Parks (Hanover, N.H.: University Press of New England, 1989), xxiv, xxv, xxx; Lawrence Buell, *New England Literary Culture from Revolution through Renaissance* (Cambridge: Cambridge University Press, 1986).

34. H. G. Jones, ed., *Historical Consciousness in the Early Republic: The Origins of State Historical Societies, Museums, and Collections, 1791–1861* (Chapel Hill: North Caroliniana Society and North Carolina Col-

lection, 1995); Michael O'Brien, *Conjectures of Order: Intellectual Life and the American South, 1810–1860,* 2 vols. (Chapel Hill: University of North Carolina Press, 2004), 2:623–653; Appleby, *Inheriting the Revolution,* 242; Stephen Nissenbaum, "New England as Region and Nation," in *All over the Map: Rethinking American Regions,* ed. Edward L. Ayers, Patricia Nelson Limerick, Stephen Nissenbaum, and Peter S. Onuf (Baltimore: Johns Hopkins University Press, 1996), 38–61; David Waldstreicher, *In the Midst of Perpetual Fetes: The Making of American Nationalism, 1776–1820* (Chapel Hill: University of North Carolina Press, 1997); Joseph A. Conforti, *Imagining New England: Explorations of Regional Identity from the Pilgrims to the Mid-Twentieth Century* (Chapel Hill: University of North Carolina Press, 2001); Hall, "Reassessing the Local History of New England," xxvi; François Weil, "John Farmer and the Making of American Genealogy," *NEQ* 80, 3 (September 2007): 415.

35. N. A. Haven to James Savage, 3 March 1823, folder 1823, JSP; John Farmer to John Kelly, 1 January 1823, box 1, folder 10, JFP; Daniel Webster, "First Settlement of New England," in *The Writings and Speeches of Daniel Webster,* 18 vols. (Boston: Little, Brown and Company, 1903), 1:181–183; John D. Seelye, *Memory's Nation: The Place of Plymouth Rock* (Chapel Hill: University of North Carolina Press, 1998), 4.

36. Weil, "John Farmer," 417–420; "Memoir of John Farmer, M.A., Late Corresponding Secretary of the New Hampshire Historical Society," *NEHGR* 1, 1 (January 1847): 9, 20. For a different view of Farmer, see Francesca Morgan, "Lineage as Capital: Genealogy in Antebellum New England," *NEQ* 83, 2 (June 2010): 250–262.

37. John Farmer, *A Genealogical Register of the First Settlers of New England* (Lancaster, Mass.: Carter, Andrews & Co., 1829), iii; Lemuel Shattuck to John Farmer, 25 February 1830, box 3, folder 13, JFP.

38. Weil, "John Farmer," 420–421; John Farmer, Diary, 1806–1838, John Farmer Papers, Rauner Library, Special Collections, Dartmouth College, Hanover, N.H.; Farmer to Kelly, 22 September 1823, box 1, folder 13, JFP.

39. Farmer to Kelly, 25 March 1825, folder 1; Samuel C. Allen to Farmer, 7 May 1825, folder 3; Francis Jackson to Farmer, 21 January 1826, folder 8, all in box 2, JFP; Weil, "John Farmer," 421-423.

40. Edward Bangs to James Savage, 3 November 1828, box 2, folder 22, JFP; Ralph Waldo Emerson to Farmer, 14 February 1829, box 3, folder 2, JFP.

41. Willard to Farmer, 9 September 1829, folder 8; William Plumer to Farmer, 20 January 1830, folder 12; Shattuck to Farmer, 25 February 1830, folder 13, all in box 3, JFP; Weil, "John Farmer," 423-424.

42. Kelly to Farmer, 25 October 1824, box 1, folder 19, JFP; Farmer to Kelly, 14 April 1825, box 2, folder 2, JFP (Farmer's emphasis); Farmer to Willard, 30 October 1826, box 2, folder 13, JFP.

43. William Sprague to Farmer, 25 April 1825, box 2, folder 2, JFP; Christopher C. Baldwin to Shattuck, 29 January 1831, box 1, folder 1831-1832, LSC; Farmer to Jedidiah Farmer, 1 December 1828, box 2, folder 22, JFP; Shattuck to Farmer, 24 June 1829, box 3, folder 6, JFP.

44. Farmer to Kelly, 25 December 1823, box 1, folder 15, JFP; Kelly to Farmer, 12 September 1826, box 2, folder 13, JFP; Mary Clark to Isaac Spalding, 22 September 1836, box 5, folder 25, JFP.

45. Weil, "John Farmer," 427; Farmer to Kelly, 11 November 1823, box 1, folder 14, JFP; Farmer to Kelly, 11 January 1827, box 2, folder 15, JFP; Kelly to Farmer, 8 January 1827, box 2, folder 15, JFP.

46. Weil, "John Farmer," 428-430; Farmer to Isaac Spalding, 9 September 1829, box 3, folder 8, JFP; Farmer to Willard, 23 October 1829, box 3, folder 9, and Willard to Farmer, 2 November 1829, box 3, folder 10, JFP; Willard to Farmer, 30 September 1832, box 4, folder 17, and 17 December 1832, box 4, folder 19, JFP.

47. Weil, "John Farmer," 430-431; Joshua Coffin to Alonzo Lewis, 23 March 1828, folder 1, Alonso Lewis Papers, Phillips Library, Peabody Essex Museum, Salem, Mass.; Mary Clark to Francis Jackson, 13 October 1822, folder 1822, Francis Jackson Papers, MHS; Alonzo Lewis to Farmer, 21 April 1826, box 2, folder 10, and 7 September 1826, box 2, folder 13, JFP.

48. Lewis to Farmer, 3 December 1834, box 5, folder 11, JFP.

49. Weil, "John Farmer," 431–432.

50. Samuel Gardner Drake, "Origins of the New England Historic Genealogical Society," *NEHGR* 9, 1 (January 1855): 9–12; William Carroll Hill, *A Century of Genealogical Progress: Being a History of the New England Historic Genealogical Society, 1845–1945* (Boston: New England Historic Genealogical Society, 1945); John A. Schutz, *A Noble Pursuit: The Sesquicentennial History of the New England Historic Genealogical Society, 1845–1995* (Boston: New England Historic Genealogical Society, 1995).

51. Samuel H. Riddel, "Mr. Charles Ewer," in *Memorial Biographies of the New England Historic Genealogical Society*, 9 vols.(Boston: New England Historic Genealogical Society, 1880–1908), 2:113–155; John H. Sheppard, "Memoir of Samuel Gardner Drake, A.M.," *NEHGR* 17 (July 1863): 197–211; David L. Greene, "Samuel G. Drake and the Early Years of the *New England Historical and Genealogical Register*, 1847–1861," *NEHGR* 145 (July 1991): 203–233; Francis J. Bosha, "A Solitary Man Arrayed in Black: The Society's Samuel Gardner Drake, 1798–1875," *NEHGR* 150 (July 1996): 299–310.

52. "Farmer's Historical Sketch of Amherst, New Hampshire," *NAR* 46, 99 (April 1838): 536–537.

53. Redfield, *Genealogical History of the Redfield Family*, iii, iv.

54. Robert M. Taylor Jr., "Summoning the Wandering Tribes: Genealogy and Family Reunions in American History," *Journal of Social History* 16, 2 (Winter 1982): 32; Lemuel Shattuck, *A Complete System of Family Registration* (Boston: W. D. Ticknor, 1841); Shattuck, *Blank Book Forms for Family Registers* (Boston: The author, 1856); William H. Whitmore, *A Handbook of American Genealogy: Being a Catalogue of Family Histories* (Albany, N.Y.: Joel Munsell, 1862); James Savage, *A Genealogical Dictionary of the First Settlers of New England, Showing Three Generations of Those Who Came before May, 1692, on the Basis of Farmer's Register*, 4 vols. (Boston: Little, Brown and Company, 1860–1862), 1:v, viii, x; "Peerages and Genealogies," *NAR* 97, 200 (July

1863): 69; James Savage to his daughter, 30 July 1867, box 3, folder 1865–1869, JSP.

55. *Sesqui-Centennial Gathering of the Clan Darlington: At the Residence of Brinton Darlington, in East Bradford, Chester County, Pennsylvania, on the 20th of August, 1853* (Lancaster, Pa.: Printed at the request of the Tribe [by E. C. Darlington, Printer], 1853), 6, 17; "Bond's Genealogies of Watertown," *NAR* 83, 172 (July 1856): 58–59.

56. Savage, *Genealogical Dictionary*, 1:x. See also Savage's many letters to Sylvester Judd beginning in 1846 in box 2 (1836–1859), JSP. Isaac W. K. Handy, *Annals and Memorials of the Handys and Their Kindred*, ed. Mildred Handy Ritchie and Sarah Rozelle Handy Mallon (Ann Arbor, Mich.: William L. Clements Library, 1992), xxix; Carlos Coolidge to H. Bond, 8 February 1850, folder 23; George A. Bowman to H. Bond, 25 October 1853, 7, 25, and 30 March, and 3 August 1854, folder 6, all in box 7, HBP.

57. Nelson A. Bixby to H. Bond, 16 December 1845 and 3 June 1846, folder 3; George A. Bond to H. Bond, 9 January 1852, folder 4; Catherine J. Bond to H. Bond, 29 October 1835, and Esther E. Bond to H. Bond, 26 December 1847, folder 4; Mary Bond to H. Bond, 22 June 1846, folder 5; Mary Bowman to H. Bond, 21 October and 31 October 1853, folder 6, all in box 7, HBP. Spelling kept.

58. "The Weeks Family," *Frontier Palladium* (Malone, NY), [1850], inserted in book Weeks Family Meeting, s.d., box 3, HSM; Jonathan Avery Shepard, "An Address Delivered at a Meeting of the Descendants and Relatives of the late Holland Weeks, at New Haven Vt, Sept 16th 1841," Weeks Family Papers, box 1, folder 1, HSM; John C. Park, *Address at a Meeting of the Descendants of Richard Haven of Lynn, at Framingham, Mass., August 29, 1844. Being the Second Centennial Anniversary of His Landing in New England* (Boston: Samuel N. Dickinson, printer, 1844); Rev. Joseph Haven Jr., *Address at the Second Meeting of the Descendants of Richard Haven of Lynn, held at Framingham, Mass., August 30, 1849* (Framingham: Boynton & Marshall, 1849); Richard Soule, *Memorial of the Sprague Family: A Poem*

Recited at a Meeting in Duxbury, of the Descendants and Connections of Hon. Seth Sprague, on the Occasion of His Eighty-Sixth Birthday, July 4th, 1846; With the Family Genealogy and Biographical Sketches in Notes (Boston: James Munroe and Company, 1847); *Sesqui-Centennial Gathering of the Clan Darlington.*

59. Circulars, 12 March 1854 and 1 January 1855, subgroup VI, series F, folder 1, Cushman Collection, NEHGS; circulars, 4 April 1855, December 1855, 1 October 1856, 16 July 1858, 1 October 1858, and 28 July 1859, folder 2, ibid.; William H. Whitmore, *The American Genealogist: Being a Catalogue of Family Histories and Publications Containing Genealogical Information Issued in the United States, Arranged Chronologically,* 3rd ed. (Albany, N.Y.: Joel Munsell, 1875), 93-94, 142.

60. Benes, "Family Representations and Remembrances," 36-39.

61. Barnhill, "'Keep Sacred the Memory of Your Ancestors,'" 60-62; Family Register, broadside (New Market, Va.: Ambrose Henkel & Comp., 1811), LCP.

62. Barnhill, "'Keep Sacred the Memory of Your Ancestors,'" 64-65; Maureen A. Taylor, "Tall Oaks from Little Acorns Grow: The Family Tree Lithograph in America," in Simons and Benes, *Art of Family,* 81.

63. Jonathan Brown Bright to Henry Bond, 7 September 1852 and 23 December 1853, box 8, folder 8, HBP.

64. See the publishers' names in Whitmore, *American Genealogist,* 9-147. John J. Latting, "A Memorial Sketch of Joel Munsell, Printer and Publisher," *NYGBR* 11, 2 (April 1880): 57, 59-60; David Simeon Edelstein, *Joel Munsell: Printer and Antiquarian* (New York: Columbia University Press, 1950).

65. H. Bromfield to James Savage, 26 September 1814, box 1, folder 1813-1814, JSP; Benjamin Savage to James Savage, 25 January 1815, box 1, folder 1815, and 15 September 1821, folder 1821, July-December, JSP; R. Farmer to John Farmer, 18 July 1820, box 1, folder 4, JFP; Nathaniel Lane Taylor, "Genealogist John Farmer Discovers His Ancestry: The Warwickshire Family of Edward[1] Farmer, Isabel[1]

(Farmer) (Wyman) (Blood) Green, and Thomas[1] Pollard, of Billerica, Massachusetts," *NEHGR* 160 (2006): 261-272; 161 (2007): 62-72, 146-155, 209-222; Alonzo Lewis to John Farmer, 3 December 1834, box 5, folder 11, JFP; Elias Loomis to Farmer, 25 April 1836, box 5, folder 22, JFP; I. Daniel Rupp, *A Brief Biographic Memorial of Joh. Jonas Rupp, and Complete Genealogical Family Register of His Lineal Descendants, from 1756 to 1875* (Philadelphia: L. W. Robinson, 1875), 14-22; circular letter of James Savage, 21 March 1842, box 2, folder 1842, January-April, JSP; Savage Diary, box 2, folder Diary 20 April-18 November 1842, JSP; "Bond's Genealogies of Watertown," 55.

66. John M. Bradbury, "Horatio Gates Somerby," *NEHGR* 28 (July 1874): 341.

67. This paragraph is based on analysis of material in several notebooks in Horatio Gates Somerby's papers: vol. 102, box 3; vols. 145 and 146, box 4, HGSP.

68. Joseph Willard, *Willard Memoir; or, Life and Times of Major Simon Willard* (Boston: Phillips, Sampson and Company, 1858), 442.

3. ANTEBELLUM BLOOD AND VANITY

1. Herman Melville, *Pierre; or, The Ambiguities; Israel Potter: His Fifty Years of Exile; The Piazza Tales; The Confidence-Man: His Masquerade; Uncollected Prose; Billy Budd, Sailor: (An Inside Narrative)* (New York: Library of America, 1984), 10, 13, 14, 15-16, 17.

2. Alice P. Kenney, *The Gansevoorts of Albany: Dutch Patricians in the Upper Hudson Valley* (Syracuse, N.Y.: Syracuse University Press, 1969); Merton M. Sealts Jr., "The Melvill Heritage," *Harvard Library Bulletin* 34, 4 (Fall 1986): 337-361; Hershel Parker, *Herman Melville: A Biography*, 2 vols. (Baltimore: Johns Hopkins University Press, 1996), 1:1-12.

3. Allan Melvill to Maria Gansevoort Melvill, 21-31 May 1818, 29 July 1818, box 304, Gansevoort-Lansing Collection, NYPL; Kenney, *Gansevoorts of Albany*, 176-177; Parker, *Herman Melville*, 1:9-12, 35; Jay Layda, *The Melville Log: A Documentary Life of Herman Melville, 1819-1891*, 2 vols. (New York: Harcourt, Brace and Company, 1951), 1:25.

4. Catharine Read Williams, *Aristocracy; or, The Holbey Family: A National Tale* (Providence: J. Knowles, 1832), vi, 53–55, 56.

5. Catharine Read Williams, *Annals of the Aristocracy: Being a Series of Anecdotes of Some of the Principal Families of Rhode-Island*, 2 vols. (Providence, R.I.: B. T. Albro, Printer, 1845), 1:3; "Who Are the Aristocrats?," *New Hampshire Gazette*, 15 January 1839.

6. François-René de Chateaubriand, *The Memoirs of François-René, Vicomte de Chateaubriand, Sometime Ambassador to England*, trans. Alexander Teixeira de Matos, 6 vols. (New York: G. P. Putnam's Sons, 1902), 1:256–257; Frederick Marryat, *A Diary in America*, ed. Sydney Jackman (New York: Alfred A. Knopf, 1962), 235.

7. Francis J. Grund, *Aristocracy in America, from the Sketch-Book of a German Nobleman* (New York: Harper, 1959), 3, 29, 57, 92.

8. "Biographical Notices of Eminent Individuals, Lately Deceased: Hon. John Randolph of Roanoke," *Knickerbocker; or, New York Monthly Magazine* 2, 2 (August 1833): 157–159; "John Randolph of Roanoke," *American Turf Register and Sporting Magazine* 4, 11 (July 1833): 574; Robert Dawidoff, *The Education of John Randolph* (New York: W. W. Norton, 1979), 91–93. For a stimulating analysis of upper-class genealogy as a cultural and social strategy of the American bourgeoisie, see Francesca Morgan, "A Noble Pursuit? Bourgeois America's Uses of Lineage," in *The American Bourgeoisie: Distinction and Identity in the Nineteenth Century*, ed. Sven Beckert and Julia B. Rosenbaum (New York: Palgrave Macmillan, 2010), 135–152.

9. "American Genealogies," *NAR* 82, 171 (April 1856): 470.

10. Margaret Hunter Hall, *The Aristocratic Journey: Being the Outspoken Letters of Mrs. Basil Hall Written during a Fourteen Months' Sojourn in America, 1827–1828*, ed. Una Pope-Hennessy (New York: G. P. Putnam's Sons, 1931), 139; Marryat, *Diary in America*, 146, 147.

11. Isaac Weld, *Travels through the States of North America and the Provinces of Upper and Lower Canada, during the Years 1795, 1796, and 1797*, 2 vols. (London: J. Stockdale, 1799), 1:13, 15; Rufus Wilmot Griswold, *The Republican Court; or, American Society in the Days of Washington*

(New York: D. Appleton and Company, 1856), 11–12, 203; Samuel Eliot Morison, *The Life and Letters of Harrison Gray Otis, Federalist, 1765–1848,* 2 vols. (Boston and New York: Houghton Mifflin Company, 1913), 1:125–127.

12. Peter Atall [Robert Waln], *The Hermit in America on a Visit to Philadelphia* (Philadelphia: M. Thomas, 1819), 115; William S. Hastings, "Robert Waln, Jr.: Quaker Satirist and Historian," *PMHB* 76 (January–April 1952): 71–80.

13. James Fenimore Cooper, *Notions of the Americans,* 2 vols. (Philadelphia: Carey, Lea & Carey, 1828), 1:303; Thomas Hamilton, *Men and Manners in America,* 2 vols. (Philadelphia: Carey, Lea and Blanchard, 1833), 1:206.

14. Hugh Swinton Legaré to A. Huger, 15 December 1834, in *Writings of Hugh Swinton Legaré,* 2 vols. (Charleston, S.C.: Burges & James, 1846), 1:218; Hamilton, *Men and Manners in America,* 2:144; Sir Charles Lyell, *A Second Visit to the United States of North America,* 2 vols. (New York: Harper & Brothers, 1849), 1:223; Charles Fraser, *Reminiscences of Charleston, Lately Published in the "Charleston Courier"* (Charleston, S.C.: John Russell, 1854), 57; Walter J. Fraser, *Charleston! Charleston! The History of a Southern City* (Columbia: University of South Carolina Press, 1989), 196; Daniel Kilbride, *An American Aristocracy: Southern Planters in Antebellum Philadelphia* (Columbia: University of South Carolina Press, 2006).

15. Nicholas B. Wainwright, ed., *A Philadelphia Perspective: The Diary of Sidney George Fisher Covering the Years, 1834–1871* (Philadelphia: Historical Society of Pennsylvania, 1967), 24; [W. L. Fisher], "The subjoined account of the family connexions of my father, THOMAS FISHER, and of my mother, SARAH FISHER, has been collected with considerable care, and is believed to be authentic," MS, 13, LCP.

16. Hugh Swinton Legaré to I. E. Holmes, 2 October 1832, in *Writings of Hugh Swinton Legaré,* 1:205; Washington Irving, "The Sketchbook

of Geoffrey Crayon, Gent.," in *History, Tales, and Sketches* (New York: Library of America, 1983), 791; Sandra Tomc, "Restyling an Old World: Nathaniel Parker Willis and Metropolitan Fashion in the Antebellum United States," *Representations* 85 (Winter 2004): 109.

17. Wainwright, *Philadelphia Perspective*, 16.

18. Daniel Walker Howe, "A Massachusetts Yankee in Senator Calhoun's Court: Samuel Gilman in South Carolina," *NEQ* 44, 2 (June 1971): 213; Caroline Gilman, *Recollections of a Southern Matron* (New York: Harper & Brothers, 1838), 10, 27, 28, 29, 90, 91, 92, 96, 166, 181; Thomas Gilpin, *Memorials and Reminiscences in Private Life of the Gilpin Family in England and America* (Philadelphia: T. K. and P. G. Collins, Printers, 1852), 14, 27, 29-31.

19. Deborah Logan, Diary, vol. 1, 1808-1814, LCP. On Logan's diary, see Karin Wulf, "'Of the Old Stock': Quakerism and Transatlantic Genealogies in Colonial British America," in *The Creation of the British Atlantic World*, ed. Elizabeth Mancke and Carole Shammas (Baltimore: Johns Hopkins University Press, 2005), 304-320.

20. Abram C. Dayton, *Last Days of Knickerbocker Life in New York* (New York: G. P. Putnam's Sons, 1897), 196, 197; Frederic Cople Jaher, *The Urban Establishment: Upper Strata in Boston, New York, Charleston, Chicago, and Los Angeles* (Urbana: University of Illinois Press, 1982), 173-175, 246-247; George Templeton Strong, *The Diary of George Templeton Strong*, ed. Allan Nevins and Milton Halsey Thomas (Seattle: University of Washington Press, 1988), 34.

21. Sands Family Genealogy, 2 vol., MS 575, HSP; Irving, *History, Tales, and Sketches*, 53, 128-129, 131-132; St. Nicholas Society of the City of New York, *An Hundred Year Record, 1835-1935* (New York: St. Nicholas Society, 1935), 68; Janice Zita Grover, "Luxury and Leisure in Early Nineteenth Century America: Saratoga Springs and the Rise of the Resort" (PhD diss., University of California at Davis, 1973), 63-75; Mary Weatherspoon Bowden, "Cocklofts and Slang-Whangers: The

Historical Sources of Washington Irving's *Salmagundi*," *New York History* 61, 2 (April 1980): 133–160.

22. Jerome Bonaparte Holgate, *American Genealogy, Being a History of Some of the Early Settlers of North America and Their Descendants, from their First Emigration to the Present Time* (Albany, N.Y.: Printed by J. Munsell, 1848), 4; Henry R. Stiles, "Anniversary Address," *NYGBR* 2 (April 1871): 92. See James Riker to Samuel Browning, 17 February 1845, and to John Van Osdall, 12 July 1845, box 13, folder 6; Riker to Rev. D. Benedict, 20 February 1847, box 13, folder 7, James Riker Papers, NYPL; James Riker, *A Brief History of the Riker Family: From their First Emigration to this Country in the Year 1638, to the Present Time* (New York: D. Fenshaw, 1851); Riker, *The Annals of Newtown, in Queens County, New York* (New York: D. Fenshaw, 1852), 267, 290, 299, 348, 358, 365, 378, 380, 393, 406.

23. Ronald Story, *The Forging of an Aristocracy: Harvard and the Boston Upper Class, 1800–1870* (Middletown, Conn.: Wesleyan University Press, 1980), 3–23; Jaher, *Urban Establishment*, 16, 19, 20–21.

24. Frances W. Gregory, *Nathan Appleton, Merchant and Entrepreneur, 1779–1861* (Charlottesville: University Press of Virginia, 1975), 1–10.

25. John Sparhawk Appleton to Nathan Appleton (hereafter NA), 23 March 1806, 3 and 5 June 1817, 15 June 1818; Jesse Appleton to NA, 15 January 1818; James Appleton to NA, 23 February 1818; Eben Appleton to NA, 20 October 1818, box 13, folder 13.13: 1795–1819, AFP.

26. Eben Appleton to NA, 20 October 1818, box 13, folder 13.13: 1795–1819, AFP.

27. See AFP, box 13, folder 13.14: 1821–1838; George Bancroft to NA, 29 October 1850, William H. Prescott to NA, October 1850, James Savage to NA, 9 November 1850, and Joseph Hunter to NA, 28 December 1850, box 13, folder 13.17: 1850, October–December, AFP; Sir Bernard Burke to NA, 21 June and 14 July 1851, box 13, folder 13.18: 1851, AFP.

28. Cromwell Pearce, Memoirs, 1855, fol. 2, HSP.

29. "The Puritan Element in the American Character," *New Englander and Yale Review* 9, 36 (November 1851): 531-544; Stephen Nissenbaum, "New England as Region and Nation," in *All over the Map: Rethinking American Regions,* ed. Edward L. Ayers, Patricia Nelson Limerick, Stephen Nissenbaum, and Peter S. Onuf (Baltimore: Johns Hopkins University Press, 1996), 38-61; Susan-Mary Grant, *North over South: Northern Nationalism and American Identity in the Antebellum Era* (Lawrence: University Press of Kansas, 2000); Joseph A. Conforti, *Imagining New England: Explorations of Regional Identity from the Pilgrims to the Mid-Twentieth Century* (Chapel Hill: University of North Carolina Press, 2001); David D. Hall, "Reassessing the Local History of New England. Part One: The Rise and Fall of a Great Tradition," in *New England: A Bibliography of Its History,* ed. Roger Parks (Hanover, N.H.: University Press of New England, 1989); John D. Seelye, *Memory's Nation: The Place of Plymouth Rock* (Chapel Hill: University of North Carolina Press, 1998).

30. Pershing Vartanian, "The Puritan as a Symbol in American Thought: A Study of the New England Societies, 1820-1920" (PhD diss., University of Michigan, 1971), 12-28; Cephas Brainerd and Eveline Warner Brainerd, eds., *The New England Society Orations,* 2 vols. (New York: Century Company, 1901); Seelye, *Memory's Nation,* 60-85; "Puritan Element," 532; Grant, *North over South,* 54-56.

31. Michel O'Brien, *Conjectures of Order: Intellectual Life and the American South, 1810-1860,* 2 vols. (Chapel Hill: University of North Carolina Press, 2003), 1:286, 309-322; William Robert Taylor, *Cavalier and Yankee: The Old South and American National Character* (New York: G. Braziller, 1961).

32. William Meade, *Old Churches, Ministers and Families of Virginia,* 2 vols. (Philadelphia: J. B. Lippincott & Co., 1857), 1:79-80, 83; 2:300.

33. George Fitzhugh, "Old Churches, Ministers, and Families of Virginia," *De Bow's Review* 26, 2 (February 1859): 121, 123, 124, 125;

George Fitzhugh, "Family History and the Philosophy of Names," *De Bow's Review* 29, 3 (September 1860): 269.

34. Robert E. Bonner, "Roundheaded Cavaliers? The Context and Limits of a Confederate Racial Project," *Civil War History* 48, 1 (March 2002): 34-43; Jan C. Dawson, "The Puritan and the Cavalier: The South's Perception of Contrasting Traditions," *Journal of Southern History* 44, 4 (1978): 597-614; Wendell Phillips to John Farmer, 9, 23, and 28 January 1833, folder 20, box 4, JFP; Phillips to Farmer, 25 February 1833, folder 21, box 4, JFP; Wendell Phillips, "Notices of the Greene Family," *NEHGR* 4, 1 (January 1850): 75; Strong, *Diary of George Templeton Strong*, 170; William Falconer, "The Difference of Race between the Northern and Southern People," *Southern Literary Messenger* 30 (June 1860): 401-408; Grant, *North over South*, 54-59; William H. Whitmore, *The Cavalier Dismounted: An Essay on the Origins of the Founders of the Thirteen Colonies* (Salem, Mass.: G. M. Whipple & A. A. Smith, 1864); "Heraldry in New England," *NAR* 100, 206 (January 1865): 186-194 (the article is not signed, but Whitmore is a likely author).

35. Charles Fenno Hoffman, *The Pioneers of New York: An Anniversary Discourse Delivered before the St. Nicholas Society of Manhattan, December 6, 1847* (New York: Stanford & Swords, 1848), 8-9.

36. Gouverneur Morris, "A Discourse Delivered before the New-York Historical Society, at Their Anniversary Meeting, 6th December 1812," in *Collections of the New-York Historical Society, for the Year 1814* (New York: Printed by Van Winkle and Wiley, 1814), 121, 128.

37. E. B. O'Callaghan, ed., *Documents Relative to the Colonial History of the State of New York*, 15 vols. (Albany, N.Y.: Weed, Parsons and Company, 1853-1887), 1:vi-viii; Gulian C. Verplanck, *An Anniversary Discourse, Delivered before the New-York Historical Society, December 7, 1818* (New York: James Eastburn, 1818), 59, 73.

38. "The St. Nicholas Society of New-York," *New-York Mirror*, 23 December 1837 and 12 January 1839.

NOTES TO PAGES 96-100

39. Edward F. De Lancey, "Original Family Records of Loockermans, Bayard, Van Cortlandt, Van Rensselaer, and Schuyler," *NYGBR* 5, 2 (April 1874): 70; Gerard Troost to Pierre Van Cortlandt, 13 October 1841, in *Van Cortlandt Family Papers*, ed. Jacob Judd, 4 vols. (Tarrytown, N.Y.: Sleepy Hollow Restorations, 1976–1981), 4:307.

40. Harriet Langdon Pruyn Price, *Harmanus Bleecker: An Albany Dutchman, 1779–1849* (Albany, N.Y.: William Boyd Printing Company, 1924); O'Callaghan, *Documents*, 1:x–xlv; Alice P. Kenney, "Neglected Heritage: Hudson River Dutch Material Culture," *Winterthur Portfolio* 20, 1 (Spring 1985): 53.

41. Irving, *History, Tales, and Sketches*, 53; De Witt Clinton, "A Discourse Delivered before the New-York Historical Society, at Their Anniversary Meeting; 6th December 1811," in *Collections of the New-York Historical Society, for the year 1814* (New York: Printed by Van Winkle and Wiley, 1814), 39; Grover, "Luxury and Leisure," 69.

42. "Ancestrel Pride," *American Masonic Register*, July 1821, 421, 422, 423.

43. Junius Henri Browne, *The Great Metropolis: A Mirror of New York* (Hartford: American Publishing Company, 1869), 596.

44. "American Genealogies," 471.

45. Grund, *Aristocracy in America*, 29, 124-128.

46. Joseph [pseud.], *New-York Aristocracy; or, Gems of Japonica-Dom* (New York: Charles B. Norton, 1851), 19.

47. George William Curtis, *The Potiphar Papers* (New York: G. P. Putnam and Company, 1853), 1–2, 149; Nathaniel Parker Willis, *The Rag-Bag, a Collection of Ephemera* (New York: Charles Scribner, 1855), 49, 54.

48. Browne, *Great Metropolis*, 596; *NYT*, 17, 20, 21, 27, and 28 July 1852; 4, 11, and 12 August 1852; 5 and 12 June 1854. See also *NYT*, 9 April 1858. Henry Hays to Charles H. Browning, 7 December 1868 and 3 February 1869, box 1, Charles H. Browning Papers, NYPL; Joseph, *New-York Aristocracy*, 19.

49. Browne, *Great Metropolis*, 598.

50. Thomas W. Gwilt Mapleson, *A Hand-Book of Heraldry* (New York: J. Wiley, 1851), 5-7.

51. Willis, *Rag-Bag*, 54, 56. For the creation of the American College, see the inside front cover of *The Chronotype: An American Memorial of Persons and Events* 1, 1 (January 1873).

52. Ball Family Papers, Joseph Ball Papers, Estate Papers, 1855-1860, HSP; Helen Hincliff, "Estate Frauds and Spurious Pedigrees," *Genealogical Journal* 19, 1-2 (1991): 22-46.

53. George O. Zabriskie, "Anneke Jans in Fact and Fiction," *NYGBR* 104 (1973): 65-72, 157-164; W. J. Parry, "The 'Heirs of Anneke Jans Bogardus' versus Trinity Church: A Chronicle of New York's Most Prolonged Legal Dispute," *NYGBR* 125 (1994): 67-73, 161-167; Willem Frijhoff, "Emblematic Myths: Anneke's Fortune, Bogardus's Farewell, and Kieft's Son," in *Myth in History, History in Myth,* ed. Laura Cruz and Willem Frijhoff (Leiden: Brill, 2009), 117-146.

54. *Bogardus v. Trinity Church,* 4 Sandf. Ch. 678, 781, 810 (June 1847).

55. Wilson Miles Cary to Joseph Lemuel Chester, 10 May 1866, vol. C, fols. 405-406, CCP; Cary to Chester, 1 October 1866, vol. C, fol. 402, CCP; Mary Jacquelin (Smith) Lee to Mary Jacquelin (Smith) Vowell, 22 April 1843, MS 6:1 J 2748:1, VHS.

56. Dudley S. Jennings to William Chapman Jennings, 11 July 1846, folder 4; Hansford Dade Duncan to William Chapman Jennings, 17 September and 12 December 1848, 14 February 1849, 22 November 1849, and 17 July 1850, folder 2, both in A10-16, section 5, MS 3J 4495 a, Jennings Family Association Papers, VHS.

57. Copy of minutes of the proceedings of the Jennings Family Convention held at Nashville, Tenn., 15-17 September 1849, A2-3, section 2, MS 3J 4495 a, Jennings Family Association Papers, VHS.

58. Minutes of meetings of Jennings Family Association, s.d. [1851 or 1852], A2-3, section 2; Hansford Dade Duncan to William Chapman Jennings, 16 July 1852, folder 2, A10-16, section 5, all in MS 3J 4495 a, Jennings Family Association Papers, VHS.

59. "The Chase Meeting," *Barre Patriot*, 26 February 1847.

60. Moses Chase to John B. Chase, 11 January 1847, vol. 3, fol. 18, Joshua Coffin Papers, Phillips Library, Peabody Essex Museum, Salem, Mass.

61. Form letter of the Houghton Association, 1846, folder 46, bMS Am 2048 (46), Henry Oscar Houghton Additional Papers, Houghton Library, Harvard University; Houghton Association, *Report of the Agent in England* (New York: Printed by Jared W. Bell, Printer, 1848); Houghton Association, *Constitution and Officers of the Houghton Association* (New York: Van Norden & Amerman, Printers, 1847).

62. Horatio Gates Somerby to Thomas Lawrence, 9 April 1852, 21 May 1852, 20 October 1852, vol. 146, box 4, HGSP.

63. Jonathan Allen to the Rev. B. Smith, 23 September 1842, folder Letters 1841–1842, box 1, CSP; William Slade to Henry Clay, 25 September 1842, folder Letters 1841–1842, box 1, CSP; Pat Orvis, "Columbus Smith, West Salisbury's Legendary Country Squire," *Burlington Free Press*, 18 July 1964; Columbus Smith, *To the Honourable the Commissioners under the Convention of February the 8th, 1853, between the United States of America and Her Britannic Majesty, for the Settlement of Claims of the Citizens of either Country upon the Government of the Other: A Statement of the Claim of William Cook, James Cook, Samuel Cook, Linus B. Cook, Patty Beach, Isaac Baker, and Maria his wife, William C. Ball, Daniel Ball, Jacob Ball, and Robert B. Moores, and Caroline his Wife, all Natives of the United States of America; with Documents in Support of the Same* (London: s.n., 1853).

64. Chester Ingraham to Columbus Smith (hereafter CS), 11 April 1845, box 3, folder 12; Orange Brittell to CS, 23 December 1846, and CS to Orange Brittell, 7 January 1847, box 3, folder 1; Joseph M. Loomis to CS, 12 May 1847, and Benjamin Chase to CS, 22 May 1847, box 4, folder 4, all in CSP.

65. *Report of a Search made in England for a Property reported to belong to the Gibbs's in U.S.A., in the years 1847–48, by Columbus Smith, Esq., Agent for the Acting Gibbs Association of Vermont. Containing a short History of*

the Gibbs's in England: likewise several Genealogies of different branches of the Gibbs Family (Middlebury, Vt.: Justus Cobb, Printer, 1848).

66. CS to Fitz Henry Warren, 27 March 1850, untitled letter book (February 1850–March 1851), box 2, folder "Account books," CSP; untitled notebook with list of correspondents, 1854–1864, box 2, folder "Account books," CSP.

67. CS to Loving May, 6 March 1850, untitled letter book (February 1850–March 1851), box 2, folder "Account books," CSP; CS to Orville Hemenway, 8 March 1854, untitled letter book (June 1853–March 1854), box 2, folder "Account books," CSP.

68. CS to David A. Morris, 14 March 1850, and to Parker Earle, 18 March 1850, untitled letter book (February 1850–March 1851), box 2, folder "Account books," CSP.

69. CS to George Hoskins, 20 February 1850, untitled letter book (February 1850–March 1851), box 2, folder "Account books," CSP.

70. CS to Josiah Houghton, 4 February 1850, to T. W. Gibbs, 5 February 1850, and to John Gibbs, 4 February 1850, untitled letter book (February 1850–March 1851), box 2, folder "Account books," CSP; "Universal Diary," 1850 (1848 on the cover), 3 June 1850, box 2, folder "Account books," CSP.

71. William H. Whitmore, *The American Genealogist: Being a Catalogue of Family Histories and Publications Containing Genealogical Information Issued in the United States, Arranged Chronologically*, 2nd ed. (Albany, N.Y.: Joel Munsell, 1868), 26, 28, 229.

4. "UPON THE LOVE OF COUNTRY AND PRIDE OF RACE"

1. "American Genealogies," *NAR* 82, 171 (April 1856): 469; George Brown Goode, *Virginia Cousins: A Study of the Ancestry and Posterity of John Goode of Whitby* (Richmond, Va.: J. W. Randolph & English, 1887), xxvi; Michael G. Kammen, *Mystic Chords of Memory: The Transformation of Tradition in American Culture* (New York: Knopf, 1991), 249; Alexander Brown, *The Cabells and Their Kin* (Boston and New York: Houghton, Mifflin & Co., 1895), iii; Wallace Evan Davies, *Pa-*

triotism on Parade: The Story of Veterans' and Hereditary Organizations in America, 1783–1900 (Cambridge, Mass.: Harvard University Press, 1955), 38.

2. Franz Boas, "This Nordic Nonsense," *Forum* 74, 4 (October 1925): 502, 503.

3. Barbara Miller Solomon, *Ancestors and Immigrants: A Changing New England Tradition* (Boston: Northeastern University Press, 1989); John Higham, *Strangers in the Land: Patterns of American Nativism, 1860–1925* (New Brunswick, N.J.: Rutgers University Press, 2002); Reginald Horsman, *Race and Manifest Destiny: The Origins of American Racial Anglo-Saxonism* (Cambridge, Mass.: Harvard University Press, 1981).

4. Samuel Osgood, "Life and Its Record in This Generation: Anniversary Address before the New York Genealogical and Biographical Society, April 11, 1878," *NYGBR* 9, 3 (July 1878): 107-108.

5. Francis Galton, *Hereditary Genius: An Inquiry into Its Laws and Consequences* (London: Macmillan and Co., 1869); "Hereditary Genius," *Appleton's Journal of Literature, Science and Art* 1, 3 (17 April 1869): 82–83; "Hereditary Genius," *Appleton's Journal of Literature, Science and Art* 3, 47 (19 February 1870): 217-218.

6. William H. Whitmore, "Hereditary Ability," *NEHGR* 23 (July 1869): 285-289; Henry R. Stiles, "Anniversary Address," *NYGBR* 2 (April 1871): 80, 81.

7. Goode, *Virginia Cousins*, xxvii; Elias Loomis, *The Descendants of Joseph Loomis* (New Haven, Conn.: Tuttle, Morehouse & Taylor, 1870); Elisha S. Loomis, *Descendants of Joseph Loomis in America, and His Antecedents in the Old World* ([Berea, Ohio]: Privately printed, 1909), 17; T. G. E. [Thomas G. Evans], "A Frisian Family," *NYGBR* 24, 4 (October 1893): 198; "Societies and Their Proceedings. New-England Historic Genealogical Society," *NEHGR* 46, 1 (January 1892): 93; Kammen, *Mystic Chords of Memory*, 220-221.

8. Alexander Graham Bell to Mabel Hubbard Bell, 16 June 1885, 17 July 1885, undated (probably 6 December) and 8 December (quotation)

1885, 22 May 1887, 21 June 1887, 28 June 1888, Alexander Graham Bell Papers, Library of Congress; "An Island of Silence," *WP*, 20 January 1895; Robert V. Bruce, *Bell: Alexander Graham Bell and the Conquest of Solitude* (Boston: Little, Brown, and Co., 1973), 409-412.

9. Henry Smith Williams, "The Lesson of Heredity," *NAR* 157, 442 (September 1893): 341, 342, 343, 344, 352; Veritas, "'Scientific' Genealogy: A Rejoinder," *Science* 19, 476 (18 March 1892): 157; Charles H. Cooley, "Genius, Fame, and Comparison of Races," *Annals of the American Academy of Arts and Sciences* 9 (May 1897): 317-358; Richard T. Ely, "Heredity and Circumstances," *Outlook* 48, 12 (16 September 1893): 505-506; "Heredity and Environment in Race Improvement," *AAAPSS* 39, 1 (July-December 1909): 3-29; Hamilton Cravens, *The Triumph of Evolution: American Scientists and the Heredity-Environment Controversy, 1900-1941* (Philadelphia: University of Pennsylvania Press, 1978).

10. Herbert Baxter Adams, *History of the Thomas Adams and Thomas Hastings Families, of Amherst, Massachusetts* (Amherst, Mass.: privately printed, 1880), 7, 19; Edward N. Saveth, *American Historians and European Immigrants, 1875-1925* (New York: Columbia University Press, 1948), 22, 23; James Kendall Hosmer, *The Last Leaf: Observations, during Seventy-Five Years, of Men and Events in America and Europe* (New York: G. P. Putnam's Sons, 1912), 188; James Kendall Hosmer, *A Short History of Anglo-Saxon Freedom: The Polity of the English-Speaking Race* (New York: C. Scribner's Sons, 1890).

11. Ethel F. Fisk, ed., *The Letters of John Fiske* (New York: Macmillan Company, 1940), 374, 442-443, 688-690; John Fiske, *Darwinism and Other Essays* (London and New York: Macmillan and Company, 1879).

12. "Genealogy Bears Out Heredity Law," *NYT,* 27 March 1910; Frederick Adams Woods, "Heredity and the Hall of Fame," *Popular Science Monthly* 82 (May 1913): 445-452; Henry Cabot Lodge, *Early Memories* (New York: C. Scribner's Sons, 1913), 3, 4, 8-9; Saveth, *American Historians and European Immigrants,* 51.

13. Charles Henry Browning, *Americans of Royal Descent* (Philadelphia: Porter & Coates, 1883). Seven new editions were published up to 1920. Browning's correspondance, box 1, Charles H. Browning Papers, NYPL; Charlotte Perkins Gilman, *The Living of Charlotte Perkins Gilman: An Autobiography* (Madison: University of Wisconsin Press, 1991), 1-2; Gail Bederman, *Manliness and Civilization: A Cultural History of Gender and Race in the United States, 1880–1917* (Chicago: University of Chicago Press, 1995), 121-169; Alys Eve Weinbaum, "Writing Feminist Genealogy: Charlotte Perkins Gilman, Racial Nationalism, and the Reproduction of Maternalist Feminism," *Feminist Studies* 27, 2 (2001): 274-285; Arthur Meredyth Burke, *The Prominent Families of the United States of America* (London: Sackville Press, 1908).

14. Philip E. Chappell, *A Genealogical History of the Chappell, Dickie and Other Kindred Families of Virginia* (Kansas City, Mo.: Hudson-Kimberly Publishing Company, 1900), 12; Roberdeau Buchanan, *Genealogy of the Roberdeau Family* (Washington, D.C.: Joseph L. Pearson, Printer, 1876), 9, 40.

15. Garland E. Allen, "The Eugenics Record Office at Cold Spring Harbor, 1910-1940: An Essay in Institutional History," *Osiris* 2 (1986): 225; Edward A. Ross, "America's Race Problems," *AAAPSS* 18 (July 1901): 85, 88; Ross's emphasis.

16. David Starr Jordan and Sarah Louise Kimball, *Your Family Tree: Being a Glance at Scientific Aspects of Genealogy* (New York: D. Appleton and Company, 1929), 9; Mark H. Haller, *Eugenics: Hereditarian Attitudes in American Thought* (New Brunswick, N.J.: Rutgers University Press, 1963), 17-20, 62.

17. Amzi B. Davenport, *A History and Genealogy of the Davenport Family, in England and America, from* A.D. 1086 *to* 1850 (New York: S. W. Benedict, 1851); William H. Whitmore, *The American Genealogist: Being a Catalogue of Family Histories and Publications Containing Genealogical Information Issued in the United States, Arranged Chronologically,* 3rd ed. (Albany, N.Y.: Joel Munsell, 1875), 65-66; Jordan and

Kimball, *Your Family Tree*, v-vi, 3-20, 198, 220-221, 312; Daniel J. Kevles, *In the Name of Eugenics: Genetics and the Uses of Human Heredity* (Cambridge, Mass.: Harvard University Press, 1995), 41-56.

18. Paul Popenoe, "Genealogy and Eugenics," *Utah Genealogical and Historical Magazine* 6 (1915): 202, 203, 204, 205, 206, 209-217; Molly Ladd-Taylor, "Eugenics, Sterilization and Modern Marriage in the USA: The Strange Career of Paul Popenoe," *Gender and History* 13, 2 (August 2001): 298-327; Alexandra Minna Stern, *Eugenic Nation: Faults and Frontiers of Better Breeding in Modern America* (Berkeley: University of California Press, 2005).

19. Popenoe, "Genealogy and Eugenics," 215; Allen, "Eugenics Record Office," 226; Stern, *Eugenic Nation*, 104-108.

20. Kevles, *In the Name of Eugenics*, 58; Allen, "Eugenics Record Office," 241; Charles B. Davenport, comp., *The Family-History Book*, ERO Bulletin no. 7 (Cold Spring Harbor, N.Y.: Eugenics Record Office, 1912); Charles B. Davenport and Harry H. Laughlin, *How to Make a Eugenical Family Study*, ERO Bulletin no. 13 (Cold Spring Harbor, N.Y.: Eugenics Record Office, 1915); Charles B. Davenport, "Family Records," *Science* 29, 750 (14 May 1909): 791; 30, 775 (5 November 1909): 646; Davenport, "The Value of Scientific Genealogy," *Science* 41, 1053 (5 March 1915): 337-342; Eben Putnam, "Tracing Your Ancestry," *Journal of Heredity* 9, 1 (January 1918): 8-14.

21. Boutwell Dunlap, "History of Organization of International Congress of Genealogy," in *Proceedings International Congress of Genealogy, San Francisco, July 28-31, 1915* (San Francisco: Organization Committee of International Genealogical Federation, 1915), 3-5; "Genealogy and Eugenics," *Journal of Heredity* 6, 2 (February 1915): 72; "International Congress of Genealogy," *Journal of Heredity* 6, 11 (November 1915): 518; Paul Popenoe, "The Relationship between Genealogy and Eugenics," in *Proceedings International Congress of Genealogy*, 63-78 (the address was republished in both the *Journal of Heredity* and the *Utah Genealogical and Historical Magazine*); Colvin B. Brown, "Address of Welcome," in *Proceedings International Con-*

gress of Genealogy, 102; Robert W. Rydell, *World of Fairs: The Century-of-Progress Expositions* (Chicago: University of Chicago Press, 1993), 38-43; Stern, *Eugenic Nation*, chap. 1.

22. Ellsworth Huntington and Martha Ragsdale, *After Three Centuries: A Typical New England Family* (Baltimore, Md.: Williams & Wilkins Company, 1935); Arthur H. Estabrook and Ivan E. McDougle, *Mongrel Virginians: The Win Tribe* (Baltimore: Williams & Wilkins Company, 1926); Nancy L. Gallagher, *Breeding Better Vermonters: The Eugenics Project in the Green Mountain State* (Hanover, N.H.: University Press of New England, 1999), 75-85; Gregory M. Dorr, *Segregation's Science: Eugenics and Society in Virginia* (Charlottesville: University of Virginia Press, 2008).

23. Phillip Payne, "The Shadow of William Estabrook Chancellor: Warren G. Harding, Marion, Ohio, and the Issue of Race," *Mid-America* 83, 1 (Winter 2001): 39-62; Francis Russell, *The Shadow of Blooming Grove: Warren G. Harding in His Times* (New York: McGraw-Hill, 1968); "Cox of Jersey Stock. Governor's Genealogy Shows Ancestors Lived in Monmouth County," *NYT*, 3 August 1920; "Haddam Home of Hardings. Five Generations from Connecticut Ancestor to Ohio Nominee," *NYT*, 22 August 1920.

24. Harry M. Daugherty and Thomas Dixon, *The Inside Story of the Harding Tragedy* (New York: Churchill Company, 1932), 58-67; "Charge Falsehoods in Ohio's Campaign: Republican Chairman Accuses Foes of Circulating Lies About Harding," *NYT*, 17 October 1920; "Candidates' Ancestors," *NYT*, 24 October 1920; "College Ousts Professor Chancellor Because of Circulars on Harding," *NYT*, 30 October 1920; "Trace Harding Back to Colonial Line. Dayton Journal Prints Results of an Investigation of the 'Whispering Campaign'," *NYT*, 31 October 1920; "An Odious Attack," *NYT*, 31 October 1920; "Harding Ignores 'Whisper' Campaign," *NYT*, 1 November 1920.

25. Merle E. Curti, *The Roots of American Loyalty* (New York: Columbia University Press, 1946), 173-199, quote on 176; Davies, *Patriotism on*

Parade; Solomon, *Ancestors and Immigrants;* Higham, *Strangers in the Land;* Cecilia E. O'Leary, *To Die For: The Paradox of American Patriotism* (Princeton, N.J.: Princeton University Press, 1999).

26. Curti, *Roots of American Loyalty,* 176; Saveth, *American Historians and European Immigrants,* 47; Stuart McConnell, "Reading the Flag: A Reconsideration of the Patriotic Cults of the 1890s," in *Bonds of Affection: Americans Define Their Patriotism,* ed. John E. Bodnar (Princeton, N.J.: Princeton University Press, 1996), 113; David W. Blight, *Race and Reunion: The Civil War in American Memory* (Cambridge, Mass.: Harvard University Press, 2001).

27. David Starr Jordan, "Heredity and Politics," *Current Literature* 16, 2 (August 1894): 139.

28. John Fiske, "Manifest Destiny," *Harper's New Monthly Magazine* 70, 418 (March 1885): 578-590; Fiske, *American Political Ideas Viewed from the Standpoint of Universal History* (New York: Harper & Bros., 1885), vi; Josiah Strong, *Our Country: Its Possible Future and Its Present Crisis* (New York: Baker & Taylor Company, 1885), 159, 165, 175, 178; Solomon, *Ancestors and Immigrants,* 61-69; Milton Berman, *John Fiske: The Evolution of a Popularizer* (Cambridge, Mass.: Harvard University Press, 1961); Paul R. Meyer, "The Fear of Cultural Decline: Josiah Strong's Thought about Reform and Expansion," *Church History* 42, 3 (September 1973): 396-405.

29. Davies, *Patriotism on Parade,* 44, 73; Joseph Thompson Dodge, *Genealogy of the Dodge Family of Essex County, Mass., 1629-1894* (Madison, Wis.: Democrat Printing Company, 1894), iv; Eugene Zieber, comp., *Ancestry: The Objects of the Hereditary Societies and the Military and Naval Orders of the United States, and the Requirements for Membership Therein* (Philadelphia: Department of Heraldry of the Bailey, Banks & Biddle Company, 1895).

30. Davies, *Patriotism on Parade,* 50; John St. Paul Jr., *The History of the National Society of the Sons of the American Revolution* (New Orleans: Pelican Publishing Company, 1962), 20, 155; Woden S. Teachout,

"Forging Memory: Hereditary Societies, Patriotism, and the American Past, 1876–1898" (PhD diss., Harvard University, 2003), 19–80.

31. Mary S. Lockwood, "Women Worthy of Honor," *WP*, 13 July 1890; Francesca Morgan, *Women and Patriotism in Jim Crow America* (Chapel Hill: University of North Carolina Press, 2005), 42–44; Teachout, "Forging Memory," 112–138.

32. Theodore M. Banta, *A Frisian Family: The Banta Genealogy* (New York, 1893); Elizabeth S. Rogers to Hayden Carruth, 2 and 17 April 1894, Elizabeth S. Rogers Papers, NEHGS.

33. Minutes of the Chapter, 7 January 1897 and 8 January and 21 May 1903, box 1, Records (1896–2008), Daughters of the American Revolution, Sarah Caswell Angell Chapter (Ann Arbor, Mich.), Michigan Historical Collections, Bentley Historical Library, University of Michigan; source's emphasis.

34. *Proceedings of the Thirty-Ninth Continental Congress of the National Society of the Daughters of the American Revolution: Washington, D.C., April 1930* (Washington, D.C.: Judd & Detweiler, 1930), 5, 149–161; Mary S. Lockwood, First Historian General, revised with additional records by Susan Riviere Hetzel, *Lineage Book of the Charter Members of the National Society of the Daughters of the American Revolution* (Washington, D.C.: National Society, Daughters of the American Revolution, 1908).

35. *Proceedings of the Thirty-First Continental Congress of the National Society of the Daughters of the American Revolution: Washington, D.C., April 1922* (Washington, D.C.: Judd & Detweiler, 1922), 10; *Proceedings of the Twentieth Continental Congress of the Daughters of the American Revolution: Washington, D.C., April 1911* (Washington, D.C.: Press of Byron S. Adams, 1911), 9.

36. *Proceedings of the Thirtieth Continental Congress of the National Society of the Daughters of the American Revolution: Washington, D.C., April 1921* (Washington, D.C.: Hayworth Publishing House, 1921), 6; Teachout, "Forging Memory," 135.

37. William L. Kingsley, "Puritan Genealogies," *New Englander and Yale Review* 51, 234 (September 1889): 234.

38. Wesley Frank Craven, *The Legend of the Founding Fathers* (New York: New York University Press, 1956), 134; Saveth, *American Historians and European Immigrants,* 203-215; Charles H. Wesley, "Racial Historical Societies and the American Heritage," *Journal of Negro History* 37 (January 1952): 11-35; John J. Appel, "Immigrant Historical Societies in the United States, 1880-1950" (PhD diss., University of Pennsylvania, 1960).

39. *Proceedings of the Scotch-Irish Congress* 8 (1896): 31; Appel, "Immigrant Historical Societies," 85, 87.

40. B. H. Dupuy, *The Huguenot Bartholomew Dupuy and His Descendants* (Louisville, Ky.: Courier-Journal Job Printing Company, 1908), 378; Charles W. Baird, "Account of Daniel Lestrange and Wife, Huguenot Immigrants," *NYGBR* 2, 4 (October 1871): 179-185; Edward F. De Lancey, "Original Family Records—Jay," *NYGBR* 7, 3 (July 1876): 110-116; William E. Du Bois and Patterson Du Bois, *Bi-centenary Reunion of the Descendants of Louis and Jacques Du Bois (Emigrants to America, 1660 and 1675), at New Paltz, New York, 1875* (Philadelphia: Press of Rue & Jones, 1876); La Fayette De La Mater, *Genealogy of the Descendants of Claude Le Maitre (Delamater)* (Albany, N.Y.: J. Munsell's Sons, 1882).

41. Charles W. Baird, *History of the Huguenot Emigration to America* (New York: Dodd, Mead & Company, 1885); Huguenot Society of America, *The Huguenot Society of America: History, Organization, Activities, Membership, Constitution, Huguenot Ancestors, and Other Matters of Interest* (New York: The Society, 1963).

42. "President's Address," *THSSC* 13 (1906): 11-12. Genealogical notes on several Huguenot families can be found in the volumes of the *Transactions,* beginning in 1897.

43. Eliza C. K. Fludd, *Biographical Sketches of the Huguenot Solomon Legaré and of His Family* (Charleston, S.C.: E. Perry, 1886), 6-7; Orra Eugene Monnette, *Monnet Family Genealogy* (Los Angeles: C. E. Bireley,

1911); John Timothée Trezevant, *The Trezevant Family in the United States* (Columbia, S.C.: Printed by the State Company, 1914).

44. "President Ravenel's Address, at the Annual Meeting, April 13, 1889," *THSSC* 1 (1889): 53; "President's Address," *THSSC* 10 (1903): 8, 9. See also "President's Address," *THSSC* 8 (1901): 5; "President's Address," *THSSC* 9 (1902): 5; "President's Address," *THSSC* 13 (1906): 10, 11; "President's Address," *THSSC* 14 (1907): 10; and "President's Address," *THSSC* 18 (1911): 9.

45. Willem Frijhoff, "Reinventing an Old Fatherland: The Management of Dutch Identity in Early Modern America," in *Managing Ethnicity: Perspectives from Folklore Studies, History and Anthropology,* ed. Regina Bendix and Herman Roodenburg (Amsterdam: Het Spinhuis, 2000), 121–141; "Letter from Edward A. Moseley, the Retiring President-General," *Journal of the American-Irish Historical Society* 2 (1899): 53; "American-Irish Historical Society," *Journal of the American-Irish Historical Society* 1 (1898): 7, 22, 23–24, 62.

46. Charles P. Daly, *The Settlement of the Jews in North America* (New York: P. Cowen, 1893); Barnett A. Elzas, *The Jews of South Carolina* (Philadelphia: J. B. Lippincott, 1905); Isidor Blum, *The Jews of Baltimore* (Baltimore: Historical Review Printing Co., 1910); *PAJHS* 1 (1893): iii; N. Taylor Phillips, "Family History of the Reverend David Mendez Machado," *PAJHS* 2 (1894): 45–61; Phillips, "The Levy and Seixas Families," *PAJHS* 4 (1896): 189–214; Elvira N. Solis, "Note on Isaac Gomez and Lewis Moses Gomez, from an Old Family Record," *PAJHS* 11 (1903): 139–144. Isidore Singer, ed., *The Jewish Encyclopedia: A Descriptive Record of the History, Religion, Literature, and Customs of the Jewish People from the Earliest Times to the Present Day,* 12 vols. (New York: Funk & Wagnalls, 1901–1906).

47. Joseph Jacobs, "A Plea for an American Jewish Historical Exhibition," *PAJHS* 9 (1901): 13, 14; J. Bunford Samuel, *Records of the Samuel Family* (Philadelphia: J. B. Lippincott, 1912).

48. Willard B. Gatewood, *Aristocrats of Color: The Black Elite, 1880–1920* (Bloomington: Indiana University Press, 1990), 69, 179–180, 227–228;

Billie E. Walker, "Daniel Alexander Payne Murray (1852-1925), Forgotten Librarian, Bibliographer, and Historian," *Libraries and Culture* 40, 1 (2005): 25-37.

49. Gatewood, *Aristocrats of Color,* 20, 45, 109-110, 113; Langston Hughes, "Our Wonderful Society: Washington," *Opportunity* 5, 8 (August 1927): 226.

50. Raymond J. DeMallie, "Fred Eggan and American Indian Anthropology," and "Kinship and Biology in Sioux Culture," in *North American Indian Anthropology: Essays on Society and Culture,* ed. Raymond J. DeMallie and Alfonso Ortiz (Norman: University of Oklahoma Press, 1994), 3-22, 125-146.

51. Circe Sturm, *Blood Politics: Race, Culture, and Identity in the Cherokee Nation of Oklahoma* (Berkeley: University of California Press, 2002); Jill Doerfler, "An Anishinaabe Tribalography: Investigating and Interweaving Conceptions of Identity during the 1910s on the White Earth Reservation," *American Indian Quarterly* 33, 3 (2009): 295-324; Katherine M. B. Osburn, "The 'Identified Full-Bloods' in Mississippi: Race and Choctaw Identity, 1898-1918," *Ethnohistory* 56, 3 (Summer 2009): 423-447; George Bird Grinnell, *The Cheyenne Indians: Their History and Ways of Life,* 2 vols. (New Haven, Conn.: Yale University Press, 1923); Fred Eggan, ed., *Social Anthropology of North American Tribes* (Chicago: University of Chicago Press, 1937); DeMallie, "Fred Eggan and American Indian Anthropology."

5. PEDIGREES AND THE MARKET

1. "The Family Sentiment in Americans," *NYT,* 18 May 1879.

2. See above, Chapter 2; John A. Schutz, *A Noble Pursuit: The Sesquicentennial History of the New England Historic Genealogical Society, 1845-1995* (Boston: NEHGS, 1995); David Simeon Edelstein, *Joel Munsell: Printer and Antiquarian* (New York: Columbia University Press, 1950).

3. Philip Quilibet, "Ribbons and Coronets at Market Rate," *Galaxy: A Magazine of Entertaining Reading* 23, 1 (January 1877): 127.

4. Thomas C. Amory, *Our English Ancestors* (Boston: D. Clapp & Son, 1872), 33. For examples of British genealogists working for Americans, see *NYGBR* 21, 2 (April 1890): back page; 23, 2 (April 1892): 93; 27, 3 (April 1896): back page.

5. John J. Latting, "Biographical Sketch of Joseph Lemuel Chester, D.C.L., LL.D.," *NYGBR* 13, 4 (October 1882): 149–156; John Ward Dean, *Memoir of Col. Joseph L. Chester, Ll.D., D.C.L* (Boston: Printed for private distribution, 1884), 1–20; Schutz, *Noble Pursuit*, 63–65; John T. Hassam, review of *Gleanings from English Records about New England Families,* by James A. Emmerton and Henry F. Waters (Salem, Mass.: Salem Press, 1880), *NEHGR* 34, 3 (October 1880): 422–424; Albert Matthews, "John Tyler Hassam, A.M.," *NEHGR* 58, 1 (January 1904): 13; James Kendall Hosmer, "Henry FitzGilbert Waters, A.M.," *NEHGR* 68, 1 (January 1914): 3–17; Henry F. Waters, *Genealogical Gleanings in England* (Boston: NEHGS, 1901).

6. Latting, "Biographical Sketch of Joseph Lemuel Chester," 151–152; Joseph L. Chester to F. J. Baigent, 30 September 1881, Additional MS 39985, fol. 113, British Library.

7. Henry M. Dexter to Joseph L. Chester, 14 September, 11 October, and 21 November 1865 and 11 February 1866, vol. D, fols. 665–668, 669–672, 677–680, 681–684, CCP; B. F. Stevens to Chester, 18 June 1880; Eliphalet W. Blatchford to Chester, 16 April and 21 May 1881 and 13 February and 6 June 1882, all in vol. B, fols. 114, 126–134, 136–138, 140–142, 148–151, CCP; Edward E. Salisbury to Chester, 1 April 1878 and 1 January and 6 February 1879, vol. B, fols. 823–830, 847–850, 865–868, CCP; Nathaniel H. Bishop to Chester, 24 November 1866 and 2 April 1867, vol. B, fols. 603–606, 607–610, CCP.

8. "He Traces Lineages," *WP*, 2 February 1894; *VMHB* 7, 2 (1899) and 7, 3 (1900), advertisement section; "Costs Her $500 for Royal Ancestry," *NYT*, 14 November 1907; "A Professional Genealogist. The Unique

Occupation Which One Woman Has Found," *NYT,* 3 February 1895;
George Preston Blow to Lucy Blacknall, 5 September 1900, and
Blacknall to Blow, 24 January 1907, folder George Preston Blow, Pe-
gram Family Papers, VHS.

9. Frederick W. Chapman, *The Chapman Family; or, The Descendants of
Robert Chapman, One of the First Settlers of Say-Brook, Conn.* (Hartford, Conn.: Case, Tiffany and Co., 1854); Frederick W. Chapman
and William A. Buckingham, *The Buckingham Family; or, The Descen-
dants of Thomas Buckingham, One of the First Settlers of Milford, Conn.*
(Hartford, Conn.: Case, Lockwood & Brainard, 1872); John Adams
Vinton, *The Vinton Memorial, Comprising a Genealogy of the Descen-
dants of John Vinton of Lynn, 1648* (Boston: S. K. Whipple and Com-
pany, 1858); Vinton, *The Upton Memorial: A Genealogical Record of the
Descendants of John Upton, of North Reading, Mass.* (Bath, Maine:
Printed for private use at the office of E. Upton & Son, 1874);
VMHB 10, 1 (July 1902): advertising section.

10. Schutz, *Noble Pursuit,* 47, 56, 62.

11. Rick J. Ashton, "Curators, Hobbyists, and Historians: Ninety Years
of Genealogy at the Newberry Library," *Library Quarterly* 47, 2
(April 1977): 150–152; Lester J. Cappon, *American Genealogical Periodicals: A Bibliography with a Chronological Finding-List* (New York: New
York Public Library, 1962), 24; *Proceedings of the Virginia Historical
Society at Its Annual Meeting Held in the Society's Building, December
18th 1894* (Richmond, Va.: Wm. Ellis Jones, 1894), vii.

12. "Genealogical Club," *Maine Historical and Genealogical Recorder* 3, 2
(1886): 138; "International Genealogical Club," *Maine Historical
and Genealogical Recorder* 3, 3 (1886): 207–209 and 3, 4 (1886):
292–294.

13. Cappon, *American Genealogical Periodicals,* 13, 15–16, 21; William H.
Whitmore, *The American Genealogist: Being a Catalogue of Family His-
tories and Publications Containing Genealogical Information Issued in the
United States, Arranged Chronologically,* 3rd ed. (Albany, N.Y.: Joel
Munsell, 1875), 317; Joseph L. Chester to William H. Whitmore,

22 July 1873, vol. 2: 1873–1880, Joseph L. Chester Correspondence, 1863–1880, NEHGS.

14. William H. Whitmore, *A Handbook of American Genealogy; Being a Catalogue of Family Histories* (Albany, N.Y.: Joel Munsell, 1862; new eds., 1868, 1875, 1897, 1900 [the editions from 1868 on were published under the title *The American Genealogist*]); Daniel S. Durrie, *Bibliographia Genealogica Americana: An Alphabetical Index to American Genealogies and Pedigrees Contained in State, County and Town Histories, Printed Genealogies, and Kindred Works* (Albany, N.Y.: Joel Munsell, 1868; new eds., 1878, 1886, 1895, 1900 [the 1895 and 1900 editions were published under the title *Index to American Genealogies*]); *American and English Genealogies in the Library of Congress* (Washington, D.C.: Government Printing Office, 1910; 2nd ed., 1919); Leslie H. Fishel Jr., "The Other Builder: Daniel S. Durrie and the State Historical Society of Wisconsin," *Wisconsin Magazine of History* 78, 4 (1995): 242–275.

15. Advertisement, *NYGBR* 26, 3 (July 1895): 66; Afro-American Historical Family Record, LCP; Howard P. Chudacoff, "The S. J. Clarke Publishing Company and the Study of Urban History," *Historian* 49, 2 (February 1987): 184–193.

16. John D. Champlin, "The Manufacture of Ancestors," *Forum* 10 (January 1891): 566–572; Albert Welles, *Address of Albert Welles, President, to the Council of Regents of the American College for Genealogical Registry and Heraldry, at the Society Library, New York* (New York: Society Library, 1879); [Albert Welles], letter to the editor, *Appleton's Journal of Literature, Science, and Art* 9, 200 (18 January 1873): 125.

17. Edgar de Valcourt Vermont, *America Heraldica: A Compilation of Coats of Arms, Crests and Mottoes of Prominent American Families Settled in This Country before 1800* (New York: Brentano Brothers, 1886); Eugene Zieber, comp., *Ancestry: The Objects of the Hereditary Societies and the Military and Naval Orders of the United States, and the Requirements for Membership Therein* (Philadelphia: Department of Heraldry of the Bailey, Banks & Biddle Company, 1895); Mortimer

Delano de Lannoy, *The Bibliography of American Heraldry* (New York: De Vinne Press, 1896); Edward Singleton Holden, *A Primer of Heraldry for Americans* (New York: Century Company, 1898); William Armstrong Crozier, *Crozier's General Armory: A Registry of American Families Entitled to Coat Armor* (New York: Published for the Genealogical Association by Fox, Duffield & Company, 1904); Crozier, *Virginia Heraldica, Being a Registry of Virginia Gentry Entitled to Coat Armor, with Genealogical Notes of the Families* (New York: Genealogical Association, 1908); advertisement by Mortimer Delano, *NYBGR* 28, 4 (October 1897): 251.

18. Sara Agnes Pryor, "A Search for an Ancestor," *Century Illustrated Magazine* 99, 6 (April 1895): 855-864.

19. Paul C. Reed, "Two Somerby Frauds; or, 'Placing the Flesh on the Wrong Bones,'" *TAG* 74, 1 (January 1999): 15-30; Samuel Pearce May, "Some Doubts Concerning the Sears Pedigree," *NEHGR* 40, 3 (July 1886): 261-268.

20. Joseph L. Chester to William H. Whitmore, 22 August and 7 November 1868, vol. 1: 1863-1872, Joseph L. Chester Correspondence, 1863-1880, NEHGS; Chester to Whitmore, 25 March 1876, vol. 2: 1873-1880, Joseph L. Chester Correspondence, 1873-1880, NEHGS; George Munroe Endicott to Chester, 10 January and 18 February 1878, vol. E, fols. 681-682, CCP; G. W. Baldwin to Chester, 25 June 1878, vol. B, fols. 321-322, CCP; Stephen Whitney Phoenix, *The Whitney Family of Connecticut, and Its Affiliations* (New York: Bradford Press, 1878); "Whitney Pedigree Correction," *NYGBR* 26, 4 (October 1895): 201-202; Paul C. Reed, "Whitney Origins Revisited," *TAG* 69 (1994): 9-14.

21. "Nebulae," *Galaxy* 2, 5 (1 November 1866): 483; "Our Taste for Genealogy," *Galaxy* 4, 6 (October 1867): 754; Adrian Schaade van Westrum, "Modern Ancestors and Armorial Bearings," *Lippincott's Monthly Magazine* 58 (November 1896): 677-681.

22. "Gustave Anjou, 78, Genealogist, Dies," *NYT*, 3 March 1942; Gordon L. Remington, "Gustave We Hardly Knew Ye: A Portrait of

Herr Anjou as a Jungberg," *Genealogical Journal* 19, 1–2 (1991): 59–70; Robert Charles Anderson, "We Wuz Robbed! The *modus operandi* of Gustave Anjou," *Genealogical Journal* 19 (1991): 47–58; "Sells Family Trees at a Cut-Rate Price," *NYT*, 12 December 1927.

23. *Harper's Weekly*, 8 November 1862, 719; 6 June 1863, 367; 30 December 1871, 1232; 12 August 1876, 662; Columbus Smith, *Index for Persons in America Claiming Properties Abroad: Either as Next of Kin, Heirs at Law, Legatees, or Otherwise* (Burlington, Vt.: Free Press Steam Book and Job Printing House, 1868).

24. Thomas Bentley Wikoff, *Anneke Jans Bogardus and Her New Amsterdam Estate* (Indianapolis, Ind.: privately published, 1924).

25. William H. Whitmore, "On Fortune-Hunting," *Galaxy* 4, 6 (October 1867): 661–665; Whitmore, *American Genealogist*, 182, 194, 195, 203, 216, 217, 232, 249, 261.

26. Helen Hinchliff, "Estate Frauds and Spurious Pedigrees," *Genealogical Journal* 19, 1–2 (1991): 22–46; "After an Immense Fortune. Gathering Heirs for the Hyde Property," *NYT*, 26 June 1879; "Editorial," *NYT*, 17 July 1879; "Heirs to Hundreds of Millions: A Prospect that the Great Hyde Estate in England Will be awarded to the American Heirs," *NYT*, 10 November 1879; "Hyde Heirs Losing Hope," *NYT*, 5 June 1880; "Pricking Many Golden Bubbles: How the Jennens Decision Affects the Hyde Estate Claimants and Others," *NYT*, 18 April 1881; "A Miserly Monte Cristo: The Enormous Wealth of William Jennings and the Great Interest Many Have Therein," *NYT*, 19 February 1882; "Those 'Estates' in England," *NYT*, 27 December 1885; "Unclaimed Fortunes in Holland for American Heirs," *NYGBR* 17, 3 (July 1886): 236; "Those Estates in the Moon," *NYT*, 18 October 1886.

27. Montgomery B. Gibbs, *A Golden Legacy to the Gibbs Family in America* (Chicago: Press of Edwin M. Colvin, 1893). "The 'Estate' Fever," *NYT*, 27 January 1895.

28. "Former Iowan Denies He Has Broken Any Laws," *Des Moines Register*, 20 February 1933; "Jury To Be Chosen for Famed 'Drake Estate'

Trial," *Des Moines Register,* 22 October 1933; "Widow Tells Risking $8 in Drake Estate," *Des Moines Register,* 27 October 1933; Hartzell v. United States, 72 F.2d 569 (8th Cir. 1934), 574.

29. John Higham, *History: Professional Scholarship in America,* 2nd ed. (Baltimore: Johns Hopkins University Press, 1989), 92–93; Ian R. Tyrrell, *Historians in Public: The Practice of American History, 1890–1970* (Chicago: University of Chicago Press, 2005).

30. Joseph L. Chester to William H. Whitmore, 30 September 1865, vol. 1: 1863–1872, Joseph L. Chester Correspondence, 1863–1880, NEHGS. See also Samuel G. Drake to Chester, 6 August and 13 September 1866, 25 January, 5 February, 15 March, 15 July, and 26 November 1867, and 3 January 1868, vol. D, fols. 1022–1023, 1024–1027, 1028–1031, 1032–1035, 1036–1039, 1040–1041, 1042–1045, 1046–1047, CCP; Albert Cook Myers, *Gilbert Cope, 1840–1928* (Philadelphia: Friends' Historical Association, 1929); James Southall Wilson, "Lyon Gardiner Tyler," *William and Mary College Quarterly Historical Magazine,* 2nd ser., 15, 4 (October 1935): 322.

31. William H. Whitmore, *The Elements of Heraldry* (Boston: Lee & Shepard, 1866), iv, v, 77.

32. Ibid., v.

33. Whitmore, *Handbook of American Genealogy,* iii.

34. Charles Sumner, "Discovery of the Home of Washington's Ancestors," *Historical Journal* 5, 2 (February 1861): 38–41; John Nassau Simpkinson, *The Washingtons: A Tale of a Country Parish in the 17th Century Based on Authentic Documents* (London: Longman, Green, Longman, and Roberts, 1860); "The Washingtons," *NAR* 93, 192 (July 1861): 275–277.

35. Isaac J. Greenwood, "The Washington Family," *NEHGR* 17, 3 (July 1863): 249–251; Joseph L. Chester to William H. Whitmore, 31 October 1863 and 15 December 1865, vol. 1: 1863–1872, Joseph L. Chester Correspondence, 1863–1880, NEHGS; Joseph L. Chester, *A Preliminary Investigation of the Alleged Ancestry of George Washington, First President of the United States of America; Exposing a Serious Error in the Existing*

Pedigree (Boston: H. W. Dutton & Son, Printers, 1866); Whitmore, *American Genealogist*, 212-213, quote on 213.

36. H. H. Clements, "The Washington Genealogy," parts 1-3, *The Chronotype* 1, 3 (March 1873): 65-70; 1, 4 (April 1873): 101-105; 1, 5 (May 1873): 133-138; William H. Whitmore, "The Washington Pedigree," *American Historical Record* 2, 18 (June 1873): 252, 255; Joseph L. Chester to William H. Whitmore, 22 July and 12 September 1873, vol. 2: 1873-1880, Joseph L. Chester Correspondence, 1863-1880, NEHGS.

37. Albert Welles, *The Pedigree and History of the Washington Family: Derived from Odin, the Founder of Scandinavia* (New York: Society Library, 1879); Welles, "Letter to the Editor: Washington's Family. A Historic Account of His Sisters and His Cousins and His Aunts," *NYT,* 31 March 1879; William H. Whitmore, "The Pedigree and History of the Washington Family," *The Nation* 29, 735 (31 July 1879): 84-85; Joseph L. Chester to William H. Whitmore, 29 August 1879, vol. 2: 1873-1880, Joseph L. Chester Correspondence, 1863-1880. NEHGS.

38. Joseph L. Chester, *John Rogers: The Compiler of the First Authorised English Bible; the Pioneer of the English Reformation; and Its First Martyr* (London: Longman, Green, Longman, and Roberts, 1861); May, "Some Doubts Concerning the Sears Pedigree," 261-262, 266-267.

39. Hosmer, "Memoir of Henry FitzGilbert Waters," 12-14.

40. William Ingraham Kip, "Traces of American Lineage in England," *NYGBR* 2, 3 (July 1871): 113-123; William H. Whitmore, "Notes on the Lawrence Pedigree," *NYGBR* 3, 1 (1872): 26-29; Watson Effingham Lawrence, "The Lawrence Pedigree," *NYGBR* 3, 3 (July 1872): 121-131; William H. Whitmore, "Notes on the Lawrence Pedigree.—No. 2," *NYGBR* 3, 4 (October 1872): 178-183.

41. Joseph L. Chester to William H. Whitmore, 31 October 1863, vol. 1: 1863-1872, Joseph L. Chester Correspondence, 1863-1880, NEHGS.

42. Whitmore, *American Genealogist*, 215.

43. David J. Russo, *Keepers of Our Past: Local Historical Writing in the United States, 1820s-1930s* (Westport, Conn.: Greenwood Press, 1988), 198.

44. Donald Lines Jacobus, *Genealogy as Pastime and Profession* (New Haven, Conn.: Tuttle, Morehouse & Taylor Company, 1930), 40; David L. Greene, "Donald Lines Jacobus, Scholarly Genealogy, and *The American Genealogist,*" *TAG* 72, 3–4 (July–October 1997): 159–180.

45. Milton Rubincam, "John Insley Coddington: An Appreciation," in *A Tribute to John Insley Coddington on the Occasion of the Fortieth Anniversary of the American Society of Genealogists,* ed. Neil D. Thompson and Robert Charles Anderson (New York: Association for the Promotion of Scholarship in Genealogy, 1980), 1–8.

46. Robert Charles Anderson, "An Interview with John Insley Coddington," in Thompson and Anderson, *A Tribute to John Insley Coddington,* 28–29; Greene, "Donald Lines Jacobus"; "ASG History," http://fasg.org/ASGHistory.html.

47. Eric Foner, *Reconstruction: America's Unfinished Revolution, 1863–1877* (New York: Harper & Row, 1988), 82–84; Michael P. Johnson, "Looking for Lost Kin: Efforts to Reunite Freed Families after Emancipation," in *Southern Families at War: Loyalty and Conflict in the Civil War South,* ed. Catherine Clinton (New York: Oxford University Press, 2000), 15–34.

48. Rutherford B. Hayes to [Uncle Scott], 4 March 1870, Rutherford B. Hayes Papers, Rutherford B. Hayes Presidential Center, Fremont, Ohio; Charles Richard Williams, ed., *Diary and Letters of Rutherford B. Hayes,* vol. 3 (Columbus: Ohio State Archæological and Historical Society, 1922), 91–92. I thank Nicolas Barreyre for providing me these references. Robert M. Taylor Jr., "Summoning the Wandering Tribes: Genealogy and Family Reunions in American History," *Journal of Social History* 16, 2 (Winter 1982): 32. These numbers are minima since most family reunions did not result in publications.

49. "Thomas Selden's Descendants," *NYT,* 23 August 1877.

50. *Reunion of the Dickinson Family, at Amherst, Mass., August 8th and 9th, 1883* (Binghamton, N.Y.: Binghamton Publishing Company, 1884), 2, 3.

51. Quoted in "The Coffin Reunion," *NYT,* 16 August 1881.

52. *Reunion of the Dickinson Family,* 22, 47.
53. James B. Allen, Jessie L. Embry, and Kahlile B. Mehr, *Hearts Turned to the Fathers: A History of the Genealogical Society of Utah, 1894–1994* (Provo, Utah: Brigham Young University, 1995), 43.
54. Ibid., 27, 33–35.
55. Ibid., 23, 43.
56. Jessie L. Embry, "Missionaries for the Dead: The Story of the Genealogical Missionaries of the Nineteenth Century," *Brigham Young University Studies* 17, 3 (Spring 1977): 355–360; Allen, Embry, and Mehr, *Hearts Turned to the Fathers,* 33–53.
57. James B. Allen and Jessie L. Embry, "Provoking the Brethren to Good Works: Susa Young Gates, the Relief Society, and Genealogy," *Brigham Young University Studies* 31, 2 (Spring 1991): 115–138.
58. Ibid., 121.
59. Ibid., 122–130.
60. Allen, Embry, and Mehr, *Hearts Turned to the Fathers,* 59–86.
61. Ibid., 91–124.
62. Ibid., 111, 112.
63. Thorstein Veblen, *An Inquiry into the Nature of Peace and the Terms of Its Perpetuation* (New York: Macmillan Company, 1917), 350.

6. EVERYBODY'S SEARCH FOR ROOTS

1. "Everybody's Search for Roots," *Newsweek,* 4 July 1977, 26, 27; William Marmon, "Why *Roots* Hit Home," *Time,* 14 February 1977; Stefan Kanfer, "Climbing All over the Family Trees," *Time,* 28 March 1977.
2. "Everybody's Search for Roots," 29, 32.
3. Alex Haley, *Roots: The Saga of an American Family* (New York: Doubleday, 1976); Maya Angelou, "Haley Shows Us the Truth of Our Conjoined Histories" *NYT,* 23 January 1977; Marmon, "Why *Roots* Hit Home."
4. Michael G. Kammen, *Mystic Chords of Memory: The Transformation of Tradition in American Culture* (New York: Knopf, 1991), 641; David A.

Gerber, "Haley's 'Roots' and Our Own: An Inquiry into the Nature of a Popular Phenomenon," *Journal of Ethnic Studies* 5, 3 (1977): 87–111; Tamara K. Hareven, "The Search for Generational Memory: Tribal Rites in Industrial Society," *Daedalus* 107, 4 (1978): 137–149; James A. Hijiya, "Roots: Family and Ethnicity in the 1970s," *American Quarterly* 30, 4 (Autumn 1978): 548–556; John Patrick Dulong, "Genealogical Groups in a Changing Organizational Environment: From Lineage to Heritage" (PhD diss., Wayne State University, 1986).

5. Kammen, *Mystic Chords of Memory*, 531–617, quote on 539; Paul S. Boyer, *By the Bomb's Early Light: American Thought and Culture at the Dawn of the Atomic Age* (New York: Pantheon, 1985); David Lowenthal, *The Past Is a Foreign Country* (Cambridge: Cambridge University Press, 1985); Lowenthal, *The Heritage Crusade and the Spoils of History* (Cambridge: Cambridge University Press, 1998).

6. John P. Hayes, "Everybody Is Climbing Their Family Tree," *NYT*, 25 July 1976.

7. "History of the Ohio Genealogical Society," www.ogs.org/about/history.php; Dulong, "Genealogical Groups"; P. William Filby, *American and British Genealogy and Heraldry: A Selected List of Books* (Boston: New England Historic Genealogical Society, 1983), 218, 220, 221.

8. Russell E. Bidlack, "Genealogy Today," *Library Trends* 32, 1 (Summer 1983): 17; Lester J. Cappon, "Genealogy, Handmaid of History," *National Genealogical Society Quarterly* 45, 1 (March 1957): 6, 8.

9. Filby, *American and British Genealogy and Heraldry*, 275; John B. Nichols, comp., *History of National Genealogical Society, 1903–1953* (Washington, D.C.: National Genealogical Society, 1955), 17; John A. Schutz, *A Noble Pursuit: The Sesquicentennial History of the New England Historic Genealogical Society, 1845–1995* (Boston: New England Historic Genealogical Society, 1995), 138, 162; *General Aids to Genealogical Research* (Washington, D.C.: National Genealogical Society, 1957); Bidlack, "Genealogy Today," 17.

10. Russell E. Bidlack, "Genealogy as It Relates to Library Service," in *ALA Yearbook, 1978* (Chicago: American Library Association, 1978), xxiv, xxix; Russell E. Bidlack, "Librarians and Genealogical Research," in *Ethnic Genealogy: A Research Guide,* ed. Jessie Carney Smith (Westport, Conn.: Greenwood Press, 1983), 6-7, 8.

11. Russell E. Bidlack, "The Awakening: Genealogy as It Relates to Library Service," *RQ* 23 (Winter 1983): 174; Bidlack, "Genealogy Today," 11; Wayne C. Grover, "Genealogy and American Scholarship," in *General Aids to Genealogical Research* (Washington, D.C.: National Genealogical Society, 1957), 6.

12. Rick J. Ashton, "A Commitment to Excellence in Genealogy: How the Public Library Became the Only Tourist Attraction in Fort Wayne, Indiana," *Library Trends* 32, 1 (Summer 1983): 92-94.

13. American Society of Genealogists, *Genealogical Research: Methods and Sources,* ed. Milton Rubincam (Washington, D.C.: [American Society of Genealogists], 1960); Jean White, "Genealogists Hunt Forebears in Records Here," *WP,* 20 July 1960; Michael V. Adams, "Ancestor Hunters Get Digging Tools," *WP,* 11 July 1968; "Jean Stephenson, Retired Editor, Dies," *WP,* 26 January 1979.

14. James B. Allen, Jessie L. Embry, and Kahlile B. Mehr, *Hearts Turned to the Fathers: A History of the Genealogical Society of Utah, 1894-1994* (Provo, Utah: Brigham Young University, 1995), 178-185.

15. Bidlack, "Genealogy as It Relates to Library Service," xxvi; Allen, Embry, and Mehr, *Hearts Turned to the Fathers,* 186-195; "Mormons to Hold World Conference on Records," *Los Angeles Times,* 2 August 1969; Wallace Turner, "Mormons Are Hosts to a World Archivists' Meeting. Church Is Interested in Keeping Record of Genealogies," *NYT,* 9 August 1969.

16. Nichols, *History of National Genealogical Society,* 28; Dulong, "Genealogical Groups," 98-154.

17. Philip Geyelin, "A Growing Business in Britain: Tracing Yanks' Family Trees," *Wall Street Journal,* 7 April 1960; John Barr, "Digging Up Roots of a Family Tree in Britain," *NYT,* 21 June 1964.

18. Dulong, "Genealogical Groups," 98–154; Mary Smith, "The Daughters Are Fighting for Members," *NYT*, 16 April 1961; Virginia Lee Warren, "D.A.R.—A New Concern with Public Image," *NYT*, 11 February 1968; "House of Agnew Gets New Heraldic Shield," *WP*, 28 December 1968; Mary Wiegers, "The Coats of Arms Race," *WP*, 12 January 1969; American College of Heraldry, http://americancollege ofheraldry.org.

19. Kammen, *Mystic Chords of Memory*, 271–277; Clyde A. Milner II, "The Shared Memory of Montana Pioneers," *Montana: The Magazine of Western History* 37, 1 (1987): 2–13; Milner, "The View from Wisdom: Region and Identity in the Minds of Four Westerners," *Montana: The Magazine of Western History* 41, 3 (1991): 2–17.

20. Matthew Frye Jacobson, *Roots Too: White Ethnic Revival in Post–Civil Rights America* (Cambridge, Mass.: Harvard University Press, 2006); Philip Nobile and Maureen Kenney, "The Search for Roots, a Pre-Haley Movement," *NYT*, 27 February 1977.

21. Alex Haley, "My Furthest-Back Person—'The African,'" *NYT*, 16 July 1972; Don Robinson, "Negro Traces Ancestors to Africa Tribe," *WP*, 6 June 1968; Hollie I. West, "Black, Looking Back," *WP*, 6 January 1971; Peggy J. Murrell, "Black Genealogy: Despite Many Problems, More Negroes Search for Their Family Pasts," *Wall Street Journal*, 9 March 1972; Michael Robbins, "Ancestors," *WP*, 28 April 1974; Mel Watkins, "A Talk with Alex Haley," *New York Times Book Review*, 26 September 1976, 2, 10, 12.

22. Watkins, "Talk with Alex Haley," 2.

23. Herbert Mitgang, "Howe Gets History Book Award," *NYT*, 12 April 1977; James Baldwin, "How One Black Man Came to Be an American: *Roots*," *New York Times Book Review*, 26 September 1976, 1; "Wolper Co. Is Sued on Topless Scene," *NYT*, 27 May 1976; Michael Kirkhorn, "A Saga of Slavery That Made the Actors Weep," *NYT*, 27 June 1976; "ABC's 'Roots' Garners a Top Nielsen Rating," *NYT*, 26 January 1977; Jacqueline Trescott, "Alex Haley: The Author of 'Roots,' astride His Moment of Fame," *WP*, 28 January 1977.

24. Watkins, "Talk with Alex Haley," 10; Barbara Garamekian, "Interest by Blacks in Genealogy Is Gaining," *NYT,* 11 October 1976; Charlayne Hunter-Gault, "'Roots' Getting a Grip on People Everywhere," *NYT,* 28 January 1977; Barbara Garamekian, "Blacks Searching for the Long-Lost Past," *NYT,* 21 February 1977; Thomas A. Johnson, "'Roots' Has Widespread and Inspiring Influence," *NYT,* 19 March 1977; John Darnton, "Kunta Kinte's Village in Gambia Takes 'Roots' Author to Its Heart," *NYT,* 14 April 1977; Mildred Bain and Ervin Lewis, eds., *From Freedom to Freedom: African Roots in American Soil; Selected Readings* (New York: Random House, 1977).

25. Murrell, "Black Genealogy"; *A Resolution to Pay Tribute to Alex Haley for the Impact of His Epic Work "Roots,"* 95th Cong., 1st sess., S.R. 112.

26. Christopher Lehmann-Haupt, "Corroborating Evidence," *NYT,* 14 October 1976; "'Roots' Grew out of His 'African,' Courlander Charges in Haley Suit," *NYT,* 24 May 1977; Arnold H. Lubasch, "'Roots' Plagiarism Suit Is Settled," *NYT,* 15 December 1978.

27. Willie Lee Rose, "An American Family," *New York Review of Books* 23 (11 November 1976): 3-4, 6; Mark Ottaway, "Tangled Roots," *Sunday Times,* 10 April 1977; Ottaway, "Doubts Raised over Story of the TV's Slave Saga," *Sunday Times,* 19 April 1977; Donald R. Wright, "Uprooting Kunta Kinte: On the Perils of Relying on Encyclopedic Informants," *History in Africa* 8 (1981): 208, 210-212.

28. Gary B. Mills and Elizabeth Shown Mills, "Roots and the New Faction: A Legitimate Tool for Clio?," *VMHB* 89, 1 (January 1981): 3-26; Elizabeth Shown Mills and Gary B. Mills, "The Genealogist's Assessment of Alex Haley's *Roots,*" *National Genealogical Society Quarterly* 72, 1 (March 1984): 37, 43.

29. Watkins, "Talk with Alex Haley," 10; Baldwin, "How One Black Man Came to Be an American," 1; Walter Goodman, "The Editorial Notebook," *NYT,* 15 April 1977; Mitgang, "Howe Gets History Book Award." See also Robert C. Maynard, "The Making of an American," *WP,* 26 September 1976.

30. Gerber, "Haley's 'Roots' and Our Own," 87–111; Hijiya, "Roots," 548–556; Hareven, "Search for Generational Memory," 137–149; Lowenthal, *Past Is a Foreign Country;* Roy Rosenzweig and David P. Thelen, *The Presence of the Past: Popular Uses of History in American Life* (New York: Columbia University Press, 1998).

31. Jennifer Fulkerson, "Climbing the Family Tree," *American Demographics* 17, 12 (1 December 1995): 42; Gerda Gallop-Goodman, "We Are Family," *American Demographics* 22, 9 (30 September 2000): 24; "Americans' Fascination with Family History Is Rapidly Growing," 9 June 2005, http://corporate.ancestry.com/press/press-releases/2005/06/americans-fascination-with-family-history-is-rapidly-growing/.

32. Michael Robbins, "Ancestors," *WP,* 28 April 1974; Garamekian, "Blacks Searching for the Long-Lost Past."

33. "History of Afro-American Historical and Genealogical Society," http://www.aahgs.org/about_history.htm; Hollie I. West, "Records of Black History," *WP,* 10 June 1973; "Genealogist James D. Walker Dies at Age 65," *WP,* 8 October 1993; "James Dent Walker Elected to National Genealogy Hall of Fame," http://www.aagsnc.org/articles/walker.htm.

34. Alondra Nelson, "Bio Science: Genetic Genealogy Testing and the Pursuit of African Ancestry," *Social Studies of Science* 38, 5 (October 2008): 763–764.

35. Michelle Burgen, "How to Trace Your Family Tree," *Ebony* 32, 8 (June 1977): 52–54, 58, 60, 62; Paul Harris, "The Genes That Build America," *Observer,* 15 July 2007; Dee Parmer Woodtor, *Finding a Place Called Home: An African American Guide to Genealogy and Historical Identity* (New York: Random House, 1999).

36. Malcolm Stern, *Americans of Jewish Descent* (Cincinnati: Hebrew Union College Press, 1960).

37. Arthur Kurzweil, *From Generation to Generation: How to Trace Your Jewish Genealogy and Personal History* (New York: Morrow, 1980); Gary Mokotoff, ed., *Every Family Has a Story: Tales from the Pages of "Avotaynu"* (Bergenfield, N.J.: Avotaynu, 2008).

38. "Searching for Ancestors Is Made a Bit Easier," *NYT*, 15 October 1989; Carolyn Battista, "Groups Seek Jews' European Roots," *NYT*, 3 June 1990; Ralph Blumenthal, "Woman Helps Jews Trace Eastern European Roots," *NYT*, 16 May 1998; Rachel E. Fisher, "A Place in History: Genealogy, Jewish Identity, Modernity" (PhD diss., University of California "at Santa Barbara, 1999).

39. Rosenzweig and Thelen, *Presence of the Past*, 19.

40. "Company Profile," http://www.genealogical.com/content/history .html; Michael DeCourcy Hinds, "Mail-Order Family Histories," *NYT*, 15 January 1983; Molly Sinclair, "'Heritage' Book Scrutiny," *WP*, 4 May 1985.

41. "Virginia Mormons Get Access to Church Archives in Utah," *WP*, 17 July 1982; Robert A. Hamilton, "Genealogy Session Attracting Experts," *NYT*, 3 July 1983; Donald B. Trivette, "Software for the Family Tree," *Wall Street Journal*, 15 July 1986; Hank Burchard, "Floppy Disks, Family Trees and Fun Data," *WP*, 22 April 1988.

42. "Cyndi's List of Genealogy Sites on the Internet," www.cyndislist .com; "Eastman's Online Genealogy Newsletter," http://blog.eogn .com/.

43. Bob Tedeschi, "E-Commerce Report," *NYT*, 23 September 2002; Bob Mims, "Provo, Utah–Based Online Genealogy Company Seeks to Expand," *Knight Ridder/Tribune Business News*, 15 April 2004; Eleanor Miller, "How Ancestry.com Makes Money," *Business Insider*, 27 January 2012, http://articles.businessinsider.com/2012-01-27 /research/30669556_1_ancestry-com-family-tree-maker-genealogy -societies; Ryan Dezember, "Ancestry.com Sets $1.6 Billion Deal," *Wall Street Journal*, 22 October 2012; "Company History," http://cor porate.ancestry.com/careers/companyhistory/; "Investor Relations," http://ir.ancestry.com.

44. Marc Peyser and Claudia Kalb, "Roots Network: Millions of Americans Seek Their Ancestors in Record Books, Cemeteries and Cyberspace," *Newsweek*, 24 February 1997, 32–33.

45. Duncan Campbell, "A Long Walk to Freedom," *Guardian,* 25 February 2001; Rachel L. Swarns and Jodi Kantor, "First Lady's Roots Reveal Slavery's Tangled Legacy," *NYT,* 8 October 2009; Edward Ball, *Slaves in the Family* (New York: Farrar, Straus and Giroux, 1998); Shirlee Taylor Haizlip, *The Sweeter the Juice* (New York: Simon & Schuster, 1994).

46. Annette Gordon-Reed, *Thomas Jefferson and Sally Hemings: An American Controversy* (Charlottesville: University Press of Virginia, 1997).

47. Eugene A. Foster, M. A. Jobling, P. G. Taylor, P. Donnelly, P. de Knijff, Rene Mieremet, T. Zerjal, and C. Tyler-Smith, "Jefferson Fathered Slave's Last Child," *Nature* 396 (5 November 1998): 27-28; Eric S. Lander and Joseph J. Ellis, "Founding Father," *Nature* 396 (5 November 1998): 13-14; Jan Ellen Lewis and Peter S. Onuf, eds., *Sally Hemings and Thomas Jefferson: History, Memory, and Civic Culture* (Charlottesville: University Press of Virginia, 1999); Joseph J. Ellis, "Jefferson: Post-DNA," *WMQ* 57, 1 (January 2000): 125-138; Peter Nicolaisen, "Thomas Jefferson, Sally Hemings, and the Question of Race: An Ongoing Debate," *Journal of American Studies* 37, 1 (2003): 99-118; Robert Eyler Coates, *The Jefferson-Hemings Myth: An American Travesty* (Charlottesville, Va.: Jefferson Editions, 2001); Thomas Jefferson Heritage Society, http://www.tjheritage.org/index.html.

48. Annette Gordon-Reed, *The Hemingses of Monticello: An American Family* (New York: W. W. Norton, 2008); Nicolaisen, "Thomas Jefferson," 117.

49. African Ancestry, http://africanancestry.com/.

50. On DNA testing procedures, see Andrew Yang, "Is Oprah Zulu? Sampling and Seeming Certainty in DNA Ancestry Testing," *Chance* 20, 1 (2007): 32-39; Susan Saulny, "A Spiraling Trail Back to Africa: DNA Is Breakthrough in Writer's Search," *NYT,* 26 February 2002; Harris, "Genes That Build America"; Ron Nixon, "DNA Tests Find Branches but Few Roots," *NYT,* 25 November 2007; Teresa Watanabe, "Called Back to Africa by DNA," *Los Angeles*

Times, 18 February 2009; Edward Ball, *The Genetic Strand: Exploring a Family History through DNA* (New York: Simon & Schuster, 2007).

51. Aravinda Chakravarti, "Kinship: Race Relations," *Nature* 457 (22 January 2009): 381.

52. John Seabrook, "The Tree of Me," *New Yorker,* 26 March 2001, 58–68; Dorothy Nelkin and Susan M. Lindee, *The DNA Mystique: The Gene as a Cultural Icon* (New York: Freeman, 1995); Nelson, "Bio Science," 767, 768; Nixon, "DNA Tests"; Deborah A. Bolnick, Duana Fullwiley, Troy Duster, Richard S. Cooper, Joan H. Fujimura, Jonathan Kahn, Jay S. Kaufman, Jonathan Marks, Ann Morning, Alondra Nelson, Pilar Ossorio, Jenny Reardon, Susan M. Reverby, and Kimberly Tallbear, "The Science and Business of Genetic Ancestry Testing," *Science* 318, 549 (19 October 2007): 399–400.

53. Keith Wailoo, Alondra Nelson, and Catherine Lee, eds., *Genetics and the Unsettled Past: The Collision of DNA, Race, and History* (New Brunswick, N.J.: Rutgers University Press, 2012).

ACKNOWLEDGMENTS

Until I started working on this project, I had never paid any attention to family history—mine or anybody else's. I came to this topic when I was working some years ago on how mid-nineteenth-century New Englanders coped with what Horace Bushnell in 1851 called a "complete revolution of domestic life and manners." My hypothesis was that they devised various strategies in order to make sense of their lives and the dramatic social transformations they were living through. I thought that one set of strategies might have been shaped by their personal or collective connection with the past, either real or imaginary. At the time I was in Ann Arbor, visiting the University of Michigan. I remember quite vividly meandering through the library stacks and stopping in the room hosting the CS section—the genealogical section according to the Library of Congress classification. For several days I pored over scores of published genealogies, which testified to the desire of many New Englanders of diverse social origins to anchor their understanding of the present in a past they could relate to. I was impressed with their candidness about their motivations, their enthusiastic research efforts in a period when documentary evidence was scant and difficult to uncover, and also their sense of gratification when they were able to reconstruct their ancestry. Genealogy helped them understand who they were and gave new depth to their sense of time. When I discovered, much to my surprise, that few historians had paid attention to genealogy, I decided to write this book. Over the following years I have contracted innumerable debts.

Archivists and librarians at the New England Historic Genealogical Society, the Massachusetts Historical Society, the New Hampshire Historical Society, the Virginia Historical Society, the Library Company of Philadelphia, the Historical Society of Pennsylvania, the University of Michigan, the University of Virginia, Harvard University, Tulane University, the New York Public Library, the Phillips Library at the Peabody Essex Museum, Middlebury College, the Henry Sheldon Museum of Vermont History, the British Library, the Henry N. Flynt Library, Historic Deerfield, the Rauner Library, Dartmouth College, and the College of Arms, London, all eased my research. I am particularly grateful to William Copeley, Danielle Courgeau, Donna-Belle Garvin, James Green, Cherylinne Pina, Frances Pollard, Jean-Marie Procious, Timothy Salls, David Smolen, Andrew M. Wentink, and R. C. Yorke. P. L. Dickinson, then Richmond Herald and now Clarenceux King of Arms, gave me access to the papers of Joseph L. Chester preserved at the College of Arms, London. In 2004 and 2006 fellowships from the New England Regional Research Consortium, the Virginia Historical Society, the Library Company of Philadelphia, and the Historical Society of Pennsylvania generously funded my research in Boston, Concord, Richmond, and Philadelphia. I thank James Green, Nelson D. Lankford, D. Brenton Simons, Conrad E. Wright, and all those who made this financial support available to me.

My home institution, l'École des hautes études en sciences sociales (EHESS), provided ideal intellectual and material conditions for researching and writing this book. I thank all the participants in my research seminar for their interest and challenging questions over the years, as well as Danièle Hervieu-Léger, then president of the EHESS, who granted me a timely sabbatical leave. At the Center for North American Studies, now headed by Cécile Vidal, Sophie Grandsire and Camille Amat provided perfect administrative support. My assistants Lydia Robin and Sabah Touiher wonderfully eased my efforts to complete this book while I served as president of the EHESS between 2009 and 2012.

I presented portions of this book to various audiences at the University of Virginia, the Massachusetts Historical Society, the New Hampshire Historical Society, the Organization of American Historians, the University of Geneva, Middlebury College, the University of Delaware, Oxford University, Tulane University, the Free University of Berlin, the French Association for American Studies, the Italian Association for North American Studies, the University of Toulouse le Mirail, the University of Avignon, the Higher School of Economics in Moscow, and the University of Bucharest. Through their questions, criticism, and suggestions, participants helped me clarify my argument.

Throughout the years, invitations to American universities—a vital need and pleasure for a French historian of the United States—provided a stimulating academic environment and access to essential library collections. I am grateful to Rebecca Scott and Terrence McDonald for inviting me in the fall of 2000 to be a visiting associate professor at the University of Michigan, where this project was born; to Patrick H. Hutton for inviting me to deliver the Samuel F. Emerson lecture at the University of Vermont in 2000; to Olivier

Zunz for bringing me to the University of Virginia in the falls of 2002 and 2008, and, along with Christine Zunz, for the warmth of their hospitality in Charlottesville; to Sylvia Frey for extending an invitation to serve as the Andrew W. Mellon Professor in the Humanities at Tulane University in the fall of 2003; to Nancy Cott and Akira Irye for bringing me back to Harvard University in the summer of 2004; and to Alan Brinkley for his invitation to Columbia University in the spring of 2008.

Chapter 2 incorporates my article "John Farmer and the Making of American Genealogy" from the *New England Quarterly* 80, no. 3 (September 2007): 408–434. I am grateful to Lynn Rhoads and the *New England Quarterly* for permission to expand this article for this book.

I discussed this project with many friends and colleagues who gave me their advice, criticism, and encouragement, particularly Robert C. Anderson, Bernard Bailyn, Nicolas Barreyre, Thomas Bender, Jean Boutier, Alan Brinkley, Jane Burbank, André Burguière, Christoph Conrad, Frederick Cooper, Nancy Cott, Raymond J. Demallie, Pierre Gervais, Nancy L. Green, David D. Hall, David J. Hancock, Gilles Havard, Jean Hébrard, Jean Heffer, Aline Helg, Richard Holway, Janet R. Horne, Romain Huret, Jean Kempf, James T. Kloppenberg, Emmanuelle Loyer, Vincent Michelot, Pierre Monnet, Evangeline Morphos, Natalia Muchnik, Pap Ndiaye, Sophie Nordmann, Peter S. Onuf, Gilles Pécout, Christophe Prochasson, Jacques Revel, Dinah Ribard, Jean-Frédéric Schaub, Paula Schwartz, Randy J. Sparks, David Thelen, Susan Tucker, James Turner, Laurel Thatcher Ulrich, Bertrand Van Ruymbeke, Maurizio Vaudagna, Cécile Vidal, Karin Wulf, Elvan Zabunyan, and Olivier Zunz. Michael Kammen, an anonymous reader for Harvard University

Press, Ariela J. Gross, and Martha S. Jones read the whole manuscript and offered timely and precious suggestions.

I was privileged to work at Harvard University Press with editor *extraordinaire* Joyce Seltzer. Joyce believed in this project from the start and over the years demonstrated the right mixture of patience and impatience that helped me write this book. I am extremely grateful to her, to her assistants Jeannette A. Estruth and Brian J. Distelberg, and to copyeditors Charles Eberline and John Donohue of Westchester Publishing Services. All have made the task of writing this book in English a pleasure as much as a challenge. Any remaining errors are, of course, my sole responsibility.

My family deserves all my gratitude. For over thirty years James F. and Jimmie Holland made their house feel like my American home and their family feel like my American family. In France, my wife, Jennifer Merchant, took time from her own research to hear about mine. Our children, Simon and Justine, grew up with this project. As becomes a book about family history, it is dedicated to them.

INDEX